Overcoming the Odds

Overcoming the Odds

High Risk Children from Birth to Adulthood

Emmy E. Werner
and
Ruth S. Smith

Cornell University Press
Ithaca and London

First published 1992 by Cornell University Press
First printing, Cornell Paperbacks, 1992

Library of Congress Cataloging-in-Publication Data

Werner, Emmy E., 1929–

Overcoming the odds : high risk children from birth to adulthood / Emmy E. Werner and Ruth S. Smith.
p. cm.
Includes bibliographical references and index.
ISBN 0-8014-2584-0 (alk. paper).—ISBN 0-8014-8018-3 (pbk. : alk. paper)
1. Children—Hawaii—Kauai—Longitudinal studies. 2. Socially handicapped children—Hawaii—Kauai—Longitudinal studies. 3. Life change events—Hawaii—Kauai—Longitudinal studies. I. Smith, Ruth S., 1923– . II. Title.
HQ792.U5W39 1992
371.96′7′0996941—dc20 91-23415

Cornell University Press strives to utilize environmentally responsible suppliers and materials to the fullest extent possible in the publishing of its books. Such materials include vegetable-based, low-VOC inks and acid-free papers that are also either recycled, totally chlorine-free, or partly composed of nonwood fibers.

Paperback printing 10 9 8 7 6 5

To Stanley and Earl—with much aloha

Contents

Tables

Figures

Acknowledgments

Our thanks and appreciation go to Robert J. Haggerty, M.D., and the board of directors of the William T. Grant Foundation, New York, for their financial support of this study (Project Grant #86-1110-86: Stress and Coping: Ten to Thirty).

We also thank the Sidney Stern Foundation, Los Angeles, for providing financial assistance in locating the individuals for this follow-up and the Christopher Smithers Foundation, New York, for support of the interviews with the adult children of alcoholics.

Additional financial support for this research was given by the University of California at Davis Faculty Research Committee and the Experiment Station of the College of Agricultural and Environmental Sciences.

Liza Cariaga, Renée Johansen-Khan, and Wanda McMaster, our research assistants, were invaluable in bringing this project to fruition. Leanne Friedman, our computer programmer, provided technical skills and never-ending patience. Curt Acredolo, Keith Barton, and Neil Pelkey gave statistical advice, and Dorothy Suhr typed several versions of this manuscript with precision and good will.

Holly Bailey, Susan Baker, Marcia Carlson, Bernhard Kendler, Helene Maddux, Marilyn Sale, and Kay Scheuer transformed our manuscript into this book. We thank them all. Mike Teruya, Free Spirit Photography, Kauai, photographed the children and their families that grace these pages. Although none of the persons depicted were members of the study, they are representative of the island community.

Our thanks go to the circuit courts in Hawaii, to the state's Department of Health and Division of Mental Health Services for their assistance in locating records, and most of all to the men and women from the 1955 birth cohort on Kauai, who shared the stories of their adult lives with us. We salute them with great respect for their valor in the face of great odds.

EMMY E. WERNER
Professor of Human Development
Division of Human Development
and Family Studies
University of California, Davis

RUTH S. SMITH
Clinical Psychologist
Koloa, Kauai

Overcoming the Odds

1

Introduction

I dwell in Possibility—
A fairer House than Prose—
More numerous of Windows—
Superior—for Doors.
Emily Dickinson (1862)

Emily Dickinson was 32 years old when she wrote these lines—about the same age as the women and men in our study. This book is about their possibilities, the doors that opened (or closed) for them at important life transitions, and the factors that contributed to their resiliency in the face of childhood adversity or to their recovery in later years.

The 505 individuals whose lives we followed from the prenatal period to adulthood were born in 1955 on the island of Kauai, the western-most county in the United States. They represent a mixture of ethnic groups—for the most part Japanese, Pilipino, and part and full Hawaiians. Their parents or grandparents came from Southeast Asia to work on the sugar and pineapple plantations of the island—with the dream of a better life for their children. Many intermarried with the local Hawaiians. Most were raised by parents who were semi- or unskilled laborers and who had not graduated from high school.

The Kauai Longitudinal Study has monitored the impact of a variety of biological and psychosocial risk factors, stressful life events and protective factors on the development of these individuals—at birth, in infancy, early and middle childhood, late adolescence, and now adulthood. The principal goals of our investigation were to document, in natural-history fashion, the course of all pregnancies and their outcomes in the entire community from birth until the offspring had reached adulthood, and to assess the long-term consequences of perinatal complications and adverse rearing conditions on the individuals' development and adaptation to life.

We need to keep in mind that the majority of the members of this birth cohort were born without complications, after uneventful pregnancies, and grew up in supportive home environments. They led lives that were not unusually stressful, and they coped successfully with the developmental tasks of childhood and adolescence. They performed adequately in school, had no serious learning or mental health problems, and did not get into trouble with the law.

One out of every three in this cohort, however, was born with the odds against successful development. These individuals experienced moderate to severe degrees of perinatal stress, grew up in chronic poverty, were reared by parents with little formal education, and/or lived in disorganized family environments. Their homes were troubled by discord, desertion, or divorce or marred by parental alcoholism or mental illness. Two out of three children in this vulnerable group (who encountered four or more such cumulative risk factors before the age of two) subsequently developed serious learning and/or behavior problems by age 10 or had a record of delinquencies, mental health problems, or pregnancies by age 18.

The Children of Kauai (Werner, Bierman, and French, 1971) documents the cumulative effects of poverty, perinatal stress, and a disorganized caretaking environment on the development of these children from birth to age 10. A second book, *Kauai's Children Come of Age* (Werner and Smith, 1977), examines the roots of the learning disorders, mental health problems, and antisocial behavior displayed by many of the high risk children in their teens, and analyzes the likelihood of the persistence of serious problems into adulthood.

Nevertheless, one out of every three of these high risk children (some 10% of the total cohort) had developed into a competent, confident, and caring young adult by age 18. A third book, *Vulnerable but Invincible* (Werner and Smith, 1982, 1989), contrasts the behavior and caregiving environments of the resilient youngsters with that of their high risk peers of the same age and sex who had developed serious coping problems in the first two decades of life. To the extent that the young men and women in this study were able to elicit predominantly positive responses from their environments, they were found to be stress-resistant, even when living in chronic poverty or in disorganized homes with disturbed parents. To the extent that they elicited negative responses from their environments, they were found to be vulnerable, even in the absence of biological stress or financial constraints. As disadvantages and the cumulative number of stressful life events increased, more protective factors in the children and their caregiving environment were needed to counterbalance the negative factors and to ensure positive developmental outcomes.

When we last interviewed these young men and women, their lives were in a transitional phase. They were about to graduate from high school, to leave their parental homes, and to enter their first full-time jobs. Their relationships with members of the opposite sex were still tentative. With the exception of the teenage mothers, they had not yet been confronted with the demands of childbearing and child rearing. The period of maximum risk for mental breakdown was still ahead of them.

This book finds these same men and women at a stage in life which provides them an opportunity to reappraise and modify the initial mode of adult living they established in the previous decade. The age-30 transition period is biologically the peak of adulthood, a time of great energy, but also among the most stressful of the adult life cycle (Levinson, 1986; Lowenthal, Thurnher, and Chiriboga, 1977). The central components of the adult life structures we reappraise at this stage are three interdependent life trajectories—work life, marriage, and parenthood (Elder, 1985).

The main objectives of our present inquiry are, first, to trace the long-term effects of childhood adversity on the adult lives of men and women who were exposed to poverty, parental discord or psychopathology, and perinatal stress; and, second, to examine the long-term effects of protective factors and processes that led most to a successful adaptation in adulthood.

Definition of Concepts

Resilience and *protective factors* are the positive counterparts to both *vulnerability*, which denotes an individual's susceptibility to a disorder, and *risk factors*, which are biological or psychosocial hazards that increase the likelihood of a negative developmental outcome in a group of people.

Researchers who study individuals exposed to biological risk factors and stressful life events have gone through several stages in their approach to understanding vulnerability and resiliency. First, they gave emphasis to the negative developmental outcomes associated with a single risk factor, such as low birth weight, or with a stressful life event, such as the prolonged absence of a parent. They then shifted from this "main effect" model of risk research to one that considered interactional effects among multiple stressors, such as the co-occurrence of parental psychopathology (e.g., alcoholism or mental illness) and poverty. The most recent phase has been marked by a lessened emphasis on negative developmental outcomes and a greater focus on successful adaptation in spite of childhood adversity. For in contrast to retrospective studies, prospective longitudinal studies have fairly consistently shown that even among children exposed to potent risk factors it is unusual for more than half to develop serious disabilities or persistent problems (Robins, 1978; Rutter, 1985).

During the mid 1970s, Anthony (1974), a child psychiatrist, introduced the concept of the "psychologically invulnerable child" into the literature of developmental psychopathology to describe children who, despite a history of severe and/or prolonged adversity and psychological stress, manage to achieve emotional health and high competence. As Rutter (1985) has pointed out, however, resistance to stress in children is relative, not absolute. Moreover, the bases of resistance are both environmental and constitutional, and the degree of resistance varies over time and according to life's circumstances. Consequently, more researchers today prefer the relative concepts of *resilience* or *stress-resistance* rather than *invulnerability* (Luthar and Zigler, 1991; Masten and Garmezy, 1985; Werner and Smith, 1982). This usage implies a track record of successful adaptation in the individual who has been exposed to biological risk factors or stressful life events, and it also implies an expectation of continued low susceptibility to future stressors.

Horowitz (1987, 1989), a developmental psychologist, has adapted a model originally used to analyze the relation of the resilience and susceptibility of an organism to bacterial infection as a guide to research on the effects of biological and/or social risk factors on the development of children. Her structural-behavioral model of development assumes that an individual's adequate development in a particular behavioral domain is the result of individual organismic factors acting in relation to aspects of the environment which can facilitate or impede development at any given period of the life cycle. Relative resiliency in this model is a constitutionally based organismic characteristic that accounts for individual differences from person to person and may have genetic or nongenetic origins. An individual with resiliency has constitutional resources such that his or her rate and quality of development in a particular (behavioral) domain will not be seriously affected even under adverse circumstances. Environments, in turn, can range on a continuum from facilitative to nonfacilitative, and they can include specific learning opportunities as well as the more complex social system and culture in which the individual is raised. The degree of facilitation by the environment at any point in time may be different for different domains. The model makes the assumption that there are points of reorganization in the life course at which the individual's vulnerability or resiliency to particular environments may change.

Whereas resilience is a characteristic that varies from person to person, *protective factors* or mechanisms are more specific and more narrowly defined. Protective factors modify (ameliorate, buffer) a person's reaction to a situation that in ordinary circumstances leads to maladaptive outcomes. A protective effect is evident only in combination with a risk variable. Either the protective factor has no effect in low risk populations, or its effect is magnified in the presence of the risk variable. Rutter (1989) suggests that the effects are catalytic: they may reduce the impact of the risk factor and/or the negative chain reactions associated with the risk situation, they may increase self-esteem and efficacy, and they may lead to the opening up of opportunities.

Related Research

Our current understanding of the roots of resilience and of factors or mechanisms that protect individuals against the psychosocial risks associated with adversity comes from a small but diverse body of literature generated by persons with various professional perspectives—predominantly psychologists, psychiatrists, and sociologists. Most of our knowledge to date comes from short-term studies in middle childhood and adolescence; investigations that have extended beyond the second decade of life are still rare (Anthony and Cohler, 1987; Werner, 1988, 1989, 1990).

Relatively few investigators have followed populations of high risk children and youths into adulthood to monitor the long-term effects of risk and protective factors that operated during the individuals' formative years. Studies with such a life span perspective are markedly heterogeneous. They vary in design (retrospective versus prospective), selection of subjects (clinic populations versus community cohorts), definitions and measures of quality of adaptation, and the timing of assessment in the individuals' lives and in the historical context that affects these lives.

In recent years, such research has demonstrated a significant shift from case studies and retrospective studies to prospective longitudinal studies. Case studies (Viederman, 1979) and retrospective accounts of adults who successfully overcame traumatic childhoods (Tress, 1986) and who demonstrated the capacity for love and intimacy despite parental abuse or neglect (O'Connell Higgins, 1985) suggest potential protective factors, whereas prospective longitudinal studies serve to document their short- and long-term effects. Definitions of risk in these studies vary with the level of organization, that is, whether researchers conceive of the risk factors as primarily residing in the individual organism, in the immediate family, or in the broader social context the individual inhabits (Bronfenbrenner, 1979).

Children Who Experienced Economic Hardships

Most numerous among prospective studies of high risk children in the United States and Europe are investigations that trace the long-term effects of chronic poverty or sudden economic misfortune, accompanied by severe income loss, on the individual's life course. These studies represent two different historical eras and two different generations: men and women born in the early 1920s and early 1930s who grew up in the shadows of the Great Depression but witnessed the post–World War II economic upturn in the United States and individuals born in the mid 1950s who grew up in the Vietnam War era and entered the adult work force during one of the worst recessions in the United States since the Great Depression.

Using the archival data of the Berkeley Guidance Study and the Oakland Growth Study, Elder and his colleagues have explored the long-term impact of economic hardship on both children and adolescents who experienced the Great Depression (Elder, 1974, 1986; Elder, Caspi, and Van Nguyen, 1985; Elder, Liker, and Cross, 1984; Elder, Van Nguyen, and Caspi, 1985). Data available on the 214 members of the Berkeley cohort born in 1928/29 (who experienced the Great Depression as preschoolers), follow them from age 21 months to 11/12, 17/18, and 30 years. Data available on the 167 members of the Oakland cohort (who experienced the Great Depression as adolescents) cover them from age 10 to 17/18, 30, 36, and 43 years. Elder's findings invite comparisons with the life course of the children of Kauai at several points in time—in childhood, late adolescence, and early adulthood.

In his book *Children of the Great Depression* (1974), Elder examines the impact of sudden financial misfortune on the 167 members of the Oakland cohort. Severe economic loss increased the power of the mother in family matters—as decision maker and emotional resource in times of stress. Sons and daughters from economically deprived homes sought more advice and companionship among persons outside the immediate family circle, for example teachers and friends, than did children unaffected by economic misfortune. For this generation personal assets, such as intelligence (for males) and physical attractiveness (for females), were buffers for adolescents whose families experienced financial hardships. Achievement motivation was more highly correlated with ability among the economically deprived youths than among the nondeprived. In adulthood, the offspring of the deprived reported more frequently that their lives had become more satisfying and abundant than did the nondeprived.

Elder, Liker, and Cross (1984) analyzed the life course of the 214 members of the Berkeley cohort. These individuals had experienced economic upheavals in their families as young children. An easy temperament (for both males and females) and physical attractiveness (for females), and positive mother-child relationships buffered the impact of father's (negative) behavior during the hard times of the Depression.

Boys in the Berkeley cohort who experienced the Great Depression as young children had more difficulties in youth and adulthood than did peers who did not experience economic hardships. In contrast, girls who suffered economic hardships in childhood did not develop any major coping problems in later life. A reverse trend was observed in the lives of the members of the Oakland cohort who experienced the Great Depression in adolescence: economic hardships pushed adolescent males into greater autonomy and early entrance into work life, but it had a negative effect on the self-concept of the girls (Elder, Van Nguyen, and Caspi, 1985).

In some circumstances, military service served as a positive turning point in the lives of economically disadvantaged men. In the Berkeley Guidance Study, low-achieving youths who had experienced economic hardships and had a low self-esteem tended to join the armed forces at the earliest possible moment, often dropping out of high school. Service in the military enabled these youths to acquire scholastic and occupational skills they would not have had otherwise. They married later in life (when they were more self-sufficient) and had generally more stable unions than did nonveterans. Follow-ups into midlife showed that their occupational achievements were significantly better than could have been expected on the basis of their background and functioning in their youth and that they had gained significantly more in psychological strength from adolescence to midlife than had nonveterans (Elder, 1986).

Children in High Crime Neighborhoods

Another cohort that grew up in the shadows of the Great Depression has been studied by Vaillant and his associates in Boston. He has traced the life course of some 450 men born in the early 1930s who spent their childhood years in the high crime neighborhoods of that city. Those men served as the nondelinquent control group of the studies on crime and delinquency conducted by Glueck and Glueck (1968). They were followed from age 14 until age 47, with major assessments at ages 25 and 31. Some 60 percent in this group were descendants of immigrants. Even though a generation separates these men from the children of Kauai, Vaillant's reports of their resiliency and upward social mobility are of considerable relevance to our own investigation (Felsman and Vaillant, 1987; Long and Vaillant, 1984; Snarey and Vaillant, 1985; Vaillant, 1983; Vaillant and Milofsky, 1980, 1982; Vaillant and Vaillant, 1981).

Vaillant and Milofsky (1980) applied Erikson's model (1959) of adult development to the life course of these underprivileged males and contrasted their findings with longitudinal data collected on privileged Harvard men (Vaillant, 1977). They noted that the stages attained in midlife (career consolidation, intimacy, generativity) appeared quite independent of childhood social class (whether poor or affluent) or education (whether high school or college graduate). Instead, psychological maturity in adulthood correlated strongly with childhood experiences that were conducive to the development of trust, autonomy, and initiative.

Vaillant and Vaillant (1981) subsequently assessed the relation between the mental health and career success of the inner-city men and their success at tasks reflecting Erikson's fourth developmental state (industry). Capacity to work in childhood (judged by regular part-time jobs, household chores, school achievement, and extracurricular participation) was strongly correlated with the career success of these underprivileged youths in adulthood. The same variable also was a stronger predictor of capacity for satisfying interpersonal relationships and adult mental health than was poverty or membership in a multiproblem family.

By midlife, males who had grown up in multiproblem families were, on the average, indistinguishable from the offspring of more stable working-class families in terms of mean income, years of steady employment, criminality, and mental illness (Long and Vaillant, 1984). For these men, childhood IQ showed a stronger relationship to upward social mobility than for the offspring of more stable homes. Many of the upwardly mobile men from multiproblem homes had joined the armed forces and had utilized the G.I. Bill of Rights for further educational and vocational training—like the Berkeley men who were children of the Great Depression.

Snarey and Vaillant (1985) extended their study of social mobility among the Boston inner-city men to three generations, including both their parents and their children. Two-thirds of the men and 60 percent of their offspring have moved from lower and working class status into the middle class. Among the major variables that captured most of the variance in social mobility in this cohort were maternal education, maternal occupation, childhood IQ, ego strength, and intellectualization, that is, the capacity to isolate ideation from affect.

Also relevant to our inquiry are findings reported by Farrington and his colleagues from the Cambridge Study of Delinquent Development (Farrington, 1983, 1987, 1989; Farrington, Gallagher, et al., 1988a, 1988b; West, 1982). This is a prospective longitudinal survey of 411 working class males from London's inner city, born in the early 1950s, who were first seen at ages 8–10 years and have now been followed to age 32. By 32, the more successful men in this group (as judged on the basis of satisfactory employment history and family relationships, as well as absence of criminal convictions and other deviant behavior) were contrasted with recidivists (males with records of frequent and continuous offenses). The more successful men were more likely to have been shy boys from homes where no parent had a criminal record and no sibling had behavior problems and, most important, where mothers had high opinions of their sons. In middle childhood, these males were already better behaved and less daring than the men considered unsuccessful in adulthood. There was a tendency for shyness to act as a protective factor against delinquency and crime for nonaggressive boys but as an aggravating factor for aggressive boys.

Another large-scale investigation that has explored both criminogenic and protective factors in childhood which may have long-term effects on adult development is the Cambridge-Somerville Project (McCord, 1979). A series of reports by McCord (1982, 1983a, 1983b, 1986) have detailed her findings from a 30-year follow-up of 506 males who were first identified between the ages of 8 and 15 as "predisposed to delinquency." Several childhood variables maximally distinguished between men who had become criminals and those who had not. Paternal aggressiveness and maternal permissiveness appeared to be particularly criminogenic, whereas father's esteem for the mother, mother's self-confidence and education, and maternal affection seemed to insulate a boy against criminogenic stresses. Two variables turned out to be particularly potent: a mother's self-confidence, coupled with consistent discipline, seemed to overcome the effects of father's absence or lack of affection; and a father's respect for the mother reduced the criminogenic impact of affectional deprivation and permissiveness.

Children Who Experienced Serious Caregiving Deficits

A few prospective longitudinal studies have also examined the adult adaptation of children who were exposed to parental psychopathology.

Among the first to keep an eye on the favorable development of the majority of such high risk children was the Swiss psychiatrist Manfred Bleuler (1978, 1984), who followed 184 offspring of schizophrenic patients from childhood into adulthood. Only 9 percent of their sons and daughters became schizophrenic themselves. Nearly three-fourths of his sample were healthy in adulthood; 84 percent of the married offspring of schizophrenics had successful marriages, and the great majority achieved a higher social status than had their parents. Among potent protective factors found in the lives of these resilient offspring of schizophrenics were childhood opportunities to receive some good parenting from the afflicted mother or father, to attach to a warm-hearted parent substitute or to the well parent, and to engage in responsible chores that offered the child or youth a sense of purpose, that is, to care for a younger sibling or for the sick parent.

Among contemporary investigators who have traced the fate of offspring of psychotic parents into early adulthood (ages 25–30 years) are Mednick and his associates, who studied 207 children of schizophrenic mothers in Denmark, and E. J. Anthony, who followed 40 children of manic-depressive and schizophrenic parents into their early 30s (Anthony, 1987; Mednick, Cudeck, et al., 1984). As in the Swiss study by Bleuler, Mednick and his colleagues found in Denmark that being reared by a caregiver less pathological than the schizophrenic mother (father, grandmother, other relatives) was associated with significantly better outcomes for the high risk males—unless the father was absent as well. Generally high risk females appeared more resistant to both biological stressors and breakdown of parenting. For high risk females, the absence of the father in childhood appeared less damaging in adulthood than for the high risk males, but maternal absence was related to daughters' antisocial tendencies in adulthood.

Anthony (1987) also reports that the majority of the offspring of manic-depressive and schizophrenic patients whom he followed from childhood and adolescence into young adulthood grew into healthy and competent adults. But some of the "invulnerables" from St. Louis appeared to pay a psychological price for their apparent immunity from psychiatric illness. They used distancing, intellectualization, and rationalization to deal with parental psychopathology—defense mechanisms that made it difficult for them to establish intimacy. This was especially true if the afflicted parent was of the opposite sex. Some adult children of psychotic parents broke relationships when there was a hint of closeness. Others searched for relationships that required the role of helper—such as working in human service professions. Still others, by joining a variety of social and religious groups, both diluted the intensity of their relationships but simultaneously received a good deal of emotional support.

Important contributions to our understanding of protective mechanisms come from two other prospective studies, one conducted in England, one in the United States. Both suggest that some psychological effects of the breakdown of parenting and divorce are relatively long lasting but can be buffered by supportive family members.

Rutter and his associates undertook a follow-up study of 94 English girls who had been reared in foster institutions since early childhood and of a comparison group of 51 women from the general population. Both groups were interviewed when they were between 21 and 27 years old, and home observations were made of those women who were mothers of young children (Quinton, Rutter, and Liddle, 1984; Rutter and Quinton, 1984; Rutter, 1987, 1989).

The level of good parenting in the foster-care women who had a supportive spouse (as reflected in a harmonious marriage characterized by a warm, confiding relationship) was as high as that in the comparison group. But in the absence of good marital support, there was a marked increase in the rate of poor psychosocial functioning and poor parenting among the institutionally reared women. The presence of marital support was less critical for good parenting in the comparison groups. The foster-care women who were good parents had exercised planning in the choice of their husbands (i.e., they did not marry for negative reasons—in order to escape from a bad home or because of pregnancy), and they had known their future spouses for at least six months. The girls who planned were much more likely to have had positive school experiences as well, either in academic subjects or in sports, drama, or arts and crafts. Rutter (1987) surmises that the experience of success at school had helped these women acquire a sense of their own worth and of their ability to control what happened to them.

The findings by Wallerstein and her associates from a longitudinal study of 113 children and adolescents from divorced families in California also suggest that some psychological effects of divorce (both negative and positive) are relatively long lasting (Wallerstein, 1985; Wallerstein and Blakeslee, 1989). Ten years after the parental breakup, most of the 19-to-29-year-old adults in her study regarded parental divorce as a continuing major influence in their lives. The women, especially, were apprehensive about repeating their parents' unhappy marriages during their own adulthood and appeared eager to avoid divorce for the sake of their children. But many described themselves as having emerged stronger as a consequence of the parental breakup. Divorce had thrust them earlier into positions of responsibility (taking care of the household and younger siblings), and they had benefited from the opportunity and developed a greater sense of independence and maturity than their peers from intact families. Siblings acted as a potent supportive network that buffered the negative impact of the family breakup and provided relationships that modeled loyalty, intimacy, and enduring love.

Teenage Mothers

Finally, a few follow-up studies of teenage mothers have examined the role of protective factors in the lives of young women who were exposed to a combination of biological and psychosocial risk factors: early childbearing, single parenthood, and poverty (Kellam, Adams, et al., 1982; Osofsky, 1990). The most extensive investigation so far has been conducted by Furstenberg and his associates, who followed some 289 Black adolescent mothers from their first prenatal visits to a Baltimore hospital until 16/17 years after their deliveries—when they were about 32 years old. These women are contemporaries of the young adults we have studied on Kauai—hence the findings of the Baltimore study are particularly relevant to our own follow-up.

In *Adolescent Mothers in Later Life* (1987), Furstenberg, Brooks-Gunn, and Morgan explored how the majority of the teenage mothers recovered and examined what part of their improvement was explained by their own competence and determination, by social support, and by educational and social services. In general, the situation of the young mothers had improved significantly over time. Only a quarter of the women were on welfare when they reached their early 30s; most job holders were regularly employed, and about a quarter had moved from poverty into the middle class. Using path analyses, Furstenberg and his associates focused on two key indicators of well-being in adulthood: economic independence and low fertility. Both indicators were strongly related to expressions of well-being voiced by the women. Among significant factors that determined the adolescent mothers' later success were parental education (10 grades or more), small family size (less than four children in family of origin), and not having been on welfare as a child. Parental education was linked to the educational performance and aspiration of the daughter. The keys to economic independence for the teenage mothers in later life were successful graduation from high school, restriction of further childbearing, and/or a stable marriage.

Protective Factors: The Evidence So Far

Despite the heterogeneity of the risk conditions studied, and despite conceptual and methodological differences in the assessment of quality of adult adaptation, one can begin to discern a common core of individual dispositions and sources of support which ameliorate or buffer a person's response to both constitutional risk factors (such as parental psychopathology) or stressful life events (economic hardship, divorce, breakdown of parenting). These findings have been replicated in different historical eras, across different generations, and in different metropolitan areas of the United States and Europe, with both Black and Caucasian populations.

An easy temperament, the ability to plan, achievement up to grade level in primary school, responsible chores in childhood and adolescence, and successful graduation from high school were protective factors in a number of different risk situations for both boys and girls. So were the role models of an educated, self-confident mother who valued her child and of supportive alternate caregivers in the family (grandparents, older siblings). Scholastic aptitude (as measured by intelligence tests in middle childhood) and military service that provided the opportunity to acquire educational and vocational skills were found to be protective for economically deprived boys; physical attractiveness and a supportive husband were found to be protective for girls who had suffered either economic hardships or serious caregiving deficits in childhood.

But just as vulnerability is relative, depending on complex interactions among constitutional factors and life circumstances, resilience is governed by a similar dynamic interaction among protective factors within the child, the family environment, and the larger social context (Cohler, 1987). Longitudinal studies that have followed high risk children to maturity find that, at each developmental stage, there is a shifting balance between the stressful life events that heighten children's vulnerability and the protective factors that enhance their resilience. This balance not only changes with the stages of the life cycle but also varies with the sex of the individual and the cultural context in which he or she matures (Werner, 1990).

Both the American and European studies reviewed here have shown that boys are more vulnerable than girls in childhood to the effects of biological insults, caregiving deficits, and economic hardships. This trend is reversed in the second decade, with girls becoming more vulnerable than boys in adolescence, especially with the onset of early childbearing. In young adulthood, the balance appears to shift back again in favor of the women (Werner, 1988).

What have we learned from earlier research that gave direction to our present undertaking?

1. We expected to find both continuities and discontinuities in the pathways from childhood to adulthood among the high risk individuals who participated in our study. We expected greater continuity in adult life for the resilient individuals who had successfully mastered the developmental tasks of childhood and adolescence. In contrast, we expected to find more discontinuities in the paths to adulthood among the high risk individuals who had developed serious problems by the time they left high school: the teenage mothers, delinquents, and youths troubled by serious mental health problems.

2. We anticipated that some of the protective factors found in earlier studies of high risk individuals would act as buffers in the adult lives of the men and women on Kauai as well. But previous investigations had focused on a more limited time span in the life course—from middle childhood or adolescence to early adulthood. We had the advantage of a data base that extended downward to infancy and preschool age. We expected to find some sturdy roots of adult resilience in those earlier years.

3. Previous research had given us some clues about turning points in later life—illustrated by the positive impact of military service on the work lives of disadvantaged men and of supportive spouses on the parenting skills of high risk women. We expected to find additional turning points in the lives of our cohort members which led them on the road to recovery. We also expected to find significant prior differences between individuals who sought or elicited such "second chance" opportunities and those who did not.

4. When we began this study, relatively little was known about the lives of adult women who successfully overcame a traumatic childhood or youth. Most of the large follow-up studies of high risk youths into adulthood had examined the lives of men. We expected that the impact of stressful life events and of protective factors would differ for men and women at different stages of their life cycles. Our large cohort and extensive data base now permit us to examine the interplay between stressful life events and protective factors for each gender at five critical periods in the life course: infancy, early childhood, middle childhood, late adolescence, and early adulthood. We wanted to trace the different pathways that led men and women from an adverse childhood to a successful adaptation in early adulthood. This we set out to do.

The Plan of This Book

In Chapter 2, we describe the social and historical context of the study and the methods we used to assess the cohort members and their families. We then give an overview of how the children of Kauai fare as adults.

In Chapter 3, we give an account of the adult status of the ordinary men and women in this cohort. Most had grown up in supportive home environments, without exposure to serious adversities, and had not developed any serious learning and/or behavior problems in childhood or adolescence. We then turn to the life stories of the high risk children who had grown into competent, confident, and caring adolescents, despite perinatal stress, poverty, or parental psychopathology. We examine how these resilient youngsters now fare as adults in Chapter 4.

We subsequently take a look at what happened in adulthood to their high risk peers who had developed serious coping problems in childhood and/or adolescence. We look at the later lives of the teenage mothers (in Chapter 5), at delinquents with and without records of adult crime (in Chapter 6), and at the men and women who had previously developed serious mental health problems in response to an accumulation of stressful life events in their childhood or youth (in Chapter 7). In Chapters 8 and 9, we examine the long-term effects of stressful life events and of protective factors that contributed to changes in life trajectories from risk to adaptation and that led to recovery in adulthood.

In Chapter 10, we summarize what we have learned about the long-term consequences of stressful life events in childhood or adolescence which exert a continuing price in adulthood, and about the positive effects of protective factors that operated at key turning points in the lives of high risk individuals. We conclude our report with a discussion of the implications of our findings for developmental research and for social policy.

To make our findings more accessible to the general reader, we have placed all tables in Appendix I. Here the interested reader can find a detailed account of the statistical analyses of our data which support the discussion in the text. This appendix also includes the path diagrams that trace the links between stressful life events and protective factors and quality of adult adaption for the men and women in this cohort.

Throughout this book, we present case histories and vignettes drawn from our extensive files and interviews to illustrate the shifting balance between vulnerability and resiliency which characterized the lives of many of the individuals in our study. For the tale is best told by the men and women who have struggled and often succeeded against the odds.

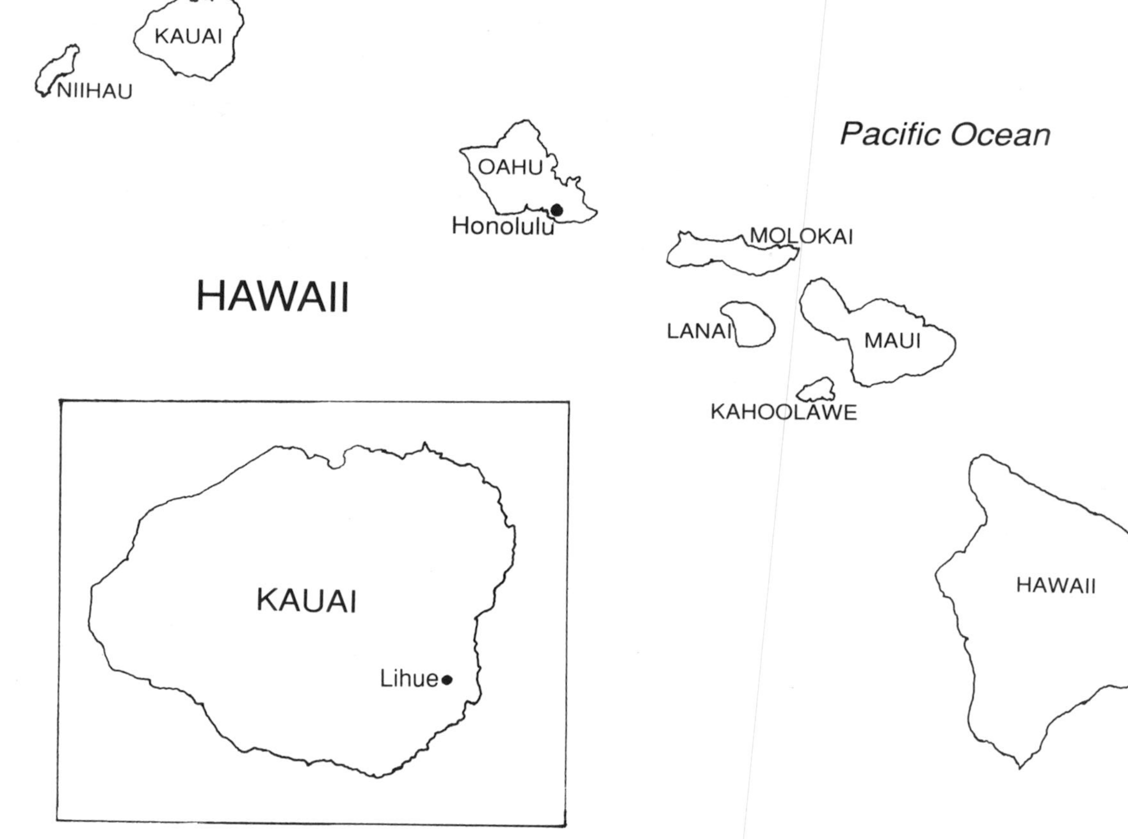
KAUAI
NIIHAU
OAHU
Honolulu
Pacific Ocean
MOLOKAI
HAWAII
LANAI
MAUI
KAHOOLAWE
KAUAI
Lihue
HAWAII

Figure 1.

2

The Context of the Study

The island of Kauai lies at the northwest end of the Hawaiian chain, some one hundred miles from Honolulu, the capital and major urban center of the fiftieth state. The island, a single shield volcano, is among the oldest in the chain and was created millions of years ago by molten lava, bubbling out of a rift in the floor of the Pacific Ocean. The ancient Hawaiians named it Kauai-a-mano-ka-lani-po—"the fountainhead of many waters from on high and bubbling up from below."

Kauai has great natural beauty and is regarded by many people—visitors and residents alike—as one of the loveliest of the Hawaiian islands. Its geology is complex, and over the centuries its 627 square miles have been shaped by the destructive forces of wind, waves, and rain and by the procreative forces of sun and water. Together these forces have created spectacular mountains and valleys, cliffs and canyons, lush rain forests and swamps, and miles of magnificent beaches.

The People of Kauai: Origins

Kauai's earliest inhabitants probably came from the Marquesa Islands around 500 A.D. and were followed, around 1000 A.D., by migrations from Tahiti. The civilizations established by these first Polynesians, with an elaborate hierarchy of royalty, priests, warriors, and commoners, would see little change for nearly a millennium. A Hawaiian creation chant tells the story of this long-distant past:

Well formed is the child, well formed now
Child in the time when men multiplied
Child in the time when men came from afar . . .
Born were men by the hundreds
Born was man for the narrow stream
Born was woman for the broad stream . . .

There was a dramatic change, however, when the British seafarer Captain James Cook "discovered" the islands in 1778. Kauai was the site of his first landing. Cook's voyage opened doors that never again closed. Traders in fur and sandalwood found the island to be a source of valuable goods and a place for refurbishing their supplies. Whalers valued the strategic location of the island for the replenishment of their food and water and for rest periods that enabled them to remain in the whaling grounds for extended periods of time.

The first Christian missionaries came to Kauai in 1820, and with them the Westernization of the island and its native people began. New Englanders set about teaching the children of royalty and, later, the common people to read and write in their native tongue and in English. Along with the religious and cultural changes set in motion by the missionaries came extensive economic changes. The newcomers and their descendants intermarried with the local Hawaiians, acquired land rights, and attempted diverse agricultural projects—growing coffee, rice, mulberries, sugar, and pineapples. The development of sugar plantations stimulated the introduction of the many ethnic groups that today, in various mixtures, constitute Kauai's polyglot population. The town of Koloa was the site of the first successful sugar plantation, established in 1835 by three Americans on about 1,000 acres of land leased to them by Kauikeaouli, king of Kauai. Koloa Plantation is still in operation today. It celebrated its 150th anniversary in 1985, when we began the 30-year follow-up of our longitudinal study.

The immigration of large numbers of Chinese, Japanese, and Portuguese (from the Azores and Madeira) as plantation laborers occurred during the second half of the nineteenth century. At the same time, Germans and Scots brought their technical skills to the growing sugar industry. During the early twentieth century, Puerto Ricans and Koreans came to Kauai, followed by large numbers of Pilipinos. Today, immigrants from the Philippine Islands constitute a large proportion of the newcomers to the island.

Economic and Social Changes

The parents of the 1955 birth cohort had been a part of these early immigrant families, some as first generation, others as second or third generation. They brought to Kauai a mixture of tongues (from Cantonese and Hakka to Japanese and Korean, from Spanish and Portuguese to Ilocano and Tagalog). They belonged to a variety of religions, from Buddhism to Shintoism, from Catholicism to Fundamentalist Protestant faiths. Their lives had been directly involved in the conflict of changing cultures.

Their children, however, have been fairly well assimilated in the local island culture. Their parents had experienced the hardships of the Great Depression and of several wars (World War II, the Korean War). The young men and women in the 1955 cohort, however, were born after the Korean War had ended, in a period of relative peace and prosperity in the United States.

On Kauai, at the time of their birth, agriculture was the principal industry; sugar and pineapple were the two most important crops. A plantation style of life predominated. People lived in small towns and plantation camps scattered around the shoreline and connected by a highway that now reaches three-quarters of the way around the island, ending in the north, where cliffs rise steeply from the edge of the Pacific Ocean.

In contrast to the mainland United States in the mid 1950s, the economy of Kauai was somewhat depressed. Pay scales were rather low at that time, and the plantations were finding it necessary to lay off workers as they mechanized their operations and turned them into "factories in the field." While unionization had greatly increased benefits for agricultural workers, competition from areas where labor was cheaper and more readily available resulted in the beginning of the decline of the sugar industry and in the eventual closing, by the end of the 1960s, of all of Kauai's pineapple plantations.

The children in our longitudinal study were in grade school when President John F. Kennedy, his brother Robert Kennedy, and Martin Luther King were assassinated and when the Civil Rights Movement and the War on Poverty captured national attention. They grew up under the shadow of the war in Vietnam, and some of their fathers and older brothers served on the battlefields in Southeast Asia. By the time they were in their mid-teens, television showed them man's first landing on the moon. The events of the 1960s in the United States presented intensity of conflict, disruption, and emotional upheaval.

During that same period, the Hawaiian islands were experiencing social and economic changes of a magnitude they had not seen since the early days of European and American contact. In August 1959, Hawaii became the fiftieth state of the union. With statehood came the biggest expansion in its history. Military spending poured millions of dollars into the island economy, making it the number-one business in the new state. By the 1960s, tourism had become the number-two industry. Both these businesses soon surpassed the sugar and pineapple industries.

The population expanded and construction boomed. Hawaii became one of the fastest-growing areas in the United States. Personal incomes rose, new educational and job opportunities became available, real estate values increased dramatically, and land issues became inseparable from politics. Thus, as they approached young adulthood, the members of the 1955 birth cohort were exposed to challenges and opportunities undreamed of by their parents.

The shift from an agricultural to a tourist-oriented economy brought with it an influx of mainlanders to Kauai—coast *haoles* (Hawaiian for strangers), mostly from California and other western states. They first came as transients, but some settled on Kauai and became long-time residents. The "hippies" of the 1960s were followed by the surfers, hotel workers, and entrepreneurs of the visitor industry in the 1970s.

In the 1970s and early 1980s, the drug scene began to develop. Kauai and the other Hawaiian islands are now famous for their high-quality marijuana crop. This nontaxable "industry" has fast become one of the major agricultural crops of the island. Cocaine use has increased as well. A number of the men and women in this cohort experimented with drugs in their teens and in young adulthood, and some now have criminal records for narcotic offenses. New waves of religious groups and fringe cults invaded the hospitable island as well and changed forever what was once a conservative traditional rural setting. Some of the more vulnerable individuals in this birth cohort were attracted to these movements.

Environmental Issues

With the growth of tourism, concern about the protection of Kauai's natural and cultural environment began to grow. The first meaningful protest against uncontrolled growth on the island took place in 1974, and among its leaders were members of the 1955 birth cohort who had recently graduated from high school. A thousand-acre coastal area on Kauai's South Shore (Mahaulepu) had been proposed for development into a resort community, featuring three hotels and several thousand condominium units. The Ohana o Mahaulepu, an organization made up primarily of young local residents, succeeded in convincing Hawaii's State Land Use Commission to reject the developers' request for redistricting. Later disclosures discredited the developer and the county mayor, and the area was "saved"—at least for the time being.

During this same decade several other environmental battles were fought on Kauai. Receiving the greatest public attention was Nukolii, a wind-swept parcel of land near Lihue, the county seat. It had been approved for development by the State Land Use Commission and by other agencies of the county of Kauai. Public protest brought about a referendum in 1980, which resulted in a 2–1 defeat of the project. Although a successful initiative campaign two years later resulted in a permit for the construction of a hotel at Nukolii, the earlier victory had done much to encourage the people of Kauai to speak out.

Although the island community was polarized by these environmental issues, the men and women in our study had learned a significant lesson in self-determination. In contrast to many of their parents, they began to perceive themselves as movers of their destiny rather than as pawns in a power game played by outsiders. These local issues probably served even more than the broader issues of the national scene—the end of the war in Vietnam, the OPEC-dominated energy crisis—to influence the attitudes of Kauai's children as they came of age.

Expansion of Educational and Social Services

Together with the dramatic economic and social changes during the past decades, there has also been a considerable expansion of educational and social services for the residents of the island. Even at birth, the children of the 1955 cohort had easy access (at no or low cost) to excellent health facilities, provided by the plantations and the territorial government. When the study began in 1955, thirteen physicians were practicing on the island; thirty years later, in 1985, there were more than sixty. Three hospitals now serve Kauai. Whereas mental health services were earlier provided by one resident social worker and an itinerant psychiatrist and psychologist, the island now has four psychiatrists, three licensed psychologists, and several social workers and counselors in private practice.

Kauai has a private Child and Family Service, as well as a Children's Mental Health Team. In- and out-patient services that meet the mental health needs of adults are provided by the state of Hawaii. Other agencies, both public and private, have specialized professional teams that serve the health, educational, and social needs of the island community. Among them are the Department of Social Services and Housing, the Department of Health, the Department of Education, the Family Court, the Division of Vocational Rehabilitation, Serenity House (for the treatment of substance abuse), and Kauai Economic Opportunity, Inc. Voluntary groups—including the Big Brothers and Big Sisters associations of Kauai, the YMCA and the YWCA, the Boy Scouts and Girl Scouts, 4-H, the Civil Air Patrol, and athletic groups such as Little League and Pop Warner—support a variety of programs with both a recreational and treatment-oriented focus.

Educational opportunities are available in Kauai institutions from preschool to college. In addition to a number of private preschools, including one where the Hawaiian language is taught, Kauai has a Headstart program, which serves about one hundred children. Some are the sons and daughters of members of the 1955 cohort. Kauai Community College (KCC), a part of the University of Hawaii system, opened its doors in 1968. In 1976 it moved to a new expanded campus, where undergraduate programs as well as adult education and other community activities are on the increase. For a substantial number of individuals in our study, KCC has provided an avenue for additional schooling after they had left high school.

Changing Social Laws

In 1970 the repeal of Hawaii's law against abortion marked a major turning point in the state's legal history, at a time when the young women in our cohort reached childbearing age. Before this time, Hawaii had a century-old criminal abortion statute. Public attitudes about abortion had begun to change in the late 1960s, when several states in the union broadened their definitions of permissible conditions for abortion. Hawaii was the first state in the union where a fundamental change in the law, rather than a simple modification of conditions, occurred. That this happened three years before the U.S. Supreme Court decision of 1973 declared restrictive abortion laws unconstitutional speaks to the capacity for social change which has come about in the islands during their short history as the youngest of the United States. Hawaii has also been one of the first states in the union to ratify the Equal Rights Amendment for women.

In Hawaii, as on the mainland, controversy about abortion still abounds. There is opposition by Right to Life movements and the Catholic Diocese of Hawaii, and many physicians exercise their right to refuse to perform abortions. In spite of continuing differences of opinion on this issue, the women in our cohort who became pregnant had a choice early on of terminating or continuing their pregnancies, and some of the pregnant teenagers in our cohort did opt for abortions.

The state of Hawaii also has a liberal no-fault divorce law that has been passed since the men and women of the 1955 birth cohort came of age. (It was last amended in 1973.) One out of six among the men and women in our study had opted for a divorce before age 30, under the affirmation that their marriage was irretrievably broken (MIB). Such a divorce becomes final in Hawaii no later than one month from the date of the decree.

If a parent is delinquent in child-support payment in an amount equal to or greater than the sum of payments that become due over one month, the courts in Hawaii can automatically order an assignment of future earnings or income in the amount adequate to ensure that past-due payments and payments due in the future will be paid. The wages of a number of delinquent parents were garnished to protect the court-ordered support payments for their children. Thus the members of this birth cohort have both options and obligations as marriage partners and parents which are different from those of earlier generations on Kauai.

Concerns about the Future of Kauai

In November 1982, Kauai was hit by Hurricane Iwa, the worst disaster in its history. The devastation caused by this severe storm resulted in millions of dollars in losses to the economy of the island; however, it also served as a catalyst in uniting people of different ethnic backgrounds and political persuasions to work for the restoration of the island's facilities and resources.

Hurricane Iwa occurred at a time when the United States had been experiencing its worst economic decline since the Great Depression, when the once-booming real estate market in Hawaii had suffered severe losses, and when competition for the declining tourist market was intense. Once the initial damage had been repaired, Kauai, under the leadership of a protourism county administration, began a campaign to entice visitors to its shores once more, especially those from the Orient.

Three years later, when our follow-up began in 1985, the men and women in our study had reached the median age of Kauai's population (30.9 years). The number of local residents had increased from 28,000 in 1955 to 45,400 in 1985. Males now exceed females by about 1,700. The number of hotel and apartment units had more than doubled from 2,628 in 1970 to 5,922 in 1985. The number of jobs generated by the tourist industry had increased in the same time from 4,450 (in 1970) to 13,120 (in 1985), and to 15,660 a year later. At any given day in 1985, every fourth person on the island was a tourist. (The 1985 census reported an average number of 11,470 visitors per day.) The island had come a long way since the first McDonald's restaurant opened in 1971 and the first urban traffic light was installed in 1973.

Meanwhile, the controversy between those on Kauai who are prodevelopment and those favoring slow or no growth continues—fueled by the projections of the chief economist of the First Hawaiian Bank that by 2010 half of the people on Kauai will be tourists and the resident population will have doubled. The coexistence of inadequate infrastructures with world-class resort hotels provokes frustration and heated debates on the island; these are duly reported by the two newspapers, the two radio stations, and a television station that are now part of Kauai's communication network. Meanwhile, more tourists arrive at the two airports, near Lihue and Princeville.

In the face of such projections, concern over the future of the island's ecosystem assumes major proportions. In 1972, Kauai's teenagers reacted to the influx of "coast haole" surfers by merely complaining, "They steal our waves." Now these young adults are taking a more active role in fighting to protect the island and its resources. They are a generation who take pride in their varied ethnic backgrounds and who want to preserve the delicate island ecosystem that is their home. That attitude represents perhaps the most significant change on Kauai in the past thirty years.

It has become a custom in recent years for the people of the island to join hands and sing "Hawaii Aloha" at the end of many group gatherings—parties, political meetings, graduations, commemorative events, and celebrations. The words of the missionary Lorenzo Lyon perhaps best reflect the common feelings the children of Kauai have developed about their island home as they grew into adults. Even those who now live on the mainland or abroad, far from their birthplace, treasure the deep ties that bind them to Kauai.

O Hawaii, my own birthplace, my own land
Our dear islands, long as mountains stand.
I will sing of truth and justice, heavenly peace
I will sing of Hawaii Nei . . .

Research Strategy

We chose the island of Kauai for a number of reasons: Here we found a population with low mobility and with coverage by medical, public-health, educational, and social services that compared favorably with most communities of similar size on the U.S. mainland. Also present was a rich opportunity to study a variety of cultural influences on child-bearing and child rearing. Kauai's unique spirit of cooperation (*kokua*) has enabled us to carry out this long-term study with a maximum of good will and a minimum of attrition. Our research enterprise relied on the skills of dedicated professionals from the University of California, the state of Hawaii, and the community agencies on Kauai.

Most of the children in the 1955 birth cohort, some three out of four, come from one of the three major ethnic groups on Kauai: the Japanese, the Pilipino, and the part and full Hawaiians. The others are ethnic mixtures that include children of parents from two different non-Hawaiian and non-Caucasian descent groups. In this birth cohort, they were mostly children of younger Japanese mothers and older Pilipino fathers. About half of the cohort (some 54 percent) grew up in poverty; they were reared by fathers who were semi- or unskilled laborers on the plantations and by mothers who had not graduated from high school. We give here a brief account of how we assessed the individual members of this cohort and their family members at each of the five stages of this longitudinal study.

The Prenatal and Perinatal Periods

Early on in the study, public health nurses recorded the reproductive histories of women who were to give birth in 1955 and interviewed them in each trimester of pregnancy, noting any exposure to physical or emotional trauma. Local physicians monitored any complications that occurred during the prenatal, labor, delivery, and neonatal periods. A clinical rating ("pre/perinatal stress score"), based on the presence of conditions thought to have had a possible deleterious effect on the fetus or newborn infant, was assigned to each child by a study pediatrician and reviewed by a second pediatrician for consistency. Appendix II gives a summary of the scoring system for pre/perinatal complications that ranged from mild (1) to moderate (2) to severe (3).

Birth–Age 2

In the postpartum period and again when the babies were one year old, public health and social workers interviewed the mothers at home. The mothers rated the infants on a number of temperamental characteristics, such as activity level, social responsiveness, and ease of handling, and reported any distressing habits, such as temper tantrums or irregular sleeping or feeding habits. The interviewers checked a series of adjectives that characterized the mother's interaction with the infant and inquired about stressful life events that had occurred between birth and the baby's first birthday.

Two board-certified pediatricians from Honolulu periodically came to Kauai to conduct a medical examination when the children were approximately age 2. A systematic appraisal of all organ systems yielded an assessment of each child's overall physical status (rated superior, normal, below normal, or retarded). Independently, two psychologists from the University of Hawaii assessed the children's cognitive development with the Cattell Infant Intelligence Scale and self-help skills with the Vineland Social Maturity Scale. They completed adjective checklists to describe the behavior of the toddler and the parent-child interactions during the testing session. They also asked the mother about any stressful life events that had occurred between the infant's first and second birthday.

The following environmental dimensions were noted to reflect intellectual stimulation, material opportunities, and emotional support available to the child from birth to age 2: (1) *mother's educational level*, based on number of years of completed schooling (from school records that also included IQ scores for 485 parents); (2) *socioeconomic status* (SES), based on father's occupation, standard of living, condition of housing, and crowding; (3) *family stability*, based on information from the home visits and interviews (at birth, age 1, and age 2) on presence or absence of the father, marital discord, alcoholism, parental mental health problems, and long-term separations of the young child from the mother without an adequate substitute caregiver. The ratings were made on a 5-point scale, ranging from very favorable (1) to very unfavorable (5). The correlation among the three ratings ranged from .33 (SES/mother's education) to .03 (mother's education/family stability).

The 10-Year Follow-up

The field staff collected existing information about each of the children in the 1955 birth cohort from records of local physicians, hospitals, the Department of Health, the Division of Mental Health Services, the Department of Social Services and Housing, and the Division of Special Services of the Department of Education.

The field staff obtained new information about each child from (1) a home interview with the primary caregiver, covering illnesses, accidents, and hospitalizations of children between ages 2 and 10 and stressful life events and behavior problems observed at home; (2) a questionnaire filled out by the current teacher, including grades in reading, writing, and arithmetic and a checklist of behavior problems observed in the classroom; (3) results of two group tests administered by a clinical psychologist—the Bender Gestalt and the Primary Mental Abilities (PMA) test—sampling reasoning, verbal, numerical, spatial, and perceptual-motor skills. Some 30 percent of the children with learning and/or behavior problems received additional diagnostic examinations from appropriate specialists.

The combined screening and diagnostic information was reviewed by a panel of the resident study staff, consisting of a pediatrician, a psychologist, and a public health nurse, who prepared a need-assessment for each child, estimating the effect of any existing handicap on school progress and the need for future care (medical, remedial education, or mental health services).

Also, when the child was age 10, public health nurses and social workers visited the home and assessed the quality of the caregiving environment from standardized interviews with the mother or mother substitute. With this information, three environmental ratings were created.

The rating of the family's *socioeconomic status* combined information on father's occupation, income, steadiness of employment, and condition of housing. It was based primarily on father's occupation, categorized into one of five levels: (1) professional; (2) semiprofessional, proprietorial, or managerial; (3) skilled trade and technical; (4) semiskilled; (5) day laborer and unskilled.

The rating of *educational stimulation* took into account opportunities provided for enlarging the child's vocabulary, the intellectual interests and activities of the family, the value the family placed on education, and opportunities for exploration of the community at large (library and recreational facilities).

The rating of *emotional support* took into account the information given in the interview on interpersonal relations between the parents and the child, availability of role models, methods of discipline, ways of expressing approval, and stressful life events encountered by the child between the ages of 2 and 10.

These three ratings were made by a clinical psychologist (independently of any knowledge of the children's earlier scores) on a 5-point scale ranging from very high (1) to high (2), adequate (3), low (4) to very low (5). The intercorrelations between the ratings ranged from .57 (SES/educational stimulation) to .37 (SES/emotional support).

The 18-Year Follow-up

When the cohort was 18, the study team searched educational, health, mental health and social service agency records, including police and family court records, for information on the entire group, and administered group tests of ability and achievement in the high schools. This screening process helped us to locate youths who had become delinquent or had developed serious mental health problems and girls who had become pregnant. In addition, a brief biographical questionnaire asking for information on educational status and plans, vocational status and plans, marital and health status, and stressful life events experienced in adolescence was mailed to each member of the 1955 birth cohort in self-addressed and stamped return envelopes.

Two psychologists from the study team also conducted an in-depth study via clinical interviews and personality tests of high risk youths with serious coping problems (repeated delinquencies, chronic mental health problems, teenage pregnancies), and of control groups without problems, matched by age, gender, ethnicity, and socioeconomic status. We used the California Psychological Inventory (CPI) to obtain (1) measures of self-assurance and interpersonal adequacy, (2) measures of socialization and responsibility, (3) measures of achievement potential and intellectual efficiency, and (4) measures of intellectual and interest modes. We used the Nowicki Locus of Control Scale to ascertain the youths' faith in the effectiveness of their own actions. The semistructured interview explored the youths' attitudes toward school, their current interests and activities, their occupational plans, and their participation in and satisfaction with work and social life. The youths were asked about their preference in friends, their perspectives on their own strengths and weaknesses, and matters about which they worried. The interview yielded a number of ratings on a 5-point scale from (1)—very high—to (5)—very low. Among the dimensions rated were overall attitude toward school, achievement motivation, realism of educational and vocational plans, overall social adjustment (with peers), overall family adjustment, and self-esteem. Reliabilities of interview ratings, made independently of the other follow-up data, ranged from the eighties to the nineties.

In the 18-year interview a number of questions dealt with the quality of the family life the youths had experienced in adolescence. We explored their attitudes toward kin and neighbors, the stressful life events they encountered in their teens, their feelings of security or conflict with regard to their families, and the degree of their identification with their fathers and mothers.

We also asked for an evaluation of the help they had received from informal and formal sources of support—such as siblings, peers, older friends, teachers, ministers, mental health professionals, and community agencies. The latter contacts were verified in the records of the local social service agencies and also provided an independent check on stressful life events that had occurred in adolescence.

The Follow-up at Age 31/32

Our principal concern in the present phase of our study has been to trace the different paths that led most men and women from an adverse childhood or youth to successful adaptation in adulthood. We wanted to examine the long-term consequences of stressful events in their earlier lives as well as the protective factors or mechanisms that contributed to their well-being and success in adulthood.

The previous follow-up stages had yielded a wealth of information on earlier stressful life events and potential buffers in the lives of these high risk individuals. We now needed to assess how well they had accomplished the transition into the world of work, marriage, and parenthood and what sources of support and inner strengths they could draw on to deal with the stressful events of their adult lives.

Perspectives and Procedures

We used two perspectives to assess the quality of adult adaptation of the men and women in our study. One was the perspective gained from a semistructured interview (questionnaire) that focused on the developmental tasks of early adulthood (Havighurst, 1972). We explored the ways in which the men and women had dealt with getting started in occupations, with selecting marriage partners or friends for a long-term commitment, their struggles with managing homes of their own, their attitudes toward bearing and rearing children, their search for congenial social groups, their concerns with civic responsibility, and their satisfaction with their accomplishments at the present stage of life (see Appendix II for a copy of the interview and questionnaire).

The responses to the interview questions permit us to make some judgment on how well a given individual has negotiated Erikson's stages of identity, intimacy, and generativity (Erikson, 1959). They allow for comparisons with the adult life course of the children of the Great Depression (Elder, 1974, 1985) and with the studies of life transitions at the University of California at San Francisco (Fiske and Chiriboga, 1990; Lowenthal et al., 1977), and they tap dimensions explored by Vaillant and his associates in the Harvard studies of adult development (Long and Vaillant, 1984; Vaillant and Milofsky, 1980).

A second complementary perspective on the quality of adult adaptation of the men and women in this cohort was gleaned from their records in the community. From the district and circuit courts on Kauai, in Honolulu, and on the other islands (Maui and Hawaii) we obtained information on every member of the 1955 birth cohort residing in the state of Hawaii who was convicted of a crime, involved as a defendant in a civil suit, or whose marriage had ended in divorce since our last follow-up. The files of the criminal, civil, and family courts (which are open to the public) contain not only records of major violations of the law but also information on domestic problems, such as delinquent child support payments and child and spouse abuse. From the state Department of Mental Health (which maintains a statewide mental health registry) we ascertained information on every member of the 1955 birth cohort who received in- or outpatient treatment for mental health problems or whose parents had such treatment. (We used code numbers to safeguard confidentiality.) From the state Department of Health we obtained records of the causes of death for members of the 1955 birth cohort who were deceased; and the Department of Social Services, Division of Vocational Rehabilitation, informed us about special services rendered to cohort members who had disabilities. Last, but not least, the U.S. Veteran's Administration provided us with information on cohort members who had served in the armed forces since they had left high school and who had received disability payments or educational benefits.

Our criteria for rating the quality of adult adaptation are based on these two perspectives: the individuals' own account of success and satisfaction with work, family and social life, and state of psychological well-being and on their records in the community. Areas included in the evaluation were achievements in school and/or work; relationships with spouse or mate; relationships with offspring; relationships with parents, in-laws, and siblings; relationships with peers; and the degree of overall satisfaction an individual expressed with his or her present state in life. A criminal record, a record of spouse or child abuse or delinquent child support, and a record of chronic substance abuse, and/or psychosomatic or psychiatric disorders were considered signs of unsuccessful adaptation to adult life. Our rating scheme is described in detail at the end of Appendix II.

We had reasons to believe from our previous follow-up studies (Werner and Smith, 1982) that the cumulative number of stressful life events an individual encountered at any given stage of the life cycle might shift the balance from resiliency to vulnerability for even the most hardy. Since the early adult and age-30 transition periods are among the most stressful in the life cycle, we needed information on life events that had been experienced by the men and women in our cohort since we last saw them at age 18. We obtained this information with a "Life Event Checklist" that included a list of events commonly perceived as stressful in adult life, such as loss of a job, breakup of a long-term relationship or marriage, illness of dependents (parents or children), personal injury, death of spouse or child (see Appendix II). Perceived stress in these areas had been shown to affect the sense of well-being among the men and women who faced incremental transitions in the *Four Stages of Life* study by Lowenthal and her associates (1977).

We also expected that some troubled adolescents, after leaving an adverse home situation, might find opportunities or supportive persons that would bolster their faith in the efficacy of their own actions and lead them on the road to recovery. We therefore asked each participant in the 31/32-year follow-up to check a list of sources of support they had encountered since we last saw them in the 18-year follow-up (see Appendix II). We also asked them to complete Rotter's Locus of Control Scale (1966), which assesses the degree to which a person believes that he or she is in control of his or her own life (internal) and the degree to which events are perceived to be a result of fate, luck, or other factors beyond personal control (external). At age 18, such a locus of control measure had differentiated significantly between high risk youths in this cohort who did and those who did not develop serious delinquencies, mental health problems, or teenage pregnancies (Werner and Smith, 1982). A follow-up of the teenage mothers in this cohort at age 26 by one of our students (Gonsalves, 1982) had shown a significant change in perceived locus of control from an external to an internal direction for young women who had gone back to school and obtained steady employment in their 20s.

We expected that these turnarounds (for better or for worse) in the adult lives of high risk individuals might be dependent on temperamental characteristics that made it easier (or harder) for a man or woman to seek or elicit new opportunities (Scarr and McCartney, 1983). Hence we asked each of the participants in our 31/32-year follow-up study to complete the EAS Temperament Survey for Adults (Buss and Plomin, 1984). It assesses dimensions of temperament (activity level, excitability, and sociability) which have shown a fair degree of stability at different stages of the life cycle (Chess and Thomas, 1984). In infancy and early childhood, these temperamental characteristics had differentiated significantly between high risk individuals in our cohort who were resilient and those who developed serious learning and/or behavior problems by ages 10 or 18. We expected that they would correlate with the quality of adult adaptation as well.

The Tracing Process

Early in 1985 we began the search for the members of the 1955 birth cohort with the help of their parents and relatives, friends, former classmates, local telephone books, city directories, and circuit court, voter registration, and motor vehicle registration records on Kauai and the other Hawaiian islands. The tracing process was complex and time consuming.

The search required a fair amount of ingenuity by the principal investigators and members of the field staff located on Kauai, in Honolulu, and on the neighboring islands. Two major changes since our last follow-up impeded our search for up-to-date addresses for individual members of the 1955 birth cohort: (1) addresses on Kauai had changed from P.O. boxes to street addresses and rural delivery, and the post office no longer made heroic efforts to locate people with insufficient addresses; (2) a high proportion of the residents of Kauai (and the state of Hawaii) had unlisted phone numbers, so that their addresses could not be checked against phone directory listings.

On the positive side, the state Department of Health in Honolulu is the central repository of all marriage certificates issued in the Hawaiian Islands. Hence we were able to trace the new addresses and names of members of the 1955 cohort who had married since our last follow-up with the help of their good offices.

The majority of the surviving members of the 1955 birth cohort still lived on Kauai. Some 10 percent had moved to other Hawaiian islands (Hawaii, Maui, Oahu)—most to Honolulu. Another 10 percent settled on the U.S. mainland and were scattered in some twenty states (from Maine to Florida, from the state of Washington to New Mexico and Texas; from New York to California). Two percent lived abroad—in Australia's Northern Territory, Japan, the Western Carolina Islands, Samoa, the Netherlands, and the Federal Republic of Germany. We noted some selective migration: by age 30, most of the individuals who had problems in school at age 10 or had records of serious delinquencies, mental health problems, or teenage pregnancies still lived on the small island of Kauai. Many still lived with parents or in-laws. In contrast, many of the resilient individuals who had coped well during childhood and adolescence, in spite of their high risk status, had moved to Honolulu and the U.S. mainland, and some lived abroad.

The most elusive among the members of the 1955 birth cohort were individuals who had developed serious mental health problems by age 18. Nearly a third could not be traced by mail, telephone, or existing records—nor was their whereabouts known by their parents, other family members, or former classmates or friends. A number of these individuals were located with the help of the mental health registry of the state of Hawaii (if they had been referred to a public agency in the islands for mental health services) and by the U.S. Veteran's Administration (if they had a record of military service and subsequently received disability or educational benefit payments).

In 1986/87, we contacted every member of the 1955 birth cohort whom we had been able to trace by repeated letters (up to three mailings) and follow-up phone conversations and invited their participation in the study. Individuals who were interviewed or who returned by mail the close-ended structured questionnaire and the tests were paid twenty dollars for their efforts. A significant number refused to accept this modest stipend and, instead, expressed their appreciation for having been included as participants in the study.

To members of the 1955 cohort who had not responded to our request for an interview and to the second mailing of the questionnaires and tests, an abbreviated biographical form was mailed early in 1988 which requested information on marital status, number of children, additional schooling, employment, a rating of satisfaction with work, marriage, and children, health problems, major worries, major sources of support, and an overall rating of life satisfaction (the questionnaire appears in Appendix II). Individuals were requested to return this form and the tests by mid-April 1988 and were paid fifteen dollars for their cooperation. At that time, the data collection process was completed.

The Participants

We have follow-up data in adulthood on 505 individuals who range in age from 31.0 to 32.4 years. They represent 82 percent of the 614 surviving members of the 1955 birth cohort for whom 1-, 2-, 10- and 18-year data are available (see Table I in Appendix I). Our attrition rate compares favorably with those reported by two major longitudinal studies on the U.S. mainland: On the East Coast, Furstenberg and his associates (1987) managed to reach 72 percent of their original target group of teenage mothers in their early 30s; and on the West Coast, Block (1971) was able to follow 70 percent of the youths from the Berkeley Guidance and Oakland Growth studies into their mid-30s.

We were fortunate to reach a relatively high proportion of the original high risk sample in our cohort, individuals who grew up in childhood poverty and in troubled families. We have data in adulthood on 88 percent of the resilient high risk individuals and on 80 percent of the high risk youths who had records of serious delinquencies, mental health problems, or teenage pregnancies. There was some overlap among the problem groups. Twenty percent of the males and 28 percent of the females among the high risk troubled teens in our follow-up had records of both juvenile offenses and mental health problems.

The individuals with previous problems on whom we have follow-up data in their early 30s do not differ significantly by gender, ethnicity, socioeconomic status, perinatal stress scores, and 10-year PMA IQ from those on whom we were unable to obtain the later data. The same holds for the individuals without previous coping problems at ages 10 or 18. On the whole, sample attrition did not appear to introduce any selective bias in our results.

3

Ordinary People

Most men and women in this cohort led ordinary lives. Their accomplishments are a tribute to their own competence and determination but also to the confidence and hope of their immigrant parents and grandparents who came to the island in search of a better life for their children and grandchildren. Most of these immigrants, though poor by material standards, kept their dreams of the "good life" while they worked on the plantations—their hopes for better education and better jobs for their children. Did their dreams materialize? Readers can judge for themselves.

Educational Accomplishments

Ninety-seven percent of the 1955 cohort had graduated from high school; only 3 percent dropped out without receiving graduation certificates. This is a remarkably low rate of educational waste when compared with a national dropout rate of 11.5 percent for the men and 11.4 percent for the women who attended U.S. high schools during the same period (*Current Population Survey*, 1986). It is a tribute to the efforts of the Kauai public school system, which reached potential dropouts through work-motivation classes, special classes for pregnant teenagers, off-campus classrooms, and outreach counselors. It is also a tribute to the parents' steadfast belief in the value of education.

Few of the immigrant parents on Kauai, with the exception of the Japanese, had themselves been high school graduates. In 1950 the median years of schooling for the mothers' generation of Kauai women 25 years or older was eight grades; median years of schooling for the fathers' generation of Kauai men 25 years or older was only six grades, an educational status reflecting the presence of the older immigrant sector of the population, especially the Pilipinos.

By age 31/32, 88 percent of the men in the 1955 birth cohort and 80 percent of the women had some additional schooling beyond high school. National rates, in contrast, were considerably lower. The U.S. Census Bureau reports that 52.7 percent of the men and 50.4 percent of the women in the same age group have some college or technical education (*Current Population Survey*, 1986).

More than half of the members of the 1955 birth cohort had attended college—either the local junior college, the University of Hawaii, or a college on the West Coast of the U.S. mainland. Nine percent of the men and 12 percent of the women went on to graduate or professional school. The proportion of men from Kauai who attended graduate or professional schools was somewhat lower than the national average of 12.6 percent for males; the proportion of women from Kauai who attended graduate or professional schools was somewhat higher than national rates of 10 percent for this age group (*Current Population Survey*, 1986).

Many youths on Kauai had worked during the summers when they were still in high school to save money for college; some had taken on loans to free their parents from expenditures that involved not only tuition but room and board and travel to the mainland. Those heading for college, if they came from poor homes, used a stepwise approach: the first two years at the Kauai Community College, the next two years at the University of Hawaii in Honolulu or Hilo, and then graduate school in Honolulu or on the mainland. Some 24 percent of the men and some 2.5 percent of the women in this cohort joined the armed forces and used their benefits to further their education. Voluntary enlistment rates in the armed forces were considerably higher for the men of Kauai than national rates for Caucasian males (13.6%) and comparable to those reported nationwide for Black males (23.9%) of the same age (*Current Population Survey*, 1986).

The local community college and the armed forces became important gateways to higher education and occupational advancement for many young men and women in this cohort who are now the first college-educated generation in their family. About half in this group (M: 48.4%; F: 54.0%) reported that they had done very well in school; some 40 percent (M: 43.3%; F: 40.2%) rated their educational accomplishment as adequate.

Two-thirds of the men and three-fourths of the women noted that additional schooling beyond high school had improved their skills and competencies for jobs. A significantly higher proportion of the women than men also appreciated the social contacts they had made with classmates and teachers (M: 22%; F: 55%).

Work Experience

About one-half of the men and women in this cohort had some work experience during high school or were working by the time they had reached age 18, a proportion comparable to that reported from surveys on the U.S. mainland (Eichorn and Stern, 1989). The jobs held by the men and women in their senior year in high school were fairly sex-typed: most of the young men were working in filling stations and garages (46%) or as plantation laborers (26%). Others worked as busboys at the local hotels, did yard work, or worked as recreation aides and tourist guides. The most common jobs for the young women in high school were in food services in the island's restaurants (44%) and as salespersons in local retail stores (26%). Others did clerical work, babysat, or served as health or recreation aides.

By the time we interviewed these same men and women at age 31/32, most were in full-time employment and satisfied with their work. Four percent of the men and 12 percent of the women were currently unemployed. Unemployment rates for the men of Kauai were lower than the nationwide average for American men in their early 30s (6.7%). In contrast, unemployment rates for the women of Kauai were higher than the national average for U.S. women of their age (6.3%) but comparable to unemployment rates of 30-year-old Black women (12.9%; *Current Population Survey*, 1986).

Most members of this cohort had held at least five jobs before their present ones. The majority had reached an occupational level above that of their parents by the time they were in their early 30s. Forty-two percent of the fathers had worked in semiskilled jobs, and 14 percent in unskilled and day labor jobs on the plantations or in the tourist industry on the island. In contrast, fewer than 15 percent of the sons and only 12 percent of the daughters in this cohort worked in semiskilled jobs, and fewer than 2 percent were unskilled day laborers—rates comparable to those reported for employed men and women of their generation on the U.S. mainland (*Current Population Survey*, 1986).

Only 7 percent of the parents had been engaged in semiprofessional, proprietary, or managerial jobs. In contrast, some 29 percent of the sons and some 18 percent of the daughters in this cohort held such jobs. While only 2 percent of the parents' generation held professional jobs, some 13 percent of the sons and some 15 percent of the daughters were now in the professions, as architects, dentists, doctors, engineers, lawyers, ministers, and teachers. The most prevalent employment on the island in this generation as in the past, however, was in the skilled and technical trades, which employed some 40 percent of the men and women in this cohort. This was in line with nationwide trends reported by the U.S. Department of Labor at that time (*Current Population Survey*, 1986).

There is certainly no indication that the members of this cohort have rejected their parents' beliefs in occupational advancement and the advantages of middle class life. Indeed, career or job success was one of the primary goals of this cohort, outdistancing more traditional objectives such as a happy marriage, children, and close relationships with family and friends. This was especially true for the women, who valued the interpersonal aspects of work more than the men did (M: 23%; F: 55%) and who more often derived self-respect from work. None of the men but 8 percent of the women felt that their work enhanced their family lives. In contrast, 10 percent of the men, but none of the women felt that their work had led to the breakup of their family lives.

Marriage

By age 32, a lower proportion of men than women on Kauai had made the transition into marriage. Some 60 percent of the men and some 76 percent of the women in this cohort had been married at least once by this time. Comparable rates nationwide were 64.7 percent for U.S. men and 68.5 percent for U.S. women in the same age group (*Current Population Survey*, 1986).

Most men and women appeared satisfied with the choice of their marriage partners and reported little conflict in their present relationships. Fifteen percent of the men and 22 percent of the women, however, did report strained relationships; and one out of six of the first marriages in this cohort had ended in divorce. The divorce rates for this cohort are higher than rates reported nationwide for men and women of the same age (M: 8.5%; F: 11.5%)—probably because Hawaiian divorce laws make the dissolution of a marriage easier than do laws in most of the United States. (see Chapter 2).

Some 4 percent of the divorced men and women in this cohort have since remarried. Ever hopeful, the majority of the men and women we interviewed still expected permanency and a sense of security from their new marriages or relationships. A significantly higher proportion of women than men expected intimacy and sharing from those relationships and valued the interpersonal aspects of marriage (M: 45%; F: 65%). A higher proportion of women than men preferred to resolve conflicts in their relationships by discussion and a joint resolution (M: 38.1%; F: 55.3%).

Children

A lower proportion of men (56%) than women (65%) in this cohort had made the transition into parenthood by age 32, but men and women were alike in their appreciation of and hopes for their children. Both mothers and fathers saw as the most positive aspect of being a parent "the pleasure of seeing the child grow." A higher proportion of women than men stressed "the opportunity to care for others" and "the belief in the future" that came with parenthood (M: 22%; F: 32.4%). The overwhelming majority of both men and women hoped that their children would acquire the competencies and skills required for economic survival (M: 64.7%; F: 62.5%), but a higher proportion of women than men stressed high achievement for their children (M: 41.2%; F: 53.1%). In contrast, a higher proportion of men than women wanted their children to be happy and satisfied with their lives (M: 35.3%; F: 28%).

Both men and women admitted that the proper discipline of their children was the most difficult aspect of being a parent. The majority reported that they had rules and regulations for their children which were negotiable (M: 61.1%; F: 68.6%). Most of the men and half of the women used both reasoning and physical punishment in disciplining their children. A higher proportion of women than men stressed early independence in their children (M: 57.1%; F: 65.6%). In contrast, a higher proportion of men than women tolerated dependence in younger children (M: 35.7%; F: 25%).

Three out of every four men but only one out of every three women reported that they divided their child-rearing responsibilities equally with their mates. Nearly half of all women still had the major responsibility for child rearing, although they were full-time workers and wives as well. What help they obtained in child care came mostly from parents, parents-in-law, and siblings, not from professionals—a trend that has been confirmed nationwide in the United States (Werner, 1984).

Social Relations

About one out of every six cohort members (M: 15.5%; F: 16.8%) had lost their fathers by the time they reached their early 30s—most had died after a prolonged illness. But nine out of ten (M: 93.7%; F: 91.9%) had mothers who were still alive and with whom they were in fairly frequent contact. More than half saw their parents regularly—visiting them in the evenings after work and on the weekends. Most of the men and women who had moved away from Kauai kept in touch with their parents by phone and visited them during major holidays, regardless of the distances involved. Only about 5 percent of the men and about 7 percent of the women had no contacts with their parents whatsoever—usually because the parents had divorced or deserted and had left Kauai when their children were still young.

Four-fifths of the men and three-fourths of the women evaluated their parents in positive tones; only one out of eight individuals could not think of anything positive to say about their parents. A majority of both men (56%) and women (60%) valued the emotional support they had received from their mothers in times of stress. A third of the men and nearly half of the women regarded their mothers as positive role models whose values they shared. For a significantly higher proportion of the women than the men, mothers provided financial support (M: 33.3%; F: 66.7%). One out of every five women relied on their mothers for child care as well. Fathers were seen as positive role models by a higher proportion of sons (37.5%) than daughters (29.3%), but more women than men valued the emotional support their fathers provided in times of stress (M: 33.3; F: 41.5%). The men, on the other hand, shared more interests and activities with their fathers than the women did.

Parents-in-law played a more positive role in the lives of their daughters- and sons-in-law than is generally surmised. A higher proportion of the men than the women evaluated their mothers-in-law in positive terms (M: 66.7%; F: 59.5%). In contrast, a higher proportion of the women than the men evaluated their fathers-in-law positively (M: 57.1%; F: 75.8%). Parents-in-law were valued for the same qualities as were the biological parents. Nearly half of the married women appreciated the emotional support provided by their mothers-in-law (47.2%) and their fathers-in-law (40%). Among the married men, the mother-in-law tended to be valued for her emotional support, the father-in-law was sought out for company and shared interests and activities during leisure time.

Parents-in-law were also important providers of child care. One out of every three mothers in this cohort relied on the help of the paternal grandmother, and one out of every five could count on the babysitting services of the paternal grandfather.

Relationships with siblings in adulthood were closer for the women than the men. Forty percent of the men but less than 20 percent of the women reported detached relationships with their brothers and sisters. A higher proportion of women than men derived emotional support from their siblings (M: 50.9%; F: 70.2%) and shared interests and activities with them (M: 39.8%; F: 57.1%).

Close friends were among the most important members of the social network for these adults. For nearly half of the men and women in this cohort, friends provided models of behavior and shared values; for two-thirds of the men and three-fourths of the women, friends were available for emotional support when needed; and for nine out of ten, friends were "good company" with whom they shared their leisure-time activities and interests—whether sports, hobbies and crafts, or other social activities.

Stressful Life Events

Levinson (1986) in his article "A Conception of Adult Development" considers early adulthood a time of rich satisfaction in terms of love, sexuality, family life, occupational advancement, and realization of major life goals. He notes that "under reasonably favorable conditions, the rewards of living in this era are enormous, but the costs often equal or exceed the benefits" (p. 5). The reports of this contemporary cohort in their early 30s bear witness to his statement. Heading the list of stressful life events for both men and women was the breakup of a long-term relationship (M: 28.3%; F: 30.6%) and financial problems (M: 28.3%; F: 28.7%). Other frequently reported stressful life events focused on work-related stress, that is, trouble with the boss (M: 21.2%; F: 19.0%) and loss of a job (M: 19%; F: 14.8%). Personal illness, illness and death of a parent—especially the father—and the death of a close friend, were experienced as stressful by nearly one out of five among the men and women in this cohort.

A higher proportion of women than men reported troubles with their in-laws (M: 8.7%; F: 14.8%) and chronic discord in their parents' families (M: 2.7%; F: 6.9%), and more women than men had experienced the death of a child by age 32 (M: 1.1%; F: 4.6%). In contrast, a higher proportion of men than women reported problems with substance abuse in their 20s and early 30s (M: 10.9%; F: 4.6%).

Among both men and women finances headed the list of current worries. Some four out of ten had incurred heavy financial obligations while their earning power was still relatively low. A significantly higher proportion of the women than the men worried about the well-being and future of their children (M: 21.3%; F: 37.4%); a significantly higher proportion of the men than the women worried about their current work situations (M: 20.8%; F: 14.2%).

More women than men worried about social issues, both in the community ("the drug scene," "teenage pregnancy," "violence"), and in their immediate families ("alcoholism," "mental illness"). The women, however, also relied on a larger network of social supports to help them cope with stressful life events and worries.

Sources of Emotional Support

Most members of this cohort turned to informal sources of support rather than to professionals in stressful times—as they had in their teens (Werner and Smith, 1982). Leading the list was the support of a spouse or mate (M: 52.2%; F: 59.3%) and the counsel of friends (M: 48.9%; F: 54.6%). Parents, siblings, and other relatives (such as grandparents) also remained important sources of emotional support for these young adults, but more so for the women than for the men.

More women than men relied on people at their workplace (coworkers, boss) to give them emotional support in difficult times, and a significantly higher proportion of women than men had sought the help of a mental health professional (M: 3.3%; F: 12%) or minister (M: 6.5%; F: 12.5%). Only 10 percent of the men, but 30 percent of the women, considered faith and prayer to be their most important help in times of stress.

Overall, women relied on a significantly larger network of social and emotional support than did the men. As a group, women had experienced more stressful life events than men in their attempts at balancing the multiple roles of full-time employee, spouse, and parent. But in spite of apparent role strains, a significantly higher proportion of women than men rated themselves as "happy and delighted" with their accomplishments by the time they had reached their early 30s.

Individuals with Serious Coping Problems: Contrasting Risk Groups

Some 18 percent in this cohort had serious coping problems by age 32; these included two or more of the following conditions: a broken marriage, a criminal record, and chronic mental health problems. Thirty-eight percent of the high risk troubled teens who had grown up in chronic poverty and in disorganized family environments were in this group of troubled adults. So were 15 percent of the high risk individuals who had not developed any problems earlier, and 10 percent of the low risk individuals who had grown up in economically secure and emotionally stable homes.

The majority of the males with a criminal record and/or serious mental health problems in adulthood came from the group of high risk youths who had already one or more serious coping problems in adolescence (including school failure, substance abuse, delinquencies, and/or mental health problems by age 18). The same was true for men with marital problems that necessitated the intervention of the family court. The proportion of troubled adult women who had been among the high risk teenagers with coping problems was also fairly high. Six out of every ten women with criminal records and/or records of serious mental health problems in adulthood had already had one or more serious coping problems in their teens, as did half of the women with marital problems that led to messy divorces or child and/or spouse abuse by age 31/32 (see Table 2 in Appendix I.

Such a retrospective look at the lives of troubled adults in this cohort may give the impression of a fair amount of continuity in maladaptive functioning from childhood to early adulthood. But a prospective view shows a different picture: of those who had multiple problems as teenagers, half or more had stable lives by age 32—especially the women (see Table 3 in Appendix I).

Few cohort members with no previous problems in their teens were among the adults who had criminal records, broken marriages, or serious mental health problems by age 32. But some 10 percent in this group (M: 22; F: 18) did have some problems in making the transition from adolescence to adulthood. They reported significantly more stressful life events between ages 18 and 32 than did their peers with good outcomes (such as financial problems, problems at work, and problems in their marriages or long-term relationships). They also scored higher than their low-risk peers on the Anger and Distress scales of the EAS Adult Temperament Survey. The women in this group scored significantly lower on the Sociability Scale as well. (See Tables 8 and 9 in Appendix I.)

In Sum

Reaching their early 30s involved a series of major life transitions among the 505 individuals in this cohort, more often for the women than for the men. Most females had made a successful entry into three major life trajectories: work, marriage, and parenthood. Many males, in contrast, were still preoccupied with the establishment and consolidation of their careers. Only about half were married and had children. This gender difference in life trajectories is not unique for our Hawaiian cohort. Magnusson (1988) has reported a similar trend for a cohort of Swedish adults who were born the same year as the children of Kauai and who grew up in a large metropolitan area.

Given the opportunity to find suitable mates, both men and women preferred intimacy over isolation, and generativity over self-absorption, but more women than men had established committed relationships with spouses and children. Although strongly career oriented, the women found more sustenance through networks of social relationships that included family, friends, and coworkers; the men's concerns focused more exclusively on their work. For a generation that came of age in hard times in the United States, the men and women in this cohort can look back with pride on their educational and vocational accomplishments. With the exception of a minority of high risk youths whose life stories we will examine in the next chapters, the majority of the ordinary people on Kauai have kept the dream of their immigrant parents for decent lives for themselves and their progeny.

Leilani

Leilani's story is typical of most women in this cohort who have made a successful transition into the adult roles of worker, wife, and mother.

Leilani (Lei) was the first child of Portuguese-Hawaiian parents who were both in their early 20s at the time of her birth. Her father had attended a vocational school, her mother had graduated from high school. Both parents held jobs in the local sugar plantation—her father in the machine shop and her mother as a clerical worker. Lei's mother worked until the sixth month of her pregnancy and, according to the records of the plantation doctor and nurse, was very careful of her health throughout this time.

Lei was born a few weeks before term, weighing 5 lbs., 14 oz., but labor was normal, and both mother and baby were healthy. Said her mother, who had been conscious during the birth, "I felt good when I got a glance of the baby. I am happy—it was worth all the trouble I went through." The attending nurse noted that the mother "felt content and was very proud of her baby." Lei's father took a vacation to help care for his infant daughter.

When Lei was age 2 the examining pediatrician described her as "a very active toddler who is normal physically and mentally." An independent examination by a psychologist characterized the behavior of the little girl with a string of positive adjectives: "agreeable, alert, confident, eager, energetic, resourceful, and responsive." He noted, "Although it was not shown on the Cattell Infant Intelligence Scales (IQ 104), I suspect above average ability." Her mother's parenting style at that time was described as "concerned, mature, responsible."

When tested again at age 10, Lei obtained a PMA IQ of 119. She was consistently receiving A's and B's at the Catholic school she had attended since kindergarten. Her achievement test scores were at or above grade level, and no behavior problems were noted by her classroom teacher. Her family provided high emotional support and adequate educational stimulation for her. Two younger siblings had been born by that time.

When Lei was in the fifth grade, her mother told us, "We are pleased with what Leilani is doing, and we hope she will keep it up. Her teacher feels she is college material, and we want her to go to college or to choose any career she wants." The mother was working part-time "to prepare for financing college." She pointed out with some pride that Lei read a lot of books and did her homework on her own, without help or supervision. The girl also participated in church-related activities, collected stamps, and took piano lessons—she had received a "superior" rating award from the National Piano Guild.

Throughout childhood and adolescence, Leilani helped care for her younger siblings and assisted with regular household chores. Her mother reported that Lei liked to be with her and that they enjoyed cooking and shopping together. She also enjoyed yard work with her father, and "tags along when he is making things. She gets along very well with him. She should have been his son." Her parents considered Lei responsible. Her mother stated, "We can depend on her. She is very neat, and keeps herself clean. She does good work at home, with her piano, and at school. I tell her I am glad. Keep it up. If she isn't doing the right thing, I tell her that too. If she listens and does her work, she gets her allowance. When we go shopping, I let her choose a gift. Her father says, 'I am proud of you—keep it up.'"

Questioned about discipline, her mother said, "My husband and I talk over our disagreements, but we don't interfere with each other's discipline at the time. Most of the time we scold or take away privileges, if need be." Questioned about problems, she noted, "I was once concerned about her overactivity, her talking a lot, and her always asking questions. . . . The public health nurse . . . told me that since Leilani was above average in intelligence, she would be high strung. Although she is usually easy to manage, she gets impatient when she can't do something right the first time." Her mother also noted that Lei was a finicky eater and a somewhat anxious child. Often at night she needed the light on while sleeping. "Her feelings are easily hurt, and she doesn't like to make mistakes. She gets frustrated and angry, and she will let you know if she is mad."

When seen again in late adolescence, Leilani had continued to maintain her high level of academic performance in most areas. Mathematics was difficult for her, with her only D in algebra, but her other grades were mostly A's and B's. With a B+ average, she was considered an honor student, but when we interviewed her on the eve of high school graduation, she was not especially satisfied with the parochial education she had received. She planned to take a business course at the local community college and then hoped to get a civil service job. Although she expected to marry eventually, she wanted to work awhile first.

At age 18, Leilani considered herself a rather outspoken person who made friends easily. She divided her free time evenly between friends and family. Her shared family activities involved household chores, picnics, and watching television. She worried somewhat about the opinion of her peers, but said, "I am independent and smart—though I keep changing my mind a lot." Although she reportedly got along well with both parents ("they try to understand me"), she felt closer to her mother. She viewed her mother as a strong person and hoped she would be like her when she grew up. She believed that her mother had influenced her the most, and encouraged her "to be what I want to be." Her father was seen as "sweet, kind, and soft." His hopes for her were "to be happy." Her own goals, at the threshold of adulthood, were for "a good job and a good life."

When we saw Leilani again in her early 30s, she was married and had three sons, ages 11, 9, and 6. She worked as a part-time secretary on Kauai and was satisfied with her job, though her work tended to interfere somewhat with her family life. She had attended secretarial school after graduating from high school and had done well. "I didn't find school stressful. I felt pressured sometimes to get good grades, but overall, I really enjoyed school. I studied a lot, but I didn't kick myself when I got a B instead of an A. Now when I look back, I have a lot of respect for people in the teaching profession."

Leilani's marriage is largely satisfying to her, although financial problems and "finding quality time" with her family present some difficulties for her and her husband. "I focus on getting through one day at a time, and I always thank God every day. I have learned that as bad as it seems sometimes, it could be worse. I try not to expect too much from my family—especially the kids. They've got responsibilities (doing household chores and babysitting), but they are still children and need time to grow. That means making mistakes." Aspects of parenthood that are most stressful for her are "trying to discipline them. Teaching them right from wrong. Trying to warn them about the bad in the world, yet trying very hard not to scare them and turn them into paranoid people who do not trust anyone. Teaching discipline is an ongoing job. I believe basically that my sons are good kids. I believe that we as parents, the schools, and TV have alerted them to the fact that it's OK to say no." Lei finds much to please her about her boys: "Almost everything they do. I always wanted sons. They are excellent students. They are in advanced programs in school. They are loving and supportive. I don't just love them; I like them a lot."

More ambivalent feelings were now expressed about her parents. "My father's mind is set on so many subjects. Trying to get him to see another side is sometimes a problem. My father is not generous with material things, although he is the first to lend a helping hand in an emergency."

Her mother's strength, which had been perceived as so admirable when Lei was in high school, was now viewed more critically. "My mother is a very strong person. There is usually only one way—hers. She is very critical and often likes to bring up mistakes from the past, though she has mellowed a little since she has had grandchildren. Although she denies favoritism, she is less critical of one of my sisters. But I have learned not to feel shattered if my mother doesn't approve of my plans. I respect my mother and father as parents and adults. I relate to them on an adult level. I don't expect too much from them. I try not to cause problems by asserting my views and beliefs, but I do share my feelings with them."

Leilani apparently gets along well with her parents-in-law, but she has some problems with a sister-in-law. "My husband has two sisters and two brothers. His mother died when he was 13, and my father-in-law was remarried to a wonderful woman who is very supportive of us. But one sister-in-law plays games with us."

Lei still enjoys playing the piano and likes to sew. She is considerably involved in the various sports activities of her boys. "At this time, my main goal is to raise my three sons to be healthy—mentally and physically. I want them to like themselves, so that no matter what they become, they can look in the mirror and feel proud. I want happiness for my family."

She worries that she or her husband could die: "What would become of our children? I have a friend fighting cancer right now. I am afraid of cancer. I also worry about losing control over the kids. I worry that I might not be as good a wife as my husband wants. I worry if people like me."

Leilani considers her strong points to be "my honesty and love for people. I am straightforward, kindhearted. I have a sense of humor. I bend over backward not to hurt people. I can get along with almost everybody." Among her weak points she considers her impulsiveness: "I talk too much when I am in an uncomfortable situation. I still feel intimidated by certain people."

Describing the most important happening in her life, Lei said, "After having my babies and staying out of the work force for seven years, I went back to work. I discovered so many qualities in myself that I didn't know I had. I am proud of myself as a person now—not just as a mommy or a wife. I receive so much fulfillment from getting my own paycheck and from my relationship with my co-workers. It has made me a better wife and mother, because I am so much happier with myself. I have grown up a lot in the past four years; I don't take anything for granted. I am so much more aware. I've become much stronger since I went back to work." She considered the period just prior to that the worst: "I went through 'burnout' at home. I felt I had hit rock bottom emotionally. I had to depend on myself to pull myself through this. I had to find the energy to get through every day. It lasted nine months. I got over it when I went back to work."

Leilani feels that the past four years, as she approached and entered her 30s, have been the best period of her life so far. "I went back to work. My children weren't babies any more. I have received so much fulfillment in being a wife, mother, and worker. I like being in my 30s. I feel I've finally grown up."

George

George's life typifies that of the "ordinary" males in this cohort. His development, the events of the various stages of his life, his aspirations and feelings about himself are shared by many young men born in the mid 1950s on Kauai.

He was the second (and last) child of Japanese-American parents who were in their late 20s at the time of his birth. Both were high school graduates, and both worked outside of the home. Their combined incomes assured them middle class status. George's mother experienced no major problems during her pregnancy. His birth was spontaneous; following his delivery his mother declared, "I feel fine." Like her first child, George was a healthy eight-pounder. His development proceeded on schedule. He was breastfed for a few weeks, but then his mother shifted him to bottle feeding since she planned to return to her job. No feeding problems were experienced by the infant; his occasional sleeping difficulties were handled by his parents by taking him in their bed. He was "spoiled" by his doting grandparents; his paternal grandmother cared for him while his mother worked. He was described by her as a "very active, good-natured, all around 'average'" baby.

The public health nurse who visited the home at 13 months found George to be a "happy, healthy boy." She noted, "Although his mother reports that her son has only been walking for a week, he appears to be very confident and sturdy on his feet. He is constantly babbling, climbing, crawling and walking all over. He seems to be a very alert infant." His mother's coping style was described as "affectionate, good-humored, responsible—she takes things in stride."

At age 2, George received high average scores on the Cattell Infant Intelligence Test and above average scores on the Vineland Social Maturity Scale. The examiners described his mother's caretaking behavior in terms similar to those used by the public health nurse. The toddler was characterized as "active, aggressive, eager, independent, and very responsive." Some restlessness was noted, but the attending pediatrician rated the boy's physical development as "above normal." A clinical psychologist rated George's intellectual development as "normal."

At age 10, George was doing well in public school. His scholastic aptitude (SCAT) and achievement (STEP) test scores were in the 85–90th percentiles. His reading and writing skills were rated "above average" by his teacher; his mathematical skills were considered "average." No behavior problems were noted. George used his time in the classroom well.

His mother still held the same job (in the school system's food services), but his father had exchanged his self-employed status for a job with the county government. The family's socioeconomic status had suffered a slight decline, to a "fair" rating, but George received adequate educational stimulation and emotional support during his childhood years. He had not been displaced by a younger sibling.

According to an interview with the mother at that time, family life was "smooth." Activities shared by George and his parents were outings, shows, and "going shopping." He liked to help his mother in the kitchen; he enjoyed golf and fishing with his father. His mother noted, "I am quite satisfied with the way he does things I ask him to do." While neither father nor mother were overly demonstrative in showing their affection, they did praise George verbally. His mother considered him "an easy child to manage." Reasoning was her primary method of discipline, followed by an occasional scolding if George did not listen.

During grade school, George attended Japanese language school for six years. He collected stamps and coins and had a close adult friend outside of the family circle with whom he "talked golf and fishing." His reading focused primarily on school requirements—"about a book a week." No serious childhood illnesses were noted, but the school nurse described him as being overweight.

In high school, George's schoolwork continued to be good. His grades were primarily B's, with an occasional A and one C. His SCAT and STEP scores remained in the upper percentiles. When interviewed just after high school graduation, he said, "Senior year was a waste—a drag. I had already done everything." Consequently, he was not satisfied with the education he had received, although he was content with his own performance in school. He had worked on the yearbook, and he enjoyed reading, swimming, and bowling. He had held part-time jobs during the summers and, occasionally, during the school years. What spare time he had left he spent with friends or "by myself." His older sister was in college, so he had little contact with her.

At age 18, in describing his mother, George said, "She is outgoing. She was the one who really pushed us to learn." His father was "working all the time." He considered his father to be more distant and felt closer emotionally to his mother. His father wanted him to be "something very solid—like an engineer." His mother encouraged him "to go do what I'll enjoy."

Looking at what he considered his strong points at that time, George commented, "I get along well with others, but I do what I feel is O.K. I don't go along with things just to please. I speak what is on my mind." He considered his outspokenness a potential weakness. "When I speak up I can be very sarcastic, and that turns some people off."

George planned to go to college, and then hoped to go on to law school to study international law. He had been influenced by his favorite teacher and also had received some help from school counselors, "mostly about school planning." "I guess my whole life has just worked up to being a lawyer. I haven't been in trouble because I didn't want to damage my reputation. I came near it, but I haven't done anything illegal ever. I got interested in the law because I wanted to help people—not really help, but protect their rights." Summarizing his goals and hopes at age 18, George concluded, "I guess I am a person with one goal in mind—just getting to the goal. I am a person who doesn't go along with people just to conform. I want to get off this rock and go to the mainland. City life holds more fascination for me."

When we saw George again at age 32, he had indeed left "the rock."

He had attended college and was working as a program/budget analyst for the National Aeronautics and Space Administration (NASA). Although he had not become a lawyer as he had originally planned, his educational and professional record clearly showed his high achievement motivation. Looking back at his college experience, he expressed satisfaction with what he had accomplished. He also noted some stress, primarily related to "being away from home, being unsure of the future, wondering how useful my degrees would be in the job market, and trying to overcome my Hawaiian way of talking."

George was married now. He had two children, ages seven and one, and considered his marriage satisfying. His wife returned to work after the birth of their second child, and they now divide household responsibilities evenly to meet their financial and family obligations. His relationship to his children is gratifying to him. "The complete trust of my children" and "seeing my children make morally right decisions" are especially satisfying aspects of parenthood for him.

He noted the financial and discipline problems that are part of his life as a father now, but he appeared to solve them in a mature and rational way. He accepted the cost of raising children as a given, and he provided them with firm discipline—"I am stricter than my wife."

The move to the U.S. mainland had placed him at a great geographical distance from his parents, but his ongoing relationship with them appeared quite satisfactory, and he looked at it realistically. He now acknowledged past difficulties with his father that he attributed to "his parochial outlook, his short temper, and his occasional drinking." He handled these by ignoring the outbursts and by trying to stay in touch with him. His mother's tendency to be somewhat secretive and her "not to worry" attitude, which had troubled him when he was younger, did not appear to affect his present life.

He had good relationships with his in-laws, his older sister, and a few close friends on the mainland, based primarily on shared values, interests, and activities. His own interests and activities included golf, woodworking, fixing up old cars, and photography. He considered his wife and coworkers, as well as his parents and sister, his main sources of emotional support in his adult life.

For George, the birth of his first child had been the most important event in his life. Asked what he would like to accomplish in his future, he said, "To raise my family in a decent and morally correct way"—a goal echoed by most "ordinary people" whom we met on Kauai, and one which his parents could be proud of.

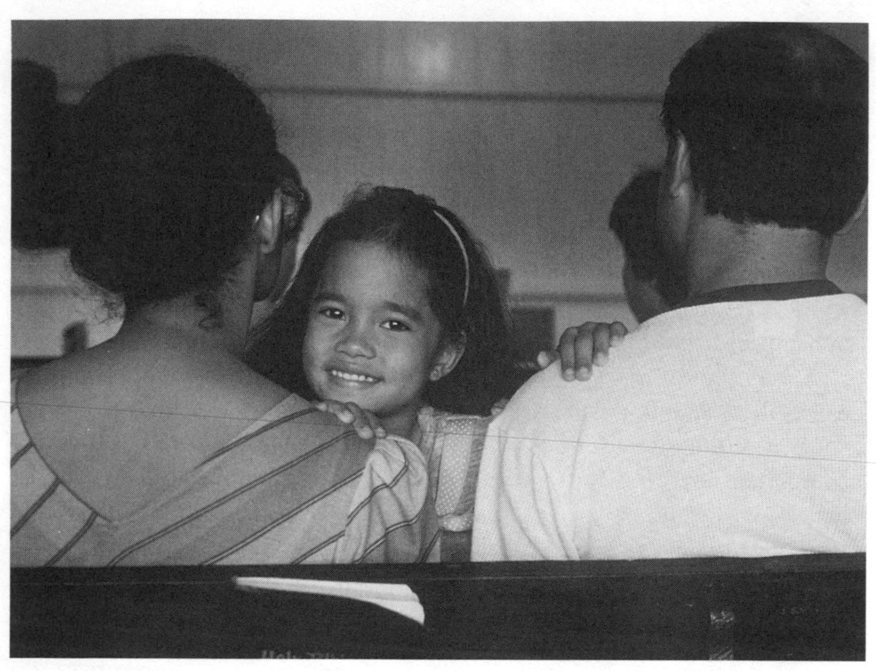

4

The Resilient Children in Adulthood

The 42 girls and 30 boys who were the focus of our book *Vulnerable but Invincible* (1982) had each encountered four or more risk factors before age 2 which were potent predictors of negative developmental outcomes for most children in this cohort. Each was born and reared in a poor family, as judged from the breadwinner's occupation, level of income, and condition of housing. Most fathers were semi- or unskilled laborers on the sugar plantations of the island. Most mothers had not graduated from high school, and about half had eight grades or less of formal education. In addition, these children had constitutional vulnerabilities: they had been exposed to moderate or severe perinatal stress, or were low-birth-weight babies, weighing less than 2,500 grams, or had physical handicaps. A significant proportion also had alcoholic or mentally ill parents.

Yet, to our surprise, these vulnerable infants managed to overcome the odds. None developed any serious learning or behavior problems in childhood or adolescence. As far as we could tell from interviews and from their records in the community, as they grew up they managed to do well in their schoolwork and in their homes and social lives; and they set realistic goals and expectations for themselves when they graduated from high school. At the end of the second decade of life they had developed into competent, confident, and caring persons who expressed a great desire to make use of whatever opportunities came along to improve themselves.

Looking back over the lives of these 72 resilient individuals, we contrasted their behavior characteristics and caregiving environments with those of high risk youths of the same age and sex who had developed serious coping problems at ages 10 or 18 (learning problems, mental health problems, serious delinquencies). We found a number of characteristics within the individuals and their families and also outside the family circle which contributed to their resilience. (For a detailed presentation of these findings, see Werner and Smith, 1982, 1989.)

Even as infants, the resilient children had temperamental characteristics that elicited positive attention from family members as well as strangers. By age one, both boys and girls were frequently described by their caregivers as "very active," the girls as "affectionate" and "cuddly," the boys as "good-natured" and "easy to deal with"—more so than the babies who later developed serious learning or behavior problems. These resilient infants also had fewer eating and sleeping habits that distressed their parents.

As toddlers, the resilient boys and girls already tended to meet the world on their own terms. The pediatricians and psychologists who examined them independently at age 2 noted their alertness and autonomy, their tendency to seek out novel experiences, and their positive social orientation. They were more advanced in communication, locomotion, and self-help skills than children who later experienced serious learning and behavior problems.

In elementary school, teachers reported that the resilient children got along well with their classmates. They had better reasoning and reading skills than the children who later developed problems, especially the girls. Although not unusually gifted, the resilient children used whatever skills they had effectively. Both parents and teachers noted that they had many interests and engaged in activities and hobbies that were not narrowly sex-typed. Such activities provided them with solace in adversity and a reason to feel proud.

By the time they graduated from high school, the resilient youths had developed a positive self-concept and an internal locus of control. On the California Psychological Inventory (CPI), they displayed a more nurturant, responsible, and achievement-oriented attitude toward life than their high risk peers who had developed problems. The resilient girls, especially, were more assertive and independent than the other girls in this cohort.

Most resilient boys and girls grew up in families with four or fewer children, with a space of two years or more between themselves and their next sibling. Few had experienced prolonged separations from a primary caretaker during the first year of life. All had the opportunity to establish a close bond with at least one caregiver from whom they received plenty of positive attention when they were infants. Some of this nurturing came from substitute parents, such as grandparents or older siblings, or from the ranks of regular babysitters. Such substitute parents played an important role as positive models of identification. Where mothers were employed, the job of taking care of younger siblings contributed to the pronounced autonomy and sense of responsibility noted among the resilient girls, especially in households where the father was absent. Resilient boys were often first-born sons who did not have to share their parents' attention with many additional children. There was usually a male in the family who could serve as a role model—if not the father, then a grandfather, older cousin, or uncle. Structure and rules and assigned chores were part of their daily routines in adolescence.

The resilient boys and girls also found emotional support outside of their own families. They tended to have at least one and usually several close friends, especially the girls. They relied on informal networks of kin and neighbors, peers and elders, for counsel and support in times of crisis. Some had a favorite teacher who had become a role model, friend, and confidant for them.

Participation in extracurricular activities played an important part in the lives of the resilient youths, especially activities that were cooperative enterprises, such as 4-H and the YMCA and YWCA. For still others, emotional support came from a youth leader or from a minister or church group. With their help the resilient children acquired a faith that their lives had meaning and that they had control over their fates.

Constitutional factors (health, temperamental characteristics) discriminated most between the resilient children and their high risk peers in infancy and early childhood. The support of alternate caregivers, such as grandparents or siblings, and the child's verbal and reasoning skills gained in importance in middle childhood. By late adolescence, personality characteristics, such as self-esteem and an internal locus of control, and the presence of external support systems differentiated most between positive and negative developmental outcomes among the high risk children. As the number of risk factors or stressful life events increased, more protective factors were needed to counterbalance the negative aspects in the lives of these vulnerable children and to ensure a positive developmental outcome.

When we last interviewed the resilient youths in their senior year in high school, they were eager to cross the threshold into young adulthood and to explore the world outside their island home. We assumed that there would be a high degree of continuity in the adaptational patterns of the resilient children as they matured into adulthood. In spite of considerable hardships, they had displayed trust, autonomy, initiative, and industry in childhood; and they had developed a strong sense of identity by late adolescence. We anticipated that their success in accomplishing the developmental tasks of childhood and adolescence would enable them to develop a sense of intimacy and generativity in adulthood.

We expected that their competence and confidence would endure and that these qualities would facilitate their entry into the world of work, marriage, and parenthood. We anticipated that they would seek and find niches in their work environment compatible with their temperament, intelligence, and interests, and that they might venture farther away from their childhood homes than most of their agemates. We also assumed that they would continue to actively recruit caregivers who would be sources of emotional support for them in adulthood—just as they had done so successfully as children. We expected that the nurturant qualities displayed by the resilient males would enable them to value the role of parent and that the assertive qualities displayed by the resilient females would enable them to value a career of their own.

The Resilient Children in Their Early 30s

We were able to obtain follow-up data in adulthood on 63 of the 72 resilient men and women in the 1955 birth cohort—88 percent of the original sample. Among our data are interviews, questionnaires, test scores, and agency records for 27 of the 30 resilient males and for 36 of the 42 resilient females. A third of the men and women in this group are of Japanese descent, a third are Pilipino, the others are part-Hawaiian.

The resilient men were about evenly divided between those who had settled on Kauai and those who left the island—to serve in the armed forces, to work in Honolulu or on the West Coast of the U.S. mainland, or to venture overseas to Japan and Europe. The resilient women had experienced even more changes of residence than the resilient men since we last saw them at age 18. We traveled thousands of miles to interview them—in their homes on Kauai, in their offices in Honolulu, and in their new residences in California, Oregon, and Washington. One of the women, a sergeant in the U.S. Air Force, was interviewed at an airfield in Colorado; another, the wife of an enlisted man, at an army base in Maryland. Some of the resilient women, in turn, traveled many miles to meet with us. Indeed, a head nurse from the state hospital at Yap had flown from her island home in the Western Carolinas to attend a conference at the University of Hawaii and to visit her kinfolk on Kauai. Her husband, a member of the legislature of the newly established state of Yap, stayed behind, caring for their two small sons.

How well did these resilient children fare in adulthood compared with men and women who had grown up under similar conditions of poverty and family instability but who had developed serious coping problems in their teens? (See Tables 4–7 in Appendix I.)

Educational and Vocational Accomplishments

Both the resilient men and the resilient women had obtained more education beyond high school than their high risk peers. Some 40 percent had attended a four-year college (M: 43.5%; F: 38.2%)—a rate more than twice as high as the national average for people their age (M: 17.2%; F: 16.0%) and significantly higher than that for men and women with coping problems by age 18 (M: 15.2%; F: 10.0%).

Equally impressive were the vocational accomplishments of the resilient men and women who entered the work force during hard economic times. When we saw them at age 31/32, only one man (a recent graduate of a textile design school in the Netherlands) and three women (all mothers of young children) were not in the labor force. Unemployment rates among the resilient individuals were lower than the national average (of 6.5%) for their age group at that time (U.S. Bureau of Labor, *Current Population Survey*, 1986).

While their fathers had been in either unskilled or semiskilled jobs, most of the resilient men and women had moved to skilled trade, technical, and managerial positions. None was in an unskilled job, and only about 10 percent held semiskilled jobs. In comparison with their peers who had developed coping problems by age 18, a significantly lower proportion of the resilient males held semi- or unskilled jobs (13.0% vs. 35.3%). A significantly higher proportion of the resilient males and females were in professional, managerial, and semiprofessional positions (M: 39.1%; F: 45.5%).

One of the resilient men was a youth minister in the state of Washington; another an engineer who designed satellites for an aircraft company in California; a third had become a career officer in the U.S. Army. Several men had entered professions related to law enforcement: one served as a deputy prosecutor; another as an adult correctional officer on Kauai. Some worked in advertising and graphic design in Honolulu; others were self-employed in construction work. Several men worked as personnel managers, foremen, or supervisors on the islands' sugar plantations; others had found employment in the tourist industry. One of the men was a commercial fisherman, another managed a local pizza parlor.

The jobs held by the resilient women ranged from the more traditional female occupations (accountant, administrative assistant, beautician, bookkeeper, clerk, insurance agent, nurse, nursery school teacher, waitress) to less traditional jobs (poet-in-residence in a school, paralegal, president of a trading company, sergeant in the U.S. Air Force, tour director, and writer of children's books).

A higher proportion of the resilient individuals than of the men and women with coping problems in adolescence reported work-related stress in their adult lives. Interpersonal difficulties with coworkers and boss were cited as the most frequently encountered stress at work by both the resilient men and women (M: 26.3%; F: 39.3%). The overwhelming majority of the resilient men and women relied on their own competence and determination in resolving such work-related difficulties (M: 73.9%; F: 61.8%).

With few exceptions (the construction workers with fluctuating income), the resilient men and women had employment that provided them with income sufficient for their styles of life. The majority relied on the income of two wage earners (spousal income was usually needed) to meet their financial needs. Career or job success was the primary goal of the resilient individuals at this stage of their lives, especially for the women.

The female poet-in-residence in a local school reflected, "Finding a career was important to me. I love the career I found, I get to structure my own work. I love working with kids and creating poetry that expresses Hawaiian values." Commented the nurse from Yap, "The work is challenging—science is fascinating and learning is fun."

While most of the resilient women stressed the cooperative aspects of work, more resilient men focused on the challenge of competition. A supervisor at the local sugar plantation said, "I am a very aggressive person—I'd rather lead than be led. I thrive on that." The young deputy prosecutor mused, "I am always competitive—there is more in life than what I am doing. I want to run for senator some day."

Marriage and Relationship with a Mate

At age 31/32, a higher proportion of resilient women than women with problems in their teens were married, but the resilient men were as reluctant to marry as were men with problems in adolescence. Four out of five among the resilient women were currently married, including 15 percent who were in their second marriage. This rate is higher than the national average (of 68.5%) for women their age. In contrast, less than half of the resilient men were married at that time. This rate is lower than the national average (of 64.7%) for men their age (*Current Population Survey*, 1986). Also, among the singles, a higher proportion of resilient men than women did not live in a committed long-term relationship (M: 21.7%; F: 8.8%). Whatever the reasons, fear of failure or fear of intimacy, there was a greater reluctance among the resilient males than among the resilient females to make commitments to a partner of the opposite sex.

A pipefitter in a navy shipyard in northern California said, "I am still single—came close to marriage, but found I am not the marrying type. There was a lot of conflict in the relationship—I had no trust in her. Now I have no headaches, no responsibilities; I'll think about marriage in another five years." Worried a free-lance graphic artist in Honolulu, "Should I wait for this one girl—date others? Maybe if I wait, she'll find someone else, and all that waiting was for nothing."

Expectations from marriage or long-term relationships differed significantly by gender. The majority of the resilient men and women wanted permanency and security (M: 57.1%; F: 73.1%), but a significantly higher proportion of the resilient females than males expected intimacy and sharing from such a relationship (M: 35.7%; F: 73.1%). These were a nurse's expectations from her marriage: "That we can always be friends first, then lovers, then husband and wife." The recently married poet said, "I make it a point to go wherever he goes. I expect my marriage to be a lifetime partnership."

Once committed, however, the resilient males worked harder at resolving conflicts in marital relationships than did males with coping problems in their teens. The overwhelming majority of the resilient men (64.7%) and about half of the resilient women (48.3%) resolved conflicts by discussion and a joint resolution. The majority reported that their caring and determination made their marriages work.

A married woman who works full time as an accountant and is the mother of two young children said, "I guess being married has its ups and downs, but we always manage to work things out." The manager of a local pizza parlor who took turns with his wife on the work shift and caring for their young children remarked, "It takes a lot of work to build a family and to have a real good relationship with one another."

Divorce and Remarriage

The divorce rates of the resilient men and women were comparable to the rates reported by their peers with coping problems by age 18 but nearly twice as high as rates reported nationwide for this generation (M: 17.4% vs. 8.5%; F: 20.6% vs. 11.5%). The resilient women, however, had higher rates of remarriage than did the resilient men (M: 8.7%; F: 14.7%).

A higher proportion of the resilient men than of the resilient women referred to the negative effects of the breakup of a long-term relationship (M: 45.5%; F: 29.4%). For the men, divorce also involved separation from children or stepchildren. A foreman who was divorced from his wife (who returned to her former husband) wrote, "When I was married I was able to relate to my stepdaughter as a friend and real father. Now [after the divorce] I have come to the realization how harsh life really is—how relationships can leave deep within hurts that don't seem to go away."

Half of the divorced men were estranged from their children; the other half reported ambivalent, off/on relationships with their offspring. In contrast, the majority of the divorced women reported that their divorces had no bearing on their present relationships with their children. They generally praised their second husbands for their caring and understanding, as well as for the acceptance of their offspring. Commented a resilient woman (who had taken an overdose of sleeping pills when her first husband deserted her), "My second husband is quiet, considerate—a good family man. He is always there to back me up. He says he likes me as I am—what's in my heart." A sales clerk, whose first marriage ended in divorce because her husband was a drug addict, told us, "My second husband is very patient, understanding—he doesn't treat my first son any differently than the other children. He is hard working and a good father."

Overall, males in this group were more reluctant than women to make long-term commitments in early adulthood, and career consolidation seemed to take precedence over intimacy. Childhood experiences of parental discord and psychopathology (especially in the mother) were reexperienced by some men in the context of the breakup of a long-term relationship, and the hurt of a divorce temporarily stunted a still-fragile feeling of trust.

Among the resilient women, there was a heightened expectation for intimacy and sharing in a long-term relationship which occasionally led to disappointments in a first marriage, but the resilient women were more willing to risk again and to enter a second and happier marriage than were resilient men. Their risk-taking in matters of the heart was also related to their greater need to find a permanent and secure home for their children.

Parenthood: Hopes and Expectations

Three out of four among the resilient women had had children by age 30, in contrast to fewer than half of the resilient men (M: 43.5%; F: 76.5%). Most had two children and did not plan to have any more. Many of their children were of preschool age or in the early elementary grades; however, some of the women who had married right out of high school already worried about their teenagers.

Although they had, on the average, a smaller number of children, the resilient men and women valued the positive aspects of parenthood more than did their peers with coping problems by age 18. Two out of three among the resilient men enjoyed the opportunity to care for their children and believed in their futures. Fewer than one out of four among the men with coping problems in adolescence had similar perspectives on parenting. Two out of three among the resilient men saw fatherhood as a sign of self-development, and a high proportion considered their spouses as helpful in their parental role—none of their high risk peers did.

There were some significant differences between the resilient men and women in their hopes and expectations for their offspring. While the majority of parents wanted their children to be competent (M: 54.5%; F: 57.1%), a significantly higher proportion of the resilient mothers expected them to achieve well in school and to be successful in a career (M: 18.2%; F: 61.9%). A loan and collection officer who is the mother of four children said, "I want them to do better than I did—go to college." Added an accountant, the mother of two preschoolers, "I hope both of them go into some kind of profession."

A significantly higher proportion of the resilient men than women considered parenthood a sign of maturity (M: 66.7%: F: 16%) and welcomed the opportunity to care for their offspring (M: 66.7%; F: 20%); a significantly higher proportion of the resilient women than men commented on the pleasure of seeing their children grow (M: 33.3%; F: 64%).

The manager of a local pizza parlor who has a 12-year-old son and a 10-year-old daughter said, "What pleases me most is just being with them—watching them grow. I am not pushing them into anything. They are their own persons. Whatever they want is fine with me—I'll do all I can to help them to succeed and be happy." Commented a supervisor in a local sugar mill, "I don't see any faults in my boy. I started a fund for him when he was born. Wherever he wants to go, I try my best to send him. He doesn't have to be successful in life—I just want him to be happy." The majority (67.7%) of the resilient women stressed early independence for their offspring, while most (62.5%) of the resilient men tolerated dependence in their young children. In spite of the obvious pride that the resilient fathers took in their children, there were still large differences between spouses in their active involvement in child rearing. Most of the resilient women reported that they had the major share of child rearing, while most of the resilient men said that both parents shared child rearing equally.

To sum up: by age 31/32, the majority of the resilient women and a minority among the resilient men had successfully mastered Erikson's (1959) stage of generativity. In spite of, or maybe because of the hardships they experienced in their own childhoods, they worked hard at being good parents who wanted the best for their young sons and daughters but also respected the individuality of their children. The resilient women (who were significantly more assertive and achievement oriented in adolescence than their peers) strove to inculcate early independence in their offspring and had high expectations for their achievement. The resilient men (who in their youth had been significantly more nurturant and sensitive than the other men in this cohort) were pleased to extend such nurturance and care to their own children.

Both the resilient men and women strove to be effective parents, in spite of their continuing frustration with their own mothers and fathers. For we could still detect some lasting effects of parental discord and psychopathology and old scars left from the breakup of their parents' marriages.

Relationships with Family and Friends

Parents

Among parental problems that excrted a continuing negative effect on the lives of the resilient men and women in adulthood were divorce, chronic family discord, parental illness, and, for the females, maternal mental illness. The overwhelming majority of the resilient men and women handled the stress of such parental problems by detachment or withdrawal, while their high risk peers continued to get enmeshed in the familial discord and pathology that was the norm for their childhoods. Some three out of four among the resilient men and women (M: 71.4%; F: 75.0%) detached themselves emotionally when difficulties arose with their mothers—in contrast to only 16 percent of the high risk men and 10 percent of the high risk women with coping problems by age 18. Two-thirds of the resilient men and women detached themselves emotionally when difficulties arose with their fathers—in contrast to only 16 percent of the high risk men and 25 percent of the high risk women with coping problems by age 18.

Comments about parents whose difficulties had caused them pain in earlier years varied from negative to ambivalent to positive. Perhaps the most critical comments came from the women who perceived themselves as abandoned by their mothers in childhood. A women who is happily married and expects to "grow old and gray" with her husband reflected on her feelings about her mother after their parents divorced when she was in junior high school. "I don't know where she is—she left us all behind. I was watching her fool around with other men. I used to be her maid—to do everything for her." Another, whose parents separated when she was three years old and who was raised by her father with the help of her paternal grandmother, said, "I don't know my real mother at all. She lives on the mainland now. When she comes for vacation to Kauai, she just goes touring around with my sisters."

Reactions to mothers who were mentally ill, and who abused their children either emotionally or physically, ranged from distant to forgiving. Said the happily married daughter of an epileptic mother who had behaved erraticly toward her, "My mom and I have never been close. I believe my mom is slow mentally—not bright—she can be very hurtful and hateful."

Nevertheless, parental illness and impending death also led to compassion and forgiveness. One of the resilient women, whose mother had been a nervous, abusive woman who had beaten her daughters savagely, said, "My mother left us several times when she had her nervous breakdowns for fear she might hurt her children. Shortly before she died from lung cancer, I was able to tell her that I loved her, and she told me that she regretted what she had done to me when I was a child."

Similar reports came from the children of alcoholics. The daughter of an alcoholic father reported, "My father used to be so erratic—he drank a lot. He was the Samurai—everything in the family's life centered around him. If he was not in a good mood, you had to walk on tiptoes. He has mellowed a bit since he got sick with cancer ten years ago." The son of an alcoholic father added, "We went through hell. It was a poor marriage—swearing, bitching all the time—my parents separated once and came back together—I grew up in all of this! My dad used to drink daily and get drunk; but two years ago, after an ulcer operation, the doctor told him that if he drank again he had to have more painful surgery. He quit smoking and drinking. Now I can sit and talk with him—now that he is on the wagon."

Parents-in-Law

In contrast to the majority of their high risk peers with coping problems, almost all of the resilient men and women who married had good relationships with their in-laws. The majority of the resilient men and women evaluated their parents-in-law positively, especially the parent-in-law of the opposite sex. A higher proportion of the men than women had good things to say about their mothers-in-law (M: 66.7%; F: 60%), and a lower proportion reported problems in their relationships with them. (M: 22.2%; F: 48.1%). Conversely, a higher proportion of the women than men gave positive evaluations of their fathers-in-law (M: 44.4%; F: 78.3%), and a lower proportion reported problems in their relationships with them (M: 54.4%; F: 26.9%).

Nearly half of the married women in this group regarded their parents-in-law as important sources of emotional support. This was especially true for women who were not particularly close to their own parents because of family discord, divorce, or psychopathology. These women recruited substitute parents among their in-laws, just as they had sought counsel and comfort from the parents of their boyfriends in their youth.

When difficulties with their parents-in-law arose, however, the majority of the resilient men and women employed the same defense mechanism they used with their own parents. They detached themselves emotionally and avoided getting enmeshed in in-law problems such as marital discord, alcoholism, or mental illness.

Siblings

The resilient men and women tended to have more satisfying relationships with their siblings in adulthood than did their peers with coping problems—a trend we had already seen in childhood and adolescence. About a third of the resilient men and nearly half of the resilient women reported continuing close relationships with their siblings in their adult lives. Those who were close to their siblings tended to value their emotional support above everything else (M: 47.6%; F: 69.7%). A much smaller proportion shared common interests and activities with their brothers and sisters (M: 14.3%; F: 30.3%), and fewer still shared common values with their siblings (M: 14.3%; F: 9.1%).

Among the group that maintained the closest sibling relationships across the years were the offspring of alcoholic or mentally ill parents. Often a resilient adult continued to play the role of comforter, counselor, or protector which he or she had assumed in late childhood or adolescence. Said a woman of Hawaiian descent who is married and the mother of two children, "My older brother is still my protector. He is in the army, but he sends his military checks to my mother for me. He stills treats me as a baby." Another woman who never knew her real father but who had grown up in the home of an alcoholic stepfather and with an emotionally distant mother, reported, "My older sister took care of me when I was pregnant because I couldn't talk to my parents who were arguing all the time." Added a divorced construction worker, offspring of an alcoholic father, "My older sister has always played a big part in my life. Whenever I get into trouble [he had problems with substance abuse], she helps me out."

The strong ties among siblings who experienced a traumatic childhood together continued, even when the resilient sibling moved away. One of the women whom we interviewed in Los Angeles said, "I am still in touch with my sister, who lives on Kauai. We hung together through the hard times when my mother beat us both. We consoled each other, and we still do."

The resilient men and women who went to college on the mainland often credited a sibling for counsel and support while away from home.

The daughter of an alcoholic father who completed a bachelor of science degree in Human Development at the University of Hawaii told us: "When I first came up to the university, my oldest brother helped me a lot—he was at the university too. I can call him if I need him—he is my counselor." A graduate in business administration from Washington State University noted, "My sister always tried to provide a family life for me when I was going to school on the mainland."

Some of the resilient women were so closely identified with the role of sibling caretaker that they had a hard time letting go. A paralegal who works in the U.S. Department of Justice said, "I am closest to the youngest. I took care of him when he was growing up. I guess I feel since I am older, he should listen." Commented another resilient big sister, "I became possessive—it is hard to release them. When I finally let go, I found my relationship became pretty good."

While most of the resilient men and women acknowledged that they now led separate lives from their siblings who have grown up, married, and have children of their own, they still felt that they could count on them in an emergency. The exceptions were those who had left behind brothers or sisters who were mired in multiple problems, similar to those their parents had to contend with: financial problems, marital problems, divorce, alcoholism, and mental illness. Most of the resilient men and women refused to get enmeshed in these problems. They often voiced disapproval—"I talk it over with them, but I can't understand their attitudes"—and they eventually detached themselves and withdrew—just as they did when they encountered similar problems with parents and in-laws.

Friends

The resilient individuals did not differ from their high risk peers in the number of friends they had or in their satisfaction with their relationships with them. In both groups, the majority of the men and women shared common interests and activities with their friends—mostly outdoor activities, family get-togethers, and shopping. The resilient individuals, however, relied on their friends less often for financial support than did their high risk peers who had been in trouble in their teens. They also shared less often a common set of values with their friends and less often mentioned their friends as role models for their adult lives.

A fairly high proportion, especially among the resilient men, acknowledged that they were loners. They could take or leave the friends with whom they shared their leisure time, and more often than not they took their own counsel when it came to major decisions in their lives. In this attitude, they differed significantly from their peers with coping problems in adolescence who depended more often on friends for emotional support in adulthood.

While most of the resilient women (63.6%) were eager to help their friends who encountered problems, the majority of the resilient men (66.7%) tended to withdraw from others' troubles. Friends acknowledged this fact and yet spoke fondly of them, as did one of the women who had gone to school with a resilient male who looked for his fortune overseas: "He was a special, multitalented person—creative, intelligent, popular. He was also strong-willed, ambitious, and moody. He had no time for a personal relationship. He was well on his way discovering the U.S.A., Mexico, Europe, and North Africa when we finally lost touch with him. I have only good wishes and thoughts for him."

Overall, the interpersonal relationships of the resilient men and women in early adulthood still revealed some of the scars of their traumatic childhoods. Although they had compassion for troubled parents and siblings who continued to struggle with alcoholism, family discord, poverty, and psychopathology, they distanced themselves from these problems, refusing to become enmeshed in them. In spite of their detachment, there was little bitterness and much forgiveness in their reflections on the hurts that had been imposed on them by quarreling, abusive, and mentally ill family members. On the whole, however, they kept their own counsel and followed a "different drummer"—the competence and determination that had led them out of poverty and misery to a more satisfying adult life of their own.

Goals and Worries

Nowhere were the differences between the resilient individuals and their peers with problems in adolescence more apparent than in the goals they had set themselves for their adult lives. Career or job success was the highest priority on the agenda of the resilient men (39.1%) and women (64.7%), but the lowest priority on the agenda of their peers with problems in adolescence. Also high on the priority list of the resilient individuals were self-development and self-fulfillment (M: 34.8%; F: 38.2%) The more traditional goals of a happy marriage, children, and having a home of one's own were mentioned by only about one out of four in this group. The lowest item in priority among their life goals were close relationships with family and friends (M: 8.7%; F: 2.9%).

At age 31/32, worries about finances were on the top of the list for both the resilient individuals and their high risk peers with problems in their teens, followed by worries about their work for the men in both groups, and by worries about their children for the women in both groups. The resilient individuals, however, worried less about their spouses than did peers of the same age and sex who had developed problems in their teens, and they worried more about social issues.

We had not anticipated the high proportion of stress-related health problems that the resilient men and women reported. These rates were more than twice as high as those mentioned by their high risk peers who had developed coping problems in adolescence. More than half of the resilient men (54.5%) and nearly half of the resilient women (41.2%) had some health problems at this stage of life. The majority of the men reported symptoms that appear to be related to stress such as chronic back problems, dizziness, fainting spells, ulcers, and problems with being overweight. Most of the health problems among the women were related to menstruation, pregnancy, or childbirth (premenstrual stress syndromes, migraine headaches, emergency D&C's, toxemic pregnancies, miscarriages, stillbirths, C-sections).

Sources of Support

In contrast to their peers with coping problems in adolescence (who relied mostly on family members and friends), the overwhelming majority of the resilient individuals considered their personal competence and determination to be their most effective resource in dealing with stressful life events (M: 73.9%; F: 61.8%). One of the resilient women, a daughter of an abusive mother, expressed her conviction succinctly: "I am a fighter—I am determined—I *will* survive. I give it 100 percent before I give up. I will never lose hope." A bookkeeper in a local construction company observed, "When things have to be done, you just *do* it. I am not the type of person to run away—no matter how difficult the problem." Said the aerospace engineer: "I don't let problems take control of myself. I just pick myself up and start all over—you can always try again."

Half of the resilient women and more than a third of the resilient men considered their spouses or mates to be important sources of support. The senior supervisor at the local sugar plantation who had lived through a traumatic childhood with a quarrelsome, alcoholic father said: "My wife is always there to listen when I have problems—she cares. That helps me to address the problem—I am not a quitter—I learn." A nursery school teacher who grew up with an alcoholic father commented: "I used to talk to my mom—now I talk to my husband—he supports me." Her twin sister said in a separate interview, "Usually, if I am really down, I talk it over with my husband and my sister. That helps it get off your chest and you feel better afterward."

Nearly half of the resilient women and one out of five among the resilient men relied on faith and prayer as an important source of support in times of difficulties (M: 17.4%; F: 41.2%). Such a faith was not narrowly confined to a particular denomination—for in this cohort there was a wide range of religious persuasions, from Buddhism to Catholicism to various mainstream Protestant denominations, and some were "born again" Christians or Mormons.

The Hawaiian head nurse who worked in a hospital in Yap summed it up: "What has helped me most in difficult times is believing in God—knowing he'd never do anything deliberately to hurt me, and knowing that something good will come out of it all. I know, after a lot of soul searching, that I, as an individual, am responsible for my own life." The part-Chinese, -Irish, -Hawaiian, -Hispanic entertainer at a Polynesian culture center expressed her belief in a very private way: "I know I have *mana* (the Hawaiian spirit)—I respect it in myself, and its effects have shown throughout my life."

The Japanese-American deputy prosecutor had his philosophy of commitment and caring: "I am not active in the church, but I am a believing person. I believe there is a reason for pain and suffering. In real stressful situations, I look at the Bible. I thank God that he gave me the power and strength to be where I am." That statement is echoed by an Assembly of God minister: "I live each day realizing that I can make anything happen when I put my faith in God."

Satisfaction with Their Current Status

Despite some continuing financial worries and the stress of multiple transitions into work, marriage, parenthood—and for some into divorce and remarriage—the overwhelming majority of the resilient men (66.6%) and women (79.4%) considered themselves to be happy or satisfied. Looking back at their lives, many of the resilient men and women commented with some surprise on their own inner strengths and accomplishments. One woman said, "I feel good about myself—actually going over a lot of hurdles—and I know now I can make it on my own." Another commented, "I like myself. . . . I surprise myself a lot with the knowledge I gained from all the jobs I have had and all the people I've met in the jobs. Lots of opportunities came my way." A man said, "The struggle to succeed gave me confidence."

Others looked forward to new challenges in their lives. One man said, "I have accomplished a lot—some of my goals I have reached, but I am always setting new goals." Another commented, "I just think I am 30 years young. I have so much more to do in my life. I can't possibly do all I want to do in 60–70 years." And a woman remarked, "I feel good—I feel that things are really rolling, moving along. It's neat to be married, to get to know a person better, to build a relationship. . . . I feel young to be 30."

A few sensed a time clock ticking away and felt that they had fallen short of the mark—in spite of considerable objective attainment. One woman responded, "Thirty? I feel that every day I am starting from new. Thirty scares me—I am not young any more. Well—I do feel 30! I look in the mirror and see the first white hair." Mused one man, "Ten years go by in a snap, sitting in my living room on my easy chair—and now I am 30. . . . I am still trying to figure out what I am supposed to accomplish. I haven't done the best I could. I can do more." From one of the brightest in this group of accomplished men came this comment: "I don't yet quite know what I am supposed to do with my life, but I am keeping my mind open. At least I try. Somehow I think it will be interesting to see where I'll be ten years from now. I hope it's better than now—I am optimistic and hopeful."

Resilient Children and Their Low Risk Peers as Adults

Measured by objective criteria, the lives of the resilient men and women who had grown up in chronic poverty were as good or better than those of their low risk peers who had grown up in more favorable economic conditions and more stable family contexts. Among the males in both groups, the unemployment rate was below the national average at the time of the follow-up (less than 5%). The majority of the men and women in both groups were in skilled technical or semiprofessional managerial positions. Their marriage rates were similar as well. In both groups, the average number of children was two—the number of offspring most parents expected to have.

Records in the community show that both the resilient men and women and their low risk peers of the same age and sex tended to be law-abiding citizens. None of the resilient men and women had run afoul of the law; only 2 percent of the low risk males and 1 percent of the low risk females had criminal records. One and a half percent of the low risk men and women had been referred for psychiatric care by age 30. None of the resilient men and only two of the resilient women had sought mental health services. In both groups, only a small minority (less than 10%) described themselves as dissatisfied with their accomplishments at the present stage of life.

Despite these similarities, a higher proportion of the resilient individuals evaluated their same sex parents negatively or had ambivalent relationships with them in adulthood. A higher proportion of the resilient individuals also reported that their parents had current problems with alcoholism and/or mental illness. Unlike their low risk peers, the majority of the resilient individuals tended to withdraw from their parents when difficulties in interpersonal relationships arose—a finding also reported by Anthony (1987) in his studies of the adult offspring of psychotic parents.

A significantly lower proportion of the resilient individuals shared common interests, activities, and values with their siblings and their friends. They also turned less often for help to family, friends, and co-workers when difficulties arose in their lives. The resilient individuals relied more exclusively on their own personal competence and determination in difficult times, but they also strove for more intimacy and sharing with spouses or mates. They were more committed to being caring, supportive parents to their own children, especially the males. A majority of the resilient males, but only a minority of their low risk peers, discussed issues with their wives and arrived at a joint resolution of their problems. Two out of three among the resilient males considered parenthood a sign of maturity and looked forward to the opportunity to care for their offspring. Few of the low risk males reported such a commitment to parenthood.

A higher proportion of the resilient individuals who had grown up in childhood poverty considered themselves "happy" and satisfied with their adult accomplishments than did their more affluent peers—a finding also reported by Elder (1974) in the *Children of the Great Depression*; but they also appear to have paid a greater price for their efforts than had their low risk peers. Stress-related health problems, possibly accentuated by constitutional vulnerabilities, were significantly higher among both the resilient men and women than among their low risk peers (M: 54.5% vs. 7.5%; F: 41.2% vs. 13.2%). A higher proportion of resilient individuals also reported serious illnesses and deaths among their parents and had siblings who were handicapped or chronically ill.

In Sum

Personal competence and determination, support from a spouse or mate, and faith were the shared qualities that characterized the resilient children as adults. With few exceptions, they worked well and loved well in contexts far different from the traumatic domestic scenes that had characterized their childhoods. Those who were married had strong commitments to intimacy and sharing with their partners and a sense of generativity which enabled them to be caring parents who respected the individuality and autonomy of their own children.

There was also, however, the need for detachment from kith and kin whose emotional and domestic problems still threatened to engulf them. The delicate balancing act between forming new attachments to loved ones of their choosing and the loosening of old ties that evoked memories of deprivation, loss, and pain, took its toll—among the men in a greater reluctance to make a definite long-lasting commitment to a mate; among the women in a sometimes exhausting tension between marriage, motherhood, and striving for success in a career. The prices they paid varied from stress-related health problems to a certain aloofness in interpersonal relationships. For in some ways they had learned to keep the memories of their childhood adversities at bay by being in the world but not of it.

When they told their tales, however, it was usually without rancor, with a sense of compassion—and above all, with optimism and hopefulness. What set them apart were life histories that revealed a "pattern of gradual mastery, restoration and recovery" (Felsman and Vaillant, 1987).

Cathy

Cathy, one of the 42 resilient women in the 1955 cohort, was the first-born child of a Chinese mother and part-Hawaiian father. Her parents had been unmarried high school students—the mother just sixteen years old and her boyfriend a high school senior. As was typical of the mid 1950s, they had few choices. Both were asked to leave school when the pregnancy was discovered. Although they wanted to marry and although the boy's family favored this move, the girl's parents opposed it. The families were on welfare, and apparently the maternal grandmother did not think they could afford to raise the infant. At first, plans were made for Cathy's mother to go to the Salvation Army Girls' Home in Honolulu and then to release the baby for adoption. But Cathy's mother had objected: "Everybody's been trying to change my mind about my boyfriend, but we've been going steady for four years and nobody can tear us apart now. The teachers want me to finish school and become a teacher, but I'll stay home and care for my baby." She continued, "The court is trying to shield me from the public, but everybody knows I'm pregnant. If I've gotten over my shame, why should anyone else be ashamed?"

The delivery of the baby, Cathy, was uneventful, and her mother reported that she was "happy and relieved" to be able to keep her infant daughter. The parents were married when Cathy was about six months old. She developed normally, although she was prone to rashes and eczema. She was described as an affectionate baby, good-natured and very active and was "spoiled" by all family members including her grandparents. There was no report of sleeping, eating, or other problems in infancy.

Environmental ratings for her first two years were low for both socioeconomic status and family stability. Cathy's mother, however, was rated high in intelligence and considered by the public health nurse to be resourceful, responsible, and self-controlled, taking life in stride. She had the primary care of her daughter during both infancy and early childhood. Developmental and psychological evaluations at age 2 found Cathy "physically and psychologically normal." The psychologist described her as an agreeable and cooperative toddler.

At the time of the 10-year follow-up, the family still lived at the edge of poverty, but emotional support and educational stimulation within the home were considered adequate. In school, a teacher indicated that Cathy was an average student who used her time well, listened carefully, and worked at grade level. She noted no behavioral problems except that Cathy tended to speak softly. The mother confessed, "I used to be annoyed when she would talk nonsense and tell her not to talk if she had nothing to say. Maybe this is why she talks so little in school." She was proud, however, of her other behaviors: "She is very dependable and can be trusted with the baby. She enjoys school and does her homework well. She's been real good." Both parents reinforced her positive behavior by praise and occasional money treats.

By this time Cathy had two younger brothers. The family enjoyed beach and yard picnics and shopping together. Cathy talked to her mother regularly about her activities, but the mother felt that Cathy preferred the father to her. She also had a close relationship with an aunt who lived nearby. She enjoyed Sunday school, 4-H, and hula lessons, was learning to sew, and had some household chores. Although the family did things together on a regular basis, Cathy often chose to be with her friends.

By the time Cathy was seen in adolescence, her parents had separated and she lived with her father. The family continued to have frequent contact with her mother, however, who worked but lived nearby; and they shared many activities together. Cathy was especially close to her youngest sibling, a second grader she helped to "mother." She saw her own mother as a firm person with definite ideas and values she respected and obeyed. As a teenager she felt closer to her mother than to her father, but these relationships changed in later years. At 18 she said of her mother, "She shows the most understanding of all—but we all get along fine. I'd like to be like my mother when I reach that age . . . she's very attractive . . . a lot of people think she's my sister." She was more inclined to talk things over with her mother but said if a matter was "really important, Dad comes in." Disagreements were minimal.

Her schoolwork was adequate, but Cathy decided to pursue a full-time job after graduation from high school. She had continued her interest in hula and had participated in several other extracurricular activities. Her goal, she said, was "just to make enough money and get married and live happily." Describing herself, Cathy said, "I can get along well with people. Since I work with people, I have talent to do things."

By 1987, Cathy, age 32, had married, divorced, and remarried. She was the mother of four children—a teenager and three preschoolers. Since high school graduation she had worked at one of Honolulu's hotels in a variety of positions, each change moving her up the career ladder. She was very satisfied with her work and viewed it as a challenge, particularly since, she said, "I never went to college and I've been accepted without a college degree, and now am being sent to advanced seminars several times a year." Stress for her was "too many bosses," but she found her husband helpful in talking things over—"he massages me and gets the headaches down! If it's really heavy, I go in and talk to the boss on a one-to-one basis." Her own competence and determination to solve any problem were quite apparent. She and her husband had recently purchased a home, a step that had initially caused some financial worry, but once the arrangements had been settled they felt financially stable.

Cathy's first marriage had lasted about three years, and she remarried five years after the divorce. Her present husband, described as a quiet, considerate man, worked in a sales position requiring early and long hours. She particularly liked the fact that he is a "family man," that he "loves me as I am" and "is always there to back me up." Any disagreements, which have been minor, were worked out in discussions. Her expectations for her marriage? "I've always prayed it would continue to grow and our family would be close, and there would not be any problem too big we could not handle. I pray daily."

This relationship contrasts strongly with her first marriage, which was marked by much distrust on her husband's part. Cathy believed that her work, which exposed her to many people, was the primary cause of this distrust and the "main downfall of the marriage." She indicated that their teenage daughter was closer to her first husband than to her, although she has had the primary care of the youngster. As a single parent she had had a difficult time financially and had received no help from the father.

Her younger children were a source of pride and pleasure to her. "I enjoy them—watching them grow up. I guess each is different in his own way." She expressed a healthy attitude in admitting that there were times she just didn't feel like being around them. Both her mother and her in-laws had been sources of support during such stressful times.

Cathy continued to have close contacts with both her parents. She viewed her father as more "mellow," and in contrast to her teen years, she felt closer to him now than to her mother, whom she saw as more controlling. Her father had been particularly supportive during her divorce. "He's always been there for me. During my divorce, when my first husband and I fought, I'd go home to him—he'd take me in. My mom felt I should work it out. He never questioned me about anything, just gave me his whole support." She described her relationships with her siblings as mutually supporting when there are problems, but their contacts were infrequent. A close friend "was always there" during her divorce.

Cathy saw herself as a giving person who got along well with anyone—the latter an evaluation consistent with her teenage appraisal of herself. Her great concern was her inability to be closer to her adolescent daughter. Bringing up her children properly, so that they feel secure at home, was of primary importance to her. She also worried lest her "marriage grow stale. . . . I always try to think of things to put life into my marriage. I don't want it to get dull and him leave—but he says he won't." She hoped to become more efficient in her job and spoke of plans for her house and yard.

The most difficult period of her life had been the breakup of her first marriage and single parenthood. An unsuccessful suicide attempt with sleeping pills after her husband deserted her had helped her to reevaluate her situation: "I believe the Lord still had a lot of things for me to do, and my life wasn't supposed to be over. He was giving me a second chance to live. I learned a lot and grew up a lot in my early 20s. Because my first marriage didn't work, I try in this marriage not to go back to the same things. I made a commitment to myself and on the Bible that this would last. Praying has helped me a lot to deal with stress."

The qualities characteristic of the resilient individuals in this cohort had enabled the adult Cathy to weather early and later trauma, to recover, and to master herself and her situation against many odds. In her early 30s she could, with strong conviction, say, "I feel good. I feel like I've accomplished what I've always wanted."

Edwin

Edwin was the fourth child of Japanese parents. His mother was 35 and his father 41 years old at the time of his birth. His Buddhist family had recently moved to Kauai from one of the other islands, where his father had worked as a mortician's helper. His work on Kauai was at a similar level, and his income very limited. He gambled a great deal and neglected his wife and children. At the time of Edwin's birth, his mother was described as of average intelligence and looking older than her years.

Labor and delivery were rapid, and the infant, who weighed nine pounds, had a slight facial cyanosis. When Edwin was two years old, pediatric evaluations and Cattell and Vineland scales placed him above average in his intellectual and social development. Examiners and observers alike noted that he was a very active toddler. The psychologist also commented on his determination, independence, and responsiveness, as well as on his distractibility and restlessness. His mother considered him to be a good-natured boy, easy to deal with, and without any distressing eating or sleeping habits.

During these years the mother did not have a job but was described as a poor housekeeper. She often visited at a neighbor's house, neglecting her own home. She seemed relaxed and easygoing, rather unemotional, and took things in stride. Their low socioeconomic status and her husband's neglect had not improved. The family lived in chronic poverty.

Edwin was referred to the orthopedic clinic of the Department of Health for his intoeing at age 2½, and he continued to receive follow-up care there until he was nearly 6 years old. Exercises were advised at first, but by age 6 he was not considered in need of further treatment. When seen for the 10-year follow-up, Edwin was somewhat obese. He had received services from the speech therapist in his first two years in school because of a tendency to lisp, and his articulation had improved.

After his biological father's desertion in Edwin's preschool years, his mother divorced; she remarried six years later. Within two weeks of the marriage, Edwin was addressing his stepfather as "Daddy." The new husband legally adopted him. The adoptive father was a part-time truck driver. Both parents did additional part-time work and also received financial help from the Department of Social Services. Environmental ratings of socioeconomic status remained low, but the family provided adequate emotional support and educational stimulation for the boy. When Edwin was in the fifth grade, his classroom teacher considered him an average student who was working at capacity. She noted that he seemed to be "more secure and happier now that he has a father."

The parents considered that Edwin could be successful at college. They read to him regularly; Edwin himself liked to read "easy books" on sports, and both parents read magazines, the daily newspaper, and church and Japanese literature. Edwin belonged to the Boy Scouts, the church Boys' Club, the local YMCA, and took Judo lessons. He was responsible for daily household chores.

The stepfather promoted family outings and often took Edwin fishing. His mother seldom did things alone with Edwin, with the exception of supervising his yard work. She commented that he sometimes talked about friends and school with her but more frequently discussed things with his stepfather. "He always talks to him. They all go to him rather than to me." She seemed unaware of what they discussed. She did feel that the stepfather "talks too rough sometimes to the children," but she kept this to herself as she did not want "to cause trouble." Discipline involved primarily the withholding of privileges; both parents praised Edwin when they were pleased.

During his high school years, Edwin had earned average school grades. No behavioral problems were noted, and sports and cars were his chief interests. He was satisfied with his school performance, being "content to get by. I did good in some, not all." His friends were a very important aspect of school, as well as of his life in general. He planned to take up auto mechanics at the local community college and then to work on Kauai.

Family relationships had been rated as poor at that time. The family did "nothing" as a unit. Edwin perceived his parents as very hard workers who insisted on a similar performance by him. He said that his stepfather had "used force" when he was young and that in later adolescence, he was not getting along well with him or his mother.

After high school graduation, Edwin had gone to Honolulu to register at a community college but was not accepted. Planning to enroll the second semester, he worked there for a while, but he did not like the city and returned home. He was back on Kauai when we interviewed him at 18 years. His return had resulted in conflict with his stepfather, who did not want him to come back and thought he should learn to live on his own. According to Edwin, "as soon as I'd reached 18, he thought I should be on my way and take care of myself." Edwin did not feel that his parents understood him, described disagreements as "a big squawk," and when asked what he did about it, said, "There's no sense. I can't win so I just go out of the house. . . . I'm helping a friend put a car back together, so I'm out every night. They go before I wake up in the morning and are sleeping when I come home." He viewed his friends as his primary source of support, but "most things I handle myself." He saw his strong point as making friends easily and his "hot temper" as a weakness. As he was completing his adolescence, his goals were still undefined. "I'm now only looking for a job; I just want to work. When the future comes, I'll take care of it."

When we interviewed Edwin on the mainland in his early 30s, his resiliency and the qualities that contributed to it were apparent. He had joined the U.S. Navy shortly after his return to Kauai, had spent three years in maintenance work—largely overseas—and was satisfied with his achievement there. "I feel I did a good job and they liked me." Later he worked on the mainland for three years, returned to Hawaii briefly, but found no suitable jobs available and came back to California, where he had worked at a naval air base for the past four years.

During his first mainland stay, he had attended night school, taking welding and math; at the time of the interview he was looking forward to further education in pipefitting and general plumbing work and in drafting. The little job-related stress he reported, he associated with his bosses and handled it by "telling them off. I bitch at them and leave, but my bosses don't want me to leave. I am too good."

Edwin initially found the adjustment to mainland living difficult. He came to know a number of island people who had moved to California, and these contacts eased his adjustment. He became involved in a relationship with a young woman, and they lived together for three years but eventually broke up. Questioned as to how he handled the stress associated with the breakup, he said, "It was difficult at first. I don't know what I did—just kept to myself." As far as future relationships were concerned: "I'll think about marriage in another five years."

Looking at his earlier relationship with his parents and his present feelings about them, he said, "I was raised strict, no TV during homework time. The only thing I hated was that they never let me play football at all. They would tell me not to play with certain people and no football—'If you play football, you move out.'" Angrily he said, "I still talk and think about it. It cannot be resolved; it's too late. If I'd found another family I could live with, I would have; but you should never stop kids from doing what they want to do. All we could play was basketball. . . . Football, I loved that sport, and for basketball I'd tell my parents not even to come and watch me play—though once in a while, they did." In spite of his feelings about his own parents' strictness, in discussing his own thoughts about raising children he said, "I'll be strict. I'll teach them respect. If you teach them when they're small, you won't have to hit them when they're older."

He had not been home in two years, but "I call my parents up on holidays." Although maintaining his distance, he described his mother as "good, really good—sensitive, quiet, and religious." As for his stepfather, "Now I look back. He taught us right from wrong. He did a good job. He taught us how to work early in life, to take responsibility. That's why I'm a good worker today." He felt closer to both parents since he'd "been away and grew up." He continued to have positive feelings about his former girlfriend's parents, whom he still saw and described as "super nice, super mellow." His contacts with his siblings were minimal. Friends continued to be important, but none was "really close." Evaluating himself, Edwin indicated that his strengths lay in getting along easily with people and in being a good listener. His primary goals in life related to job success and tenure, and the few worries he had were job-related: "If outside contractors bid on our work, will I lose my job?"

Looking at himself at age 32, in spite of the adversities that had contributed to his vulnerability in childhood and adolescence, he was able to say, "I think I did pretty good after high school. I made it on my own over here. I had no problem finding jobs. I've been pretty much on my own. I don't talk to people about problems. I keep them to myself. I guess the biggest thing that happened was staying out here after the service. I guess the most important thing that helped me cope was the way I was brought up, to have to learn to earn things and work for what you want. I'm much better than when I was a teenager. Now I don't have too much hatred or prejudice. You know growing up in Hawaii, I was fighting with the *haoles* (Caucasians). Now I see the good and bad in any race. I have all kinds of friends now. I learned after the service. I'm a simple person. I just mellowed out. I'm easy going now. I guess one day I just grew up."

5

Teenage Mothers in Later Years

In our book *Kauaï's Children Come of Age* (1977), we introduced the teenage mothers in this cohort after we had interviewed them at age 18. The 28 girls who bore live children in their teens (one additional female had an abortion) represented 8 percent of the women born on the island in 1955.

The teenage mothers, as a group, had scored within the normal range of intelligence on developmental tests at ages 2 and 10. Only a minority (N: 5) had been considered in need of remedial education in the elementary grades. But by the time we saw these young women in late adolescence, nearly half had developed some problems in school. One-third had come to the attention of the police and/or mental health agencies because of repeated truancies, sexual misconduct, or substance abuse in their teens. In contrast to the positive anticipation of the future which characterized most interviews with their peers, the responses of the teenage mothers at age 18 told a depressing tale of lack of opportunities, lack of faith in the efficacy of their own efforts, and, most of all, lack of self-esteem.

Three out of four among the teenage mothers had grown up in families with four or more children. Most of their parents had not graduated from high school, and there was little educational stimulation at home when they were children. About a third of the teenage mothers had mothers who had borne their daughters when they were adolescents themselves and had been single mothers, rearing their children with the help of grandparents. Girls of Hawaiian descent tended to repeat this pattern. They kept their babies or "hanaied" them to their parents, grandparents, close relatives, or friends—practicing an informal adoption custom that has persisted in the islands across generations.

Although the young women were not altogether lacking in emotional support, the interviews with the teenage mothers at age 18 had not revealed an encouraging outlook for their future. In contrast to peers of the same age, sex, and social class, the majority of the pregnant teenagers had been content to just get by in school (61% vs. 19%). Few expressed any satisfaction with their educational achievement (30% vs. 73%). The majority did not plan to go beyond high school (52%). Vocational plans were undefined or unrealistic for most (59%). Only about a third (35%) had some specific occupational goals. Most planned to marry—and to work to earn money—but were not committed to a job or a career. By age 18, about half of the teenage mothers were married; the other half were still living with their parents.

Married or not, the teenage mothers worried a lot, mostly about money. Very few (less than one out of four) thought highly of themselves at this stage of life or felt that they could control their futures. Although most wanted a better life for themselves and their children, they feared that the door to adult life which was opening to their peers had already shut for them.

One young woman, age 18, with a one-year-old baby and another on the way, summed up what the majority of the teenage mothers tried to tell us in our interviews: "I always wanted things to be perfect: get married, get my own place, be happy; but nothing seems to be going smoothly. I feel life is so hard, and now we are going to have two children, and I don't want them to go through what I went through." Nevertheless, there was determination and a glimmer of hope as well when she concluded the interview: "I want to get a better life for myself and my kids. I want to straighten out and get things right for the children."

Transition into Adulthood

At age 32, the same woman wrote, "I am happy. . . . I think I have accomplished everything that I want. I have a good position at work; my children are older and soon will be on their own; I am in the process of buying my own home, and I look forward to the future."

Asked about the best period of her life so far, she replied, "Age 30—I became more settled down and my children were easier to handle. I decided to go for a career. I was married and had two sets of children (three from her first husband, whom she had married in her teens; two more from her second husband, whom she had married in her mid-20s). Now I have a good job and can advance in my position."

Not every one of the teenage mothers had accomplished as much as this woman, but by age 32 the majority reported that their lot had considerably improved since we first met them at the threshold of adulthood. Our information on their experiences in adulthood is based on two sets of data, collected at age 26 (when their children were in the early elementary grades) and at age 31/32 (when their offspring were teenagers themselves).

By the time this cohort was age 31/32, we had follow-up data on 90 percent of the teenage mothers (26 out of 29), data that include interview and personality questionnaires as well as agency records from the courts, the Departments of Health and Social Services, and the mental health register of the state of Hawaii (see Tables 5 and 7 in Appendix I). One of the teenage mothers had died at age 28 from respiratory distress after a bout with cancer (carcinoma of the tongue) that had spread to her neck and chest.

Our sample of teenage mothers is small and differs in ethnic makeup from the samples in other follow-up studies of adolescent mothers, notably those by Furstenberg, Brooks-Gunn, and Morgan (1987) and Osofsky (1990). Half of the women in this group are of Hawaiian descent; the other half is about evenly divided between women of Japanese, Pilipino, and mixed ethnic heritage. All had come of age and made the transition into adulthood on a small rural island. Yet our findings are strikingly similar to those of the large-scale study of Furstenberg and his associates (Furstenberg et al., 1987, 1989) for a predominantly Black population of teenage mothers in Baltimore and to findings reported by Osofsky from both Caucasian and Black samples in New Orleans and Topeka, Kansas.

Education

By the time of the 26-year follow-up, some 90 percent of the teenage mothers in our cohort had graduated from high school. The high school completion rates of the teenage mothers on Kauai were higher than those commonly reported on the mainland (*Current Population Survey*, 1986; Furstenberg et al., 1987), in part because of extensive outreach programs for potential dropouts at the three high schools on the island; these include special night classes and programs for pregnant teenagers, tutors, outreach counselors, and special off-campus classrooms. All of the teenage mothers we interviewed at the 31/32-year follow-up, had managed to earn a high school diploma or its equivalent.

As was the case in Furstenberg's study, much educational activity took place in the second follow-up phase of our study, between ages 26 and 32, when the women's children were launched in grade school. By age 31/32, the majority of the adolescent mothers on Kauai had obtained additional schooling beyond their high school diploma. Twenty percent had attended the local community college and had obtained associate's degrees (in accounting, the computer sciences, nursing, or tourism/management); another 20 percent had received training through federally sponsored programs such as the Comprehensive Employment and Training Act (CETA). Three of the women had bachelor's degrees from four-year colleges, and one woman had obtained an M.S. degree in social work (gerontology). Others (some 14%) had sought technical training in secretarial work and word processing or attended assertiveness classes in night school.

In comparison with their low risk peers from the same cohort who had postponed their childbearing, however, a significantly higher proportion of the teenage mothers had no additional education beyond high school (40.9% vs. 8.5%), and a significantly lower proportion had attended a four-year college (9.1% vs. 43.8%) by the time they reached age 32. Almost a decade and a half after they crossed the threshold into adulthood, the delayed childbearers in this cohort were still ahead of the teenage mothers in educational attainment—but not as far ahead as they had been six years earlier.

Employment

By their early 30s, the women who had been mothers in their teens had made considerable strides toward economic self-sufficiency. Again, the picture, though not altogether rosy, was not as bleak as we had anticipated when we saw them in adolescence and had improved for most between their mid-20s and their early 30s. By age 26, when the women had barely launched their children into grade school, the majority had worked either in unskilled or semiskilled jobs in the local hotels and restaurants (as cashiers, cooks, maids, and waitresses), and some 20 percent were unemployed. Only one out of five (those who had obtained some college education, either at the local junior college or at a four-year college off the island), worked in a technical, semiprofessional, or managerial position. But even then, only 10 percent (two women) obtained some form of public assistance—mostly to tide them over in family emergencies associated with the breakup of an earlier marriage. One woman had to rely on public welfare; the other received unemployment insurance.

By the time the teenage mothers reached age 31/32, their employment picture was much more positive. Only two of the women, mothers of young preschool children, were currently unemployed and none received welfare payments. In part because of additional education and training, there had been a significant decrease among those in unskilled and semiskilled jobs and a significant increase among women who now worked in technical, semiprofessional, and managerial positions—as accountants, administrative assistants, bookkeepers, insurance sales women, licensed practical nurses, medical and dental assistants, retail buyers, social workers, statisticians, and managers of small businesses. The improvement in the islands' economy (with a booming tourist business) had, no doubt, made this transition easier—but it was noteworthy that most of the jobs the women held in their early 30s were *not* related to tourism and entertainment—as they had been when they were in their early 20s.

Still, some 40 percent of these mothers continued to worry about finances at age 31/32, as they had in their mid-20s. The worries had shifted from survival to housing and entertainment expenses for their offspring, who were now teenagers themselves. There was still a significantly higher proportion of these mothers in unskilled or semiskilled jobs than among low risk women in this birth cohort who had not borne and reared children in their teens (27.3% vs. 9.3%), and a significantly lower proportion were in professional jobs (4.5% vs. 20.9%). Nevertheless, the employment experience of these mothers refuted the popular stereotype of teenage mothers as chronic welfare recipients. As with the cohort of predominantly Black women whom Furstenberg and his associates (1987) followed across a similar time span, we found that the rate of employment of the teenage mothers on Kauai had risen steadily during the course of the study and that their levels of employment had increased with educational opportunities sought out by the mothers once their children were of school age.

An important gateway for better opportunities for them were the day and night classes offered (at little expense) by the local junior colleges; however, it was the drive and determination of the majority of the women "to better themselves for the sake of their children" which made the difference in whether they used the educational facilities available in the community. Osofsky (1990) has also observed in her samples of teenage mothers in Topeka and New Orleans that the mothers' ability to use available community resources made a difference in their lives as did their motivation and capacity to have goals. For as a 32-year-old single mother of five children (ranging in age from 5 to 15 years) told us, "I set a goal at what I wanted—what I believed in—and I didn't stop or give up until I got what I wanted."

Marital Relationships

When we first interviewed the teenage mothers at age 18, about half were married; the other half were not. The same can be said about the marital status of the adolescent mothers at age 26 and at age 32: a little more than half were married; the others were single mothers who had survived one and sometimes two marital breakups. As in the Baltimore study of Black adolescent mothers, about half of the teenage mothers on Kauai had married or remarried in their 20s, while some 40 percent had separated or divorced. By age 32, some 55 percent of the Asian and Polynesian females on Kauai were married, in contrast to only 34 percent of the Black women studied by Furstenberg and his associates (1987).

In comparison with national trends at that time, the proportion of teenage mothers who were married was lower than the norm for U.S. women in their age groups (54.5% vs. 68.5%); but the proportion who were already divorced by age 32 was higher (40.9% vs. 11.5%) (*Current Population Survey*, 1986). In contrast to the low risk women in this birth cohort who waited to have children at a later stage in life, a significantly higher proportion of teenage mothers were unmarried at age 32 (44.5% vs. 30.7%). Of those married, a higher proportion were dissatisfied or felt ambivalent about their marital relationships (55.0% vs. 13.9%). A third of the teenage mothers (33%) had had "messy" divorces, as documented in the files of the family courts. Some had been abused by a spouse or their children had been abused; others' husbands had been delinquent in child support payments.

One woman, in response to the question, "What has been the worst period of your life?" wrote, "My marriage. For we got married too young, and it was hard raising the kids and trying to keep the relationship together. Also, his abusing was horrible. So I ended up at the

Women's Center and got a divorce." Another woman wrote in response to the same question, "My marriage was the worst period [age 16–21] of my life so far. I was beaten by my husband repeatedly. Most of the time he was unemployed and we had severe financial difficulties." Added another, "The worst period of my life was between age 24 and 26. I was divorced and had a relationship with a paranoid schizophrenic and I didn't know it."

The majority of the teenage mothers whose marriages later ended in divorce had reported in the 18-year interviews that they never or only infrequently talked to their fathers (58%), and about half believed that their fathers had little or no influence on them. Nearly half of the teenage mothers had told us that their fathers did not understand them and were unconcerned about them. In contrast, a significantly higher proportion of the teenage mothers with stable marriages or satisfying long-term relationships at age 26 had had good relationships with their fathers in their teens (80% vs. 40%). Marital stability was also related positively to educational and economic achievements when the women were in their mid-20s and early 30s.

Children

As in the Baltimore study of Black teenage mothers, almost all of the young mothers on Kauai had grown up in large families. Fifty-five percent of the adolescent mothers had a second child before age 19, and 10 percent of the young mothers had a third child before 21. The second and third follow-up phases of the study, however, found that the vast majority had been able to control their fertility—as had the teenage mothers in Baltimore (Furstenberg et al., 1987).

Overall, two-fifths of the women had had only one more child; less than a third had had two additional children, and less than one out of four (23.2%) had three or more children. Most of the additional births had occurred when the young mothers were between the ages of 18 and 25, as found in the first follow-up phase. The modal number of live-born children for the adolescent mothers on Kauai by age 32 was two, about half the number of the children they had grown up with in their own families, and the number preferred by most parents in the 1955 birth cohort. These results, for the Asian and Polynesian women in rural Kauai, were very similar to those reported for contemporary Black teenage mothers in metropolitan Baltimore.

In May 1971, when these young women were still in their teens, Hawaii became the first state in the union to allow abortions on the request of the woman. Although the young women of Hawaiian descent were responsible for nearly half (43%) of all the teenage pregnancies, they contributed to only 20 percent of the abortions among the women in our study, in contrast to members of other subcultures such as the Japanese (14% of the teenage pregnancies, 60% of the abortions) and the Caucasians, who were more apt to choose to abort. The choice of abortion seemed more strongly related to the instability of the relationship with the putative father of the child than to conflicting educational and career goals (Gonsalves, 1982).

Significant in their attitudes toward their own offspring was the fact that many of the adolescent mothers on Kauai came from a subculture that valued a nurturant maternal role and prized children highly—a characteristic that still distinguishes contemporary Hawaiians from other American ethnic groups. This pride in their children was very obvious in the spontaneous comments the young mothers made when we interviewed them at ages 26 and 31/32. Said one woman, "My husband and I are better parents now, with the energy to play and surf with our boys, than if we had waited until we were older to start our family." All the women interviewed at age 26 (when their children were in grade school) agreed that it was hard to start a family as an adolescent mother, but none would trade their children for an easier time then or now.

Similar statements recurred when the women were in their early 30s, and their children were now teenagers themselves. Wrote a single mother of five who by age 32 managed a small computer business of her own, "Growing up with my children, being young and energetic, helped me to become a friend and yet a mother to four sons and one daughter. We enjoy each other's company." A social worker, mother of three, who now lived and worked in southern California with her husband added, "The most satisfying thing about being a parent has been receiving unconditional love from my children and seeing the personal growth in each child." Another came right to the point, "What's been most satisfying is when they say 'Love you, Mom' and when their faces show their excitement." A mother of four, who worked as a janitor for the local Headstart program, wrote with great pride, "The best period of my life so far was when my 14-year-old daughter (born when she herself was 17 years old) went to play community basketball and made it. It's a boys' basketball team, and she is on the first string. She made two winning baskets for her team with only five seconds to go and the team won."

Sources of Child Care

How had they managed to balance the demands of child care, schooling, and part- or full-time employment—these adolescent mothers who were barely out of childhood themselves?

Most of the teenage mothers on Kauai, like most adolescent parents from working and lower class homes, had relied on informal support networks of kith and kin rather than on formal day care (Werner, 1984). In some 80 percent of the cases, the teenage mothers had relied on relatives. Major providers of such child care when their children were young were the parents of the teenage mother (45%), other relatives of the young woman such as older sisters, aunts, and maternal grandparents (20%), in-laws (10%), and babysitters in their own homes (20%), who were mostly drawn from the ranks of trusted neighbors. Only four women used nonrelatives as babysitters on a regular basis. Only two teenage mothers reared their children by themselves.

In one out of five cases, the child was reared exclusively by a relative (usually the maternal grandmother) during the first five years, while the young mother finished her education. In about a third of the cases, a relative provided regular full-time child care during the day (or night shift) while the young mother worked. In a third of the cases, relatives rotated in providing part-time care while the teenager worked. In about one out of five cases, relatives were also available for occasional babysitting. Those among the teenage mothers who relied on professional child care were exceptions rather than the rule and would have preferred a domestic arrangement with family members had it been available. These were women who had moved away from the island to complete their education. In most cases, grandparents and in-laws did a good job of rearing the children, but the emphasis on the positive aspects of the grandparents' role should not obscure the possibility of occasionally undesirable consequences. Dell and Applebaum (1977) have used the term *trigenerational enmeshment* to describe the conflict that can result as teenage mothers play overlapping roles of parent and child. Their offspring may have difficulty in differentiating between parent, stepparent, and grandparent, as one might note in this example of a married teenage mother we interviewed at age 18:

Actually when I was born, my mother wasn't married to my father, so I was adopted by my grandparents, my mother's parents. Then my mother got married to a guy. We all lived in a three-bedroom house—three families living in one house. I lived with them till I was about 10. Then my mother divorced and got married to this other guy, and she and my younger brothers and sisters moved to Honolulu . . . and I stayed on in Kauai, and my grandmother, my stepfather, and my cousins and me, we moved to another house. When I was younger I used to have fights with my brothers and sisters, and my real mother would feel bad because they were my brothers and sisters and I shouldn't do that. But then my grandparents used to spank me, and she would feel bad also, and she would say she shouldn't have put me up for adoption, and if she didn't, I would be in Honolulu with her right now. I guess she felt real bad. . . . When I was about 12 years old, I found out I was adopted. Then I remembered when I was small, there was this guy who would come over and be with me, and he was my real father, and my grandmother (my adopted mother) would call me in the house and ask what he was telling me, and I would tell her he was my father, but she said my stepfather was my real father who took care of me. . . . Then after I got pregnant and got married [at age 17], my godmother told me that this guy—my real father—was going back to the Philippine Islands. So I tried to find out where he lived and I saw him the day before he left, and he cried. He didn't really want to go. . . . I wrote to him for a couple of months, and the last time I wrote to him, he didn't answer. . . ." [Question: "You've had so many parents and parent substitutes, how do you feel about that?"] I feel that all my life I've been moved here and moved there, and I guess I'll never be able to understand it all. Guess I'll never be able to settle down; even now that I have a baby of my own.

Personality Characteristics of Teenage Mothers at Ages 26 and 31/32

Independent samples *t* tests, used to compare mean scores on the California Psychological Inventory (CPI) of the adolescent mothers at ages 18 and 26, revealed significant differences on the subscales which had differentiated the teenage mothers from their peers at age 18 (Werner and Smith, 1977). The teenage mothers at age 26 scored significantly higher on Capacity for Status, Social Presence, Responsibility, Socialization,

Tolerance, Achievement via Independence, and Intellectual Efficiency than they had at age 18. They appeared to be more poised, self-confident, nonjudgmental, responsible, socially mature, and independent than they had been in late adolescence; above all, they tended to have a greater faith in the efficacy of their own actions than they had expressed at age 18. On both, the Nowicki Locus of Control Scale at age 26 and on the Rotter's Locus of Control Scale at age 31/32, the adolescent mothers tended to show significantly higher internal control than they had at age 18. In their early 30s, they were significantly more inner-directed than were low risk women of the same age who had not become mothers at such an early age (see Table 7 in Appendix I).

The majority of the teenage mothers felt more in charge of their own lives at age 31/32 than they had at age 18. In response to our question, "What do you consider your strong points?" they tended to give answers such as "Aggressiveness. If I want something, I make sure that I do my utmost to achieve what I want and usually nothing stops me" (from a single mother of five who was a cost technician with a large construction firm); or "I am assertive, innovative, not afraid to go out on a limb for ideas I believe can work" (from a woman who was now a vice president of a real estate company that managed small shopping centers); or "I keep on trying even when the going gets rough" (from a licensed practical nurse who was happily married and the mother of four children).

When we asked these young women about the most important thing that had happened to them in their lives so far, a number pointed with pride to their personal achievements. "I went from teenage unwed motherhood to accomplishing my goal of completing a master's degree which enabled me to support myself and my daughter," wrote the social worker who has specialized in gerontology. "When I first moved here [to California], all I had was my clothes. But now I've got a job, a car, and a place to stay, and lots of friends"—wrote a divorced mother of three—"I am trying to learn more things so I can better myself. I am always looking for challenges for my future," added a teenage mother whose marriage has lasted for fourteen-plus years. "A lot has changed since I attended different seminars for self-improvement," wrote a sales representative and operation supervisor of a local credit union. "Most of all, I have changed and I see and do things in a positive way."

For some teenage mothers, an internal locus of control was the result of a painful struggle. One woman escaped an abusive husband and struck out on her own with her two sons. "It took me a while to like myself—after my marriage," she commented. "But I am really a pleasant person.

For a long time I couldn't stand up for myself. . . . I was terrified of my husband, but he taught me a lot. . . . I finally realized what kind of a person I wanted to be; now I have succeeded." In contrast, another woman attributed her confidence and belief in herself to a very supportive husband and success in her career: "I learned I can really do what I want. . . . I became more ambitious and independent because my husband and my boss kept telling me I can be anything I want to be."

The shift from dependence on others to an appreciation of their own competence and determination was also evident in the sources of support the women enumerated at ages 26 and 31/32. In their mid-20s, the majority had relied on the support of spouses and mates in times of difficulties, or they had sought help from friends, parents, and older siblings. In their early 30s, a higher proportion of the women relied on their own determination and competence. The proportion who relied on the men in their lives had dramatically declined, and so had the proportion of women who still depended on the elders in their family.

Major Worries

Finances were the issue that had worried teenage mothers the most—at the time we first interviewed them at age 18 and again at ages 26 and 31/32 (40.0% and 42.9%). At both follow-ups, a significant proportion also worried about problems of other family members—discord, divorce, and health problems of parents and siblings (40.0% and 38.1%). By age 31/32, a higher proportion of these young women worried about their children than at age 26 (20% vs. 38.1%)—especially about the company they kept and the possibility they might associate with other teenagers who experimented with drugs. These worries may be well founded: Furstenberg and his associates (1987) reported that a large proportion of the children of the teenage mothers in their Baltimore study (over 40%) drank alcohol and smoked marijuana.

Protective Factors

We had detailed interview data on 20 of the 28 teenage mothers when they reached age 26. At that time, 10 of the young women had established stable relationships with a spouse or mate, were employed, and were satisfied with their work. The other 10 were either divorced or separated, had only intermittent employment in unskilled positions, and reported serious financial worries. Looking back over the first two and a half decades of their lives, we found some significant differences in both the behavior characteristics and caregiving environment of these two subgroups of teenage mothers (see Table 10 in Appendix I). Our numbers are small, so we need caution in generalizing from our results, but our findings with a Pacific Asian group of adolescent mothers tend to complement those of the large Baltimore study of Black women reported by Furstenberg et al. (1987).

Teenage mothers whose lot had improved had had less anxious, insecure relationships with their caregivers as infants and a stronger feeling of security as part of their families in adolescence than had teenage mothers whose lot had not improved by their mid-20s. A higher proportion of the more successful teenage mothers had had mothers who had held a steady job when they were children, and a smaller proportion had had problems in their relationship with their father in adolescence. A more internal locus of control at age 18 and a more nurturant, responsible, and flexible attitude in their mid-20s characterized the teenage mothers whose lot had improved by age 26. The unimproved group tended to consist of women who were more anxious, dependent, and inhibited and who believed that events happened to them as a result of fate, luck, or other factors beyond their control.

While the mothers whose lot had improved went to school, their sources of child care differed from those of the adolescent mothers who had not sought further education and who, at age 26, were found mostly in unskilled or semiskilled positions. A higher proportion of teenage mothers whose lot had improved by their mid-20s relied on help by siblings, friends, or in-laws; among those whose lot had not improved, child care was mostly in the hands of the women's parents, possibly increasing their dependency. The more positive outcomes by age 26 were related to a balance of high social support and a moderate number of stressful life events reported by the women.

We had additional interview data on 24 of the 28 teenage mothers at age 31/32. By that time, some 60 percent reported that they were in stable relationships, had work that satisfied them, had good relationships with their children and other family members, and could rely on several sources of support in times of difficulties. Women in this group rated themselves as happy or satisfied with their present stage of life. In contrast, some 40 percent of those who had borne children in their teens felt ambivalent or dissatisfied with their present status in life.

When we contrasted these two subgroups among the teenage mothers, we found significant differences among them which dovetail with the findings of the Baltimore study (Furstenberg et al., 1987). Both the fathers and the mothers of the more successful teenage mothers at age 31/32 had achieved higher levels of education—an average of ten grades—than had the parents of the less successful teenage mothers (whose fathers, on the average, completed only seven grades and whose mothers, on the average, had nine grades of schooling). The more successful teenage mothers had had significantly higher mean scores on the Reasoning factor of the Primary Mental Abilities (PMA) test when they were age 10 (109.4 vs. 97.5), had participated more in school activities during their teens, and had identified more with their fathers than had the less successful teenage mothers. By age 26, a significantly higher proportion in this group had already worked in skilled, semiprofessional, and/or managerial positions (87.8% vs. 14.3%).

The more successful adolescent mothers at age 31/32 also had a higher proportion of stable marriages and/or relationships (75.0% vs. 33.3%) and reported a significantly lower number of stressful life events since age 18 than did the teenage mothers who were ambivalent or dissatisfied with their status in life.

In Sum

On the whole, the teenage mothers on Kauai appeared in a more favorable light when we compare their status in their early 30s with their status at ages 18 and 26. In almost all respects, except for marital stability, they were better off than when we had seen them in their late teens and in their mid-20s. Some six out of ten had obtained additional schooling, some nine out of ten were gainfully employed, and eight out of ten were in skilled, technical, and managerial positions. On the average, they had fewer children than their families of descent—about the same numbers that were anticipated by the women in their cohort who started their childbearing later. Only one of ten in this group were unemployed in their early 30s; only one among them relied on public welfare. Indeed, a higher proportion of the teenage mothers rated themselves as happy in their early 30s than did low risk women in this cohort who had not been early childbearers (52.9% vs. 31.5%).

The paths that led to improvement for the majority of the teenage women on Kauai related to differences in competence and motivation, parental education, support and role models (especially the fathers), and to the emotional support provided by a spouse or mate in a stable union. The development of the woman's personal resources, the support of kith and kin, and the encouragement and support of the husband all acted as protective buffers that contributed to positive changes in their life trajectories from high risk pregnancy to successful adult adaptation. One of the young women summed it up succinctly, "I am currently enjoying the best part of my life, and I know it is getting better. I have a great relationship which we are both willing to work at; I have a pretty good job, lots of opportunities for advancement. Most of all, I am allowed to be independent in what I decide to do with my life, and I feel pretty confident, responsible, and in control of my life."

Jennie

Among the teenage mothers in our cohort whose lot had improved by their mid-20s and early 30s is Jennie, whose life trajectory shifted from the path of high risk pregnancy to successful adult adaptation.

Jennie's parents were in their early 30s at the time of her birth. Her Japanese mother and Portuguese father had three older girls. Her mother had had two prior miscarriages, and so she was particularly careful during this pregnancy. Delivery was normal and the baby welcomed, although her parents had hoped for a boy. The only difficulty noted by her parents was a mild feeding problem. By the time of the one-year follow-up, Jennie was reported to be getting along well, and her mother was described as intelligent, stable, responsible, and self-confident. She was affectionate and calm in her handling of the baby.

Jennie, at age 2, was a solemn child, somewhat stubborn and uncommunicative. She was judged "physically OK" but of slightly below average intelligence. The family lived in poverty, but home visitors perceived her mother to be affectionate and contented, and family stability was rated as high.

At the 10-year follow-up, the family's socioeconomic status was still low. The parents provided adequate emotional support but little educational stimulation. Both parents had only an eighth-grade education, and although her mother reported that she "read a lot," the children were not read to, nor did they read at home themselves. Jennie attended Japanese-language school and participated in 4-H activities, but her mother was concerned that she was below grade level and "slow." Her school record showed academic retardation by that time. She reported that Jennie "tries to get away from doing homework and we let her because she doesn't like pressure." In spite of these comments, her mother saw no real problems and found Jennie "easy to manage." Her father was uncommunicative and seldom commented on her behavior. The family shared few activities together.

By age 18, Jennie, whose PMA IQ at 10 years was 97 and who had already been considered academically retarded in grade 5, was receiving C's in all her school subjects and had achievement test scores in the lowest quartile. Her school record noted frequent tardiness. Jennie tended to "take things as they come." Pregnancy late in her senior year did not prevent her from graduating from high school.

When Jennie was interviewed at age 26, she was described as an enthusiastic, warm, and open person willing to participate in the follow-up interview. By then she had two children and also had experienced a miscarriage. She expressed the wish to have one more child in a couple of years and then return to work. Her husband had a supervisory job in a bank, and Jennie did odd jobs in merchandising and insurance. Her interests centered on her children, and she liked outdoor recreation and, for herself, reading. She hoped to give her children things she had never had—travel experiences and other activities. She did not want to be as strict as her parents had been and tried to let her children "explore things by themselves, help them find out on their own."

She had lived with her husband for about five years before her marriage. He was not the father of her first child, and she had "wanted him to know my son first; it was a 'package deal.' He had to take both of us . . . and he's like a friend to my son" (who still carried the natural father's name in spite of the fact that the latter had visited the boy only three times in seven years). "It was his father's wish to have his name carried on."

Jennie hoped to "understand myself more, develop the inside of me and bring it outside." She viewed herself as aggressive in meeting people and getting things started but as having difficulty "telling someone off." She had experienced a period of marital difficulty, including financial problems, and had gotten help from a coworker. She reported things to be going well at this time and indicated that her husband was her chief source of advice and support.

Seen again in her early 30s, Jennie was back to work as an accounting and claims clerk in an insurance office. She was very satisfied with her job, although it did interfere with family life to some extent. She still had only two children and now expressed no wish for more. Although basically satisfied with her husband, she did express some ambivalence about her marriage—primarily related to needing more time together and "more understanding about child upbringing." Although her husband was "very open with the kids" and continued to relate well to his stepson, she felt that she often needed to "interpret the kids to him." She described her husband as a "very understanding man, very intelligent—but sometimes he's stubborn."

Looking back at her teenage pregnancy, Jennie recalled:

> I was 18. I've put it out of my past already. We were dating. He wanted a sexual relationship; I didn't; I wanted to save myself. "I like being a virgin," I told my friends. I had a lot of platonic relationships with boys. When I met Kimo, he was a sweet talker like I'd never met before. He could sweet talk anyone. We went together six months 'til we did it. I didn't enjoy it. I was unhappy. When I found I was pregnant and told him, he left the island without telling me. I was going to Honolulu to have an abortion, as I felt I wasn't mature enough to be a single parent. I wasn't financially responsible. My sister talked me out of it, and my mother said it was against God's will. They said I could have the child and give it up for adoption. The social worker could guarantee a family. At birth they let me see him and they had the paper ready, but I decided to keep him. I've never regretted that decision. That's when I became closer to religion. . . . Being married to my husband and starting our own family and being a family is the most important thing that's happened in my life.

For her children, Jennie's hopes were "that they'll make the best of their education. Their education is important and their self-esteem—what they think of themselves. I hope they can come to me if they have a problem. I want to try to have good communication." When asked about the most positive aspect of being a parent, she said, "Just being with my kids. What's been most satisfying is when they say 'Love you, Mom' and when their faces show their excitement."

Jennie's mother was still alive, but her father had died several years earlier. She indicated that she had been a somewhat rebellious teenager and that it had been difficult living with her mother, particularly after her first pregnancy:

> We didn't get along very well. She didn't think the way I was raising my son was right. She said, "Just let him go, don't discipline him." But we

are good friends now when we aren't too close to one another. Now we can talk on the phone or set a date to have lunch. Now it's like talking to a friend. We have mutual respect, but back in high school, I couldn't talk to her. My father was really a quiet man who worked all his life. The only time he ever scolded me was when I learned how to smoke cigarettes, and my sister squealed on me. He had never raised his voice before then. . . . It was stressful helping take care of him when he was ill.

Her relationships with her in-laws were very positive, and she described them as "generous, loving, and kind."

Jennie continued to enjoy reading and outdoor activities (especially shoreline fishing) when there was time. She turned to her husband first in times of stress and had a particular friend to talk with "if he can't help me." Although she was not an active churchgoer, she believed that "religion has really helped. Picking up the Bible and reading a passage—it helps when there is no escape."

In her early 30s, she saw her strong points as "being a good listener, getting along with almost anyone, being able to strike up a conversation even with the quiet ones, making others feel comfortable and being nonjudgmental." Her weakness? "I feel scatterbrained sometimes, trying to do things all at once and not planning." She apparently no longer felt the need to "tell someone off," as she had at age 26.

The best period of her life? "My 31st year, which is this year. I just seem to have everything come together now. I like myself—I do—most of the time I like myself."

Martha

The path from teenage pregnancy to early adulthood was less successful for Martha, but her life had improved as well in the period between her mid-20s and early 30s.

Martha was the first-born child of a part-Hawaiian mother and Portuguese father. Martha's mother was 18 years old at the time of her birth and had completed only the ninth grade. During the pregnancy, the public health nurse described Martha's mother as very quiet and unresponsive. She lived with her husband's family, and the mother-in-law had taken over the preparation for the baby's arrival. Martha's mother reportedly "kept to herself." Although we have no confirming medical data, one wonders to what extent she may have been depressed.

The pregnancy and delivery were considered to be uneventful, and Martha's paternal grandmother had the major responsibility for the care of the baby. When she was 20 months, the pediatrician found her to be a "normal female infant." Martha scored significantly above average on the Vineland Social Maturity and Cattell Infant Intelligence scales and was described by the psychologist as a bright, alert child, very responsive to adult attention—"cheerful, independent, and sociable." Her mother, in contrast, was noted to be "indifferent, but relaxed and easy-going—overshadowed by the dominant personality of the mother-in-law." The public health nurse saw Martha as "spoiled by her grandparents and treated like a doll."

By the time Martha was 10, her parents had four younger children. Martha, who had been with her grandmother since infancy, lived separately with her paternal grandparents in an otherwise all-adult household. In spite of chronic poverty, Martha was given adequate emotional support. The grandparents worked, but they took care of Martha at their place of business. She visited her natural parents, and they visited her, but according to her birth mother, she was happy with the grandparents and wanted to stay there. The grandmother reported no problems with the girl. She said that she liked to read and be read to. Martha enjoyed Hawaiian dances as she grew older and became part of an entertainment group at a local hotel. The family enjoyed singing, camping, and activities on the beach, and Martha helped with household chores. She was considered a helpful child who was easy to manage.

Although her grandmother reported that schoolwork was easy for Martha, school records indicated that she was below grade level in all subjects. She had poor school attendance, but her classroom teacher noted no behavioral or emotional problems. She was considered an "attractive child, friendly but brusque."

At age 18, Martha was interviewed shortly after high school graduation. She was already married and had a 6-month-old child. She had lived with her grandmother, whom she considered to have been the most influential person in her life until her last year of high school. Now she and her husband were living with her own parents. She said that she "just didn't care for school, had been in a special project for those 'who didn't like school,'" and that education "really wasn't important" to her. She had no plans for additional schooling and "wanted to be a housewife." She worked part-time in restaurants and hotels.

Speaking of her pregnancy she said, "I decided to have the baby because of my [grand]father [her "adopted" father]. I figured if I got pregnant, I would have to get married, and then I could do what I wanted. He was always picking on me, wouldn't let me go out. I know it's not supposed to be that way, but it's working out OK." She had no special goals. She just wanted a "happy life."

When Martha was seen again at age 26, she was living in a run-down, one-room shack with her siblings. She had been married for eight years, but was currently separated from her husband and involved in a custody battle over their child. She had been beaten by her husband on occasions and was afraid of him. She had adopted the attitude of "let the judge decide" about the custody of her child. Her husband was unemployed, and she worked in a hotel. They had had previous help from social welfare agencies.

She had experienced a series of additional stresses in the intervening years—her father's death, serious quarrels with relatives, health problems, and involvement with the police. In spite of her troubles, she impressed the interviewer as "friendly, confident, bright, and quick with her answers." She had had two miscarriages by that time. She had another boyfriend and was particularly interested in her hotel work. She indicated that she "would consider going to school for that. Work is very important. I want to work. My boss likes me and believes in me. They can depend on me. If it wasn't for them, I would be nothing. But, I'm invaluable to them. They need me." She believed one of her strong points to be her self-reliance and ability to get along with people. "When there was no money and I wasn't working, I didn't ask for help. I sold vegetables, fruit, fish on my own. And then I worked as a maid."

Interviewed again in her early 30s, Martha was reunited with her husband and had another child. "I guess our problem was understanding. I never liked to listen at first to what he wanted to tell me. I learned from that. At that time we never used to talk—that was our problem. We got no outside help. We solved it ourselves when we got together again." Her evaluation of her husband at this stage of life was as "helpful—everything you could find in a man—though he picks on our oldest sometimes. He's basically a good parent."

Both Martha and her husband used prayer when confronted with difficulties on the job and in their marriage. "I don't really go to church. But I know if you do pray, you're going to get help, get the answers. That's what we do. It always works as long as you've got faith."

Martha was not working at the time of the most recent interview, but work was still of prime importance to her. She had been head housekeeper at a hotel and eventually wanted to return to work. "I guess I just like to work. I enjoy it. I stopped recently to stay home with the baby until she's bigger."

Looking back at her relationship with her parents, she was able to express more tolerance of her father than she had earlier. He was no longer alive, but she could say, "We had some bad times and some good times. We disagreed a lot and he drank a lot, but he was a happy-go-lucky man." Her mother was perceived as understanding and always there for them. Her grandparents had died. As for her in-laws: "We have no relationship. My mother-in-law doesn't like me, but that's her problem, not mine. She's there [mainland], I'm here. She left her kids. I guess she didn't like her son marrying me; she hardly talked to me when she did visit." Martha did have a good relationship with her siblings. They helped one another and had played an important part in her life. She did not have any close friends. "I try not to. I would rather stay home and mind my own business than get involved with people. Before, when I had friends, it was too much trouble, and I don't like that kind, so I just mind my own business."

Martha had experienced some additional health problems, including three miscarriages and a recent tubal pregnancy. Although she expressed the wish for three or four children, the doctor had said she had only a limited chance of having more offspring. She was philosophical about this, commenting that "what will be, will be." She continued to enjoy sports. As for her future goals: "The only goal I have is to get my own place. We've been here five years" (a small rental unit near her mother's place).

Martha had difficulty evaluating herself at the close of the interview. She did not know what her strong points might be, but "I try to be a good mother and I try to help people." She generally felt good about herself at this stage of her life. "I was really terrible before this. I cut school. I was involved in drinking, but not drugs. I got involved with troublemakers. I regret the things that happened in high school." Occasionally she thinks of going back to school for further training, perhaps in nursing. When the interviewer commented that it was never too late, she could at least tentatively agree.

6

Delinquents with and without Records of Adult Crimes

On the basis of the police and family court records available in Kauai and the other district courts in Hawaii, we identified 77 males and 26 females in this birth cohort who had been involved in their teens in larceny, burglary, car theft, malicious injury, assault and battery, possession and abuse of drugs, or sexual misconduct (Werner and Smith, 1977). A number of these youths had also repeatedly run away from home, violated curfew regulations, hunted unlawfully, or had been truant from school over extended periods. Excluded from our count were youngsters with only records of traffic citations or occasional trespassing of property (see Table 11 in Appendix I).

Nearly three times as many males as females on Kauai had an official delinquency record (M: 25%; F: 8.5%). Similar gender differences have been documented in other studies. Magnusson (1988) found in his longitudinal study of an urban Swedish cohort, born in 1955, that 28.5 percent of the males, but only 9.0 percent of the females, had been registered for criminal acts before age 18. A generation earlier, Havighurst, Bowman, Liddle, Mathews, and Pierce (1962) followed some 500 youths in a midwestern city in the United States from grade 6 through high school and noted that about a third of the males, but only 8 percent of the females, had some contact with the police during adolescence.

Most of the youths with delinquency records in our cohort had had problems in school before they were in trouble with the police. By age 10, one out of two had been considered in need of remedial education or special class placement, and one out of five had been in need of mental health services. The combined rates of educational and mental health problems for these children by age 10 was twice as high as the rates for the cohort as a whole.

There were significant differences in exposure to stressful life events between youths with delinquency records and same sex peers without delinquency records and/or mental health problems. Among both sexes, a significantly higher proportion of youngsters with delinquency records had been exposed to stressful life events that disrupted their family units, such as serious discord between parents, father absence, parental separation, desertion, or divorce. A higher proportion of males with police and/or family court contacts had been exposed to such stressful life events in childhood, while a higher proportion of females had been exposed to such stress in adolescence. About a third of the delinquent males had fathers with criminal records; delinquent females had a high proportion of family members (parents, siblings) with handicaps and learning and/or behavior problems (Werner, 1987).

The female delinquents had had more multiple problems in the second decade of life than had the male delinquents. By age 18, half of the females, but only one out of four among the males with delinquency records, had serious mental health problems necessitating in- or out-patient treatment. A third of the teenage mothers were among the delinquent females, although they constituted only 8 percent of the women in this cohort.

Predictors of Delinquency

The Men

The single most powerful predictor among the early childhood data for the boys in this cohort was a low rating of family stability (r = .19). When we combined all of our follow-up data available for the males at age 2, the multiple correlation rose to a R = .32. A low level of maternal education and a low standard of living, the presence of a congenital defect, and the mother's rating of a high activity level for her one-year-old infant, as well as below average self-help skills (low Vineland SQ) at age 2, contributed most of the added predictive power for the boys.

The two most powerful predictors of delinquency in boys at age 10 was a PMA IQ below 90 (r = .24) and a recognized need for remedial education (r = . 24). The addition of other diagnostic data obtained at age 10 raised the multiple correlation to an R of .46 for the boys, with most of the added predictive power contributed by a low socioeconomic status, a low level of maternal education, and the presence of a physical handicap at age 10. The addition of the data available by age 2 to the data from the 10-year follow-up raised the multiple correlation for the boys from R = .48 to R = .79.

The Women

The most powerful predictors of delinquency among the early childhood data for the girls was a Cattell IQ score below 80 at age 2 (r = .38) and the presence of a congenital defect (r = .37). The multiple correlation coefficient (measuring the relationship between a combination of all the variables available by age 2 with the outcome variable) rose to an R of .44 for the girls, with most of the predictive power contributed by a low level of maternal education (8 grades or less), the presence of a moderate to severe degree of perinatal stress, distressing feeding or sleeping habits, and temper tantrums noted by the mother at age 1 or by the psychologist during the 2-year examination.

The single most powerful predictor of delinquency in girls at age 10 was a recognized need for mental health services, with a correlation of r = .30. When we added the other diagnostic data obtained at age 10, we obtained a multiple correlation of R = .74. A low socioeconomic status rating, a low PMA IQ score (below 90), and a recognized need for remedial education at age 10 added most of the predictive power to the multiple correlation for the girls. The addition of the results from the 2-year examination to the 10-year data raised the multiple correlation for the girls from R = .74 to R = .81.

For both sexes, predictions of delinquency in adolescence increased from modest correlations at year 2 to high multiple correlation coefficients by year 10. Variables that were predictive of delinquency in girls in adolescence reflected the presence of behavior problems and a need for mental health services in the early elementary grades. In contrast, most boys who were to become delinquent had learning problems and were in need of remedial education (especially in reading) by age 10. Predictions improved when we took into account the family's socioeconomic status (low), the mother's level of education (low), and the presence of a congenital defect or a physical handicap by age 10. Predictions were best when birth, 2-year and 10-year data were combined.

The Delinquents in Their Early 30s

We have follow-up data in adulthood on 73 percent of the delinquents in the 1955 birth cohort who were still alive by age 31/32 (M: 50; F: 22). These data included everyone who had a record with the criminal, civil, and family courts of the state of Hawaii, the statewide mental health register, the Department of Social Services and Housing, the Division of Vocational Rehabilitation, and the U.S. Veterans Administration (for individuals who had enlisted in the armed forces).

Five males with police records had died since our last follow-up, accounting for half of all the male deaths in this cohort since age 18. Three men had died in their early 20s—one in a car crash and two from accidental drowning. A fourth, a skin diver, had an accident when free diving at thirty feet for tourists under a glass-bottom boat off the Kona Coast of the Island of Hawaii. The fifth casualty was a young man who had suffered from AIDS and who died from respiratory arrest and cryptococcal meningitis at age 30. As a teenager, he had been involved in car theft and substance abuse. He had joined the U.S. Marines at age 18 and received an honorable discharge after one year's service.

Twenty-one individuals (M: 18; F: 3) with delinquency records were among the 31 surviving members of the 1955 birth cohort who had criminal records by the time they reached age 32. Most prevalent in young adulthood were violations of narcotic laws, violent crimes (including murder, forcible rape, robbery, and aggravated assault), possession of stolen property, and disorderly conduct (see Table 12 in Appendix I).

Seventy percent of the males arrested for criminal offenses had a delinquency record, as did 66 percent of the female adult offenders. Such a retrospective look at the lives of persons who committed adult offenses may give the impression of a considerable amount of stability in criminal behavior. When we took a prospective view, however, we found that only 28 percent of the male delinquents and only 10 percent of the female delinquents in this cohort were convicted for any adult crimes. Most juvenile offenders avoided arrest after reaching adulthood; this was especially true for individuals with only one or two offenses before age 18.

Our findings with a Pacific Asian sample on rural Kauai dovetail with those reported from other longitudinal studies of contemporary cohorts of young adults on the U.S. mainland and in Europe. Wolfgang, Thornberry, and Figlio (1987) reported from Philadelphia that only 28 percent of white males who were taken into custody as juveniles were arrested as adults (but for Blacks the percentage was 54). A study of a Swedish birth cohort, born the same year as the children of Kauai, found that only a third of the male offenders in childhood and adolescence had any record of adult criminal activity by age 29 (Magnusson, 1988). A follow-up of a birth cohort in Great Britain (Wadsworth, 1979) also noted that more delinquent boys than girls became recidivist.

Characteristics of Persistent Offenders

Three out of four among the small group of juvenile offenders (N: 21) who committed further crimes in adulthood had grown up in chronic poverty as children. Two out of three had PMA IQs below 90. Half came from families broken by desertion, separation, or divorce, and one out of three had a father with a criminal record. Four out of five in this group had been considered in need of remedial education by age 10, before their delinquent careers began. On the average, these persistent offenders had been arrested four times prior to age 18 (mean: 3.6).

By age 32, nearly half in this group (45%) had broken marriages. Their divorce rate was twice as high as that for delinquents who did not engage in criminal activity as adults, and three times as high as that for the cohort as a whole. This group also contained the highest proportion of men who were delinquent in child support payments and who had a history of family abuse (i.e., who battered spouses and children). A third of the men had been referred to state mental health agencies for diagnosis and (more rarely) treatment.

With the exception of property crimes, there was not much consistency in the type of offenses these individuals committed as juveniles and as adults. Only 20 percent of the individuals convicted on narcotic drug offenses in young adulthood had been arrested for substance abuse as teenagers; only a third who were involved in crimes of violence (assault, rape, attempted murder) between the ages of 18 and 32 had been arrested for assault and battery or malicious injury in adolescence. But nearly two-thirds (63%) of the men and women who were engaged in theft and burglary or car theft in young adulthood had been arrested for larceny, burglary and/or car theft in their teens as well.

Our findings with this small group of delinquents turned criminals on a rural Hawaiian island are similar to those reported by Wolfgang and his associates from a large cohort of white and Black males in Philadelphia, by Farrington (1989) from a cohort of British working class youth, and by Magnusson (1988) from a cohort of Swedish men and women born in the same year as our study children.

Farrington (1989) reported that the majority of the 65 London men who were first convicted before their twenty-first birthday and went on to commit further crimes up to age 32 came from low income homes, scored low on intelligence tests in middle childhood, had experienced "poor child rearing," and had a parent who had been convicted for a crime. These characteristics were quite similar to the backgrounds of the persistent offenders on Kauai who were descendants of Asian and Polynesian immigrants.

Wolfgang, Thornberry, and Figlio (1987) reported from a sample of 975 Philadelphia males (representing 10 percent of the original cohort studied) that serious offenses were committed by a relatively small number of offenders and that males with four or more arrest records before age 18 had a much higher probability of arrests for adult crimes by age 30 than those with only one or two juvenile offenses. Among the minority of Swedish males whose criminal activities persisted from adolescence to adulthood, about half also had other adjustment problems, such as alcoholism or mental health problems (Magnuson, 1988). The story is the same for the persistent offenders on Kauai.

However, we found significant sex differences between male and female delinquents whose antisocial behavior persisted into adulthood (see Table 13 in Appendix I). A higher proportion of female than male delinquents who were engaged in criminal acts in adulthood had congenital defects (M: 14.3%; F: 37.5%), had parents who were alcoholic, mentally ill, or retarded (M: 19%; F: 75.0%), and had siblings with developmental disabilities (M: 4.8%; F: 71.5%). Our numbers are small, but our findings are in agreement with other American and European research reviewed by Widom and Ames (1988), findings that suggest that chronic female offenders may have a greater biological predisposition to antisocial behavior than male offenders. This issue needs to be addressed more systematically in prospective studies of delinquency and crime.

Latecomers to Crime

Ten individuals (8 men and 2 women) from this cohort were first arrested for adult crimes after age 18 without having had a record of previous juvenile offenses. All but one had been convicted for only one criminal offense before age 32. The exception was a male who was first convicted for first-degree rape at age 19 and subsequently arrested for assault (at age 26) and terrorist threats and harassment of a public servant (at age 28). The offenses of the newcomers were similar to those of the persistent offenders, ranging from the most frequent offense, promotion of dangerous drugs, to assault, property crimes, and driving under the influence of alcohol.

The socioeconomic class distribution of the newcomers to crime resembled that of the birth cohort as a whole: half came from poor homes, the other half from middle class homes; but like the persistent offenders, 80 percent of the newcomers to crime in young adulthood had been in need of remedial education as early as grade 5. Seventy percent had PMA IQs below 90 at age 10 and had been considered either slow learners, learning disabled, or borderline mentally retarded. Low intelligence was also one of the few childhood predictors found in the Cambridge Study of Delinquent Development that differentiated the latecomers to crime from the other working class males who had not committed any juvenile or adult offenses by age 32 (Farrington, 1989).

Delinquents and Their Low Risk Peers in Adulthood

How well did the delinquent youths fare in adulthood in comparison with low risk peers of the same age and sex who had not been arrested for juvenile offenses and who had no other serious coping problems by age 18?

The Men

A significantly higher proportion of men with than without a delinquency record had taken some technical training in the local community college or in the armed forces to prepare themselves for their work (62.1% vs. 21.3%). A significantly lower proportion had gone on to a four-year college (13.8% vs. 53.7%). None had gone to a graduate or professional school. Most of the men with records of previous delinquencies tended to be blue collar workers. A significantly lower proportion of the men with than without records of juvenile offenses held semiprofessional or managerial positions (13.3% vs. 40.7%), and a significantly higher proportion were in semiskilled jobs (30% vs. 8.3%). Among their ranks were bartenders, carpenters, communication technicians, construction workers, electricians, factory mechanics, fire-equipment operators, plumbers, security guards, tractor and truck drivers, treatment-plant operators, warehouse workers, and welders. Several had made the army a career—one was a recruitment officer. Another worked as a correctional officer for the state of Hawaii. One former delinquent was a car salesman, another an insurance agent. None of the men with records of juvenile offenses was unemployed.

A significant minority of the men with juvenile offenses were dissatisfied with their current jobs, especially in their relationship with bosses and union officials. Wrote a tractor operator for the county of Kauai, "There is too much politics in the system, too many unfair rules. There is union corruption, poor leadership. The whole system stinks." Most of those who felt dissatisfied reported that problems on the job remained unresolved and continued to frustrate them. Wrote another union member, a plumber, "I saw the mayor; wrote to the union president; saw a lawyer; talked to the Labor Board. Nothing helped." A truck driver added, "There is nothing much we can do except grumble among ourselves." These men had also significantly higher mean scores on the Anger Scale of the EAS Temperament Survey for Adults than did men without records of juvenile offenses.

A significantly lower proportion of the men with than without delinquency records shared common values with their siblings and friends and used them as positive role models. A significantly higher proportion of the men with than without delinquency records worried about their work (36.7% vs. 17.3%), their wives (26.7% vs. 9.6%), and their children (33.3% vs. 20.2%).

Some who had problems with spouses or mates referred to lack of fidelity. The army recruiter wrote, "The problem which led to my divorce was her being caught in bed with another man when I returned from Granada." "My wife fooled around," said a divorced truck driver. The security guard complained, "Minor things turn into a major verbal war." The treatment plant operator added, "My wife and I simply cannot get along. I am working on it and thinking about a divorce." A recently divorced carpenter with a new mate said, "My girlfriend has a very, very spoiled daughter. I always end up in a stressful argument with her." Grumbled a truck driver, "I can't agree with my wife working. We talk about it, but she is so stubborn—we can't come to an agreement."

About his children, a man who held only part-time employment at the local sugar plantation wrote, "The thing that is difficult is children nowadays don't know the value of money." Some of the paternal worries of the former delinquents had to do with enforcing rules and regulations. A worker in the sugar mill wrote, "It is difficult to teach them respect and responsibility." Others were concerned with proper parental supervision. A factory mechanic added, "It is hard to keep a watchful eye on the kids." Wrote a welder, "I am trying hard to raise them the best way I can, and hope it is not the wrong way." A truck driver worried, "I have not enough patience in teaching them."

Even though they still harbored a residue of anger, most of the men who were juvenile offenders had not gone on to a criminal career, and most were satisfied with their accomplishments by the time they reached their early 30s. Wrote a fire equipment operator who was happily married and the father of a teenage boy and girl, "The best period of my life so far is between age 25 and now. Why? Because I am financially stable and the family is set and stable." A factory mechanic optimistically added, "There are always better moments in life 'cause there will always be better things that happen in the future that make you happy."

The Women

The 26 women with records of juvenile offenses had a higher proportion of mental health problems in adolescence than did the men with juvenile records. Two females had been runaways from foster homes. One of the women had been raped (at 12) by her father, who was subsequently incarcerated for incest. Another was molested by her father's friend (at age 16). One of the delinquent women had made a suicide attempt at age 15, after a "misunderstanding" with her parents; another was committed to a local hospital at age 15 in an acute state of anxiety and depression. Two of the women with juvenile offenses had been diagnosed as schizophrenic in their teens: one was a borderline psychotic with paranoid delusion (at age 16); the other was admitted to the state mental hospital with an acute schizophrenic episode at age 18 (and was readmitted in her mid-20s).

In spite of the preponderance of multiple problems among the females with juvenile offenses, only three (10%) of the women with delinquency records in this birth cohort had been arrested for adult crimes by age 32. Of the 26 female delinquents, only three could be found in the criminal records of the district courts on Hawaii: two had been arrested for theft, the other for criminal contempt of court (vagrancy). Not only were there fewer women than men who became delinquent, there were also fewer delinquent women who became persistent offenders and who had committed more than one criminal act by age 32; however, when we compared the responses of the women who had been juvenile offenders with those of their low risk peers without delinquency records, we still noted some significant differences in their adult lives.

Forty percent of the women with records of juvenile offenses had not obtained any additional schooling beyond high school—in contrast to only 8.5 percent of the women without delinquency records. None had gone on to a four-year college or graduate school, and none held a professional position by age 31/32.

A significantly higher proportion of women with than without records of juvenile offenses were unemployed (35.7% vs. 9.3%) or worked in jobs with a high turnover rate, such as as bartenders, cocktail waitresses, counterpersons in fast food restaurants, dime store clerks, or janitors.

The proportions of women who were married by age 32 (about two-thirds) were similar for both groups. Significantly higher proportions of women with than without delinquency records, however, were dissatisfied with their marriages or worried about their spouses. Women with records of juvenile offenses had, on the average, a larger number of children by age 32 than did women without such records (2.13 vs. 1.24); but a higher proportion of the former delinquents felt ambivalent or were dissatisfied in their relationships with their offspring (27.3% vs. 11.3%).

A significantly lower proportion of women who had been delinquent in adolescence shared common interests and activities with their brothers and sisters (42.9% vs. 69.1%), and a significantly lower proportion reported that they received emotional support from siblings (35.7% vs. 78.2%) or friends (42.9% vs. 87.5%). A lower proportion of the women with than without records of juvenile offenses relied on their personal competence and determination in difficult times (33.3% vs. 63.1%). They also turned less often to parents, friends, coworkers, or prayer for support in times of difficulties than did their low risk peers. A sizable proportion, some 40 percent, felt ambivalent about their status in life at age 31/32.

"Just making it in life is my personal goal," wrote a female former delinquent who worked for a zoo. "I hope to get married yet," wrote another woman (in criminal contempt of court because of vagrancy), who struggled as a single mother to raise a 13-year-old girl and a 6-year-old boy. "My husband is going to jail," worried a third—who tended bar to support a teenage son and a 6-year-old daughter.

These women also had significantly higher scores on the Anger, Fear, and Distress scales of the EAS Adult Temperament Survey for Adults than did their low risk peers (see Table 7 in Appendix I). There was still a residue of internal problems which emerged in the self-reports of these female delinquents. In the next section, we shall see how they tried to cope with their current cares, which focused mainly on economic survival, children, and their mates—the same concerns that the delinquent males shared at this stage of life.

Protective Factors and Turning Points

There were a number of protective factors and turning points in the lives of the delinquent youths who did not go on to commit any adult crimes (see Table 14 in Appendix I).

Personal Characteristics

Delinquents who did not go on to commit any adult crimes had significantly higher mean scores on the Cattell IQ at age 2 than did the persistent offenders (96.3 vs. 89.4). They were also significantly more advanced in self-help skills in early childhood (mean SQ: 117) than were juvenile offenders who later were arrested for adult crimes (mean SQ: 108).

By age 10, there were no significant mean differences in PMA IQs between juvenile delinquents who did not go on to commit adult crimes and those who did (96.0 vs. 94.0). Only a small proportion of the desisters (12.7%), however, were considered in need of mental health services by age 10, in contrast to a significant minority (35.7%) of the persistent offenders. A significantly higher proportion of youths who were to become persistent offenders in adolescence and young adulthood were described by their classroom teachers as having temper tantrums and uncontrollable emotions and as being extremely irritable. Among delinquents who went on to commit adult crimes were also a significantly higher proportion who were considered classroom bullies and frequent liars by both their teachers and their parents in independent evaluations. These same traits also characterized the chronic offenders among the British boys in the Cambridge Study of Delinquent Development who were first evaluated by their teachers at ages 8 and 10 and who have now been followed to age 32 (Farrington, 1989).

Family

The presence of an intact family unit in childhood, and especially in adolescence, was a major protective factor in the lives of delinquent youths in this birth cohort who did not commit any offenses in early adulthood. Only one out of four in this group grew up in a home where either the mother or the father was absent for prolonged periods of times because of separation, desertion, or divorce. In striking contrast, five out of six among the delinquents who went on to commit adult crimes came from families in which one parent was absent for prolonged periods of time during their teens.

Police and court records also revealed that among the delinquent youths who did not go on to criminal careers the parents or other elders (grandparents, aunts) were more actively involved in their rehabilitation process than were the parents of later offenders. Parents would appear with the youths in court, assist in restitution where it was called for, and attend, with their sons and daughters, the counseling sessions provided by the family court. In some cases, the parents expressed embarrassment and shame over the behavior of their offspring—they felt that they had "lost face."

In contrast, most delinquent youths who went on to become persistent offenders had parents who were too involved in their own emotional and marital problems to cooperate actively with the family court and schools. Some left the island (for Honolulu and the mainland) to remarry and start a new family. Foster home placement and the Hawaii Youth Correctional Facility did not prove to be adequate parent substitutes for the persistent offenders in this group. For some, however, a promising alternative appeared to be enlistment in the military or marriage to a stable spouse.

Military Service

Both Glueck and Glueck (1968) and Elder (1986) have shown that a personal history of disadvantage, poor grades, and self-inadequacy increased the appeal of military service for earlier generations of youth who joined the armed forces during World War II and the Korean War. The same can be said for a subgroup of delinquent youths in this birth cohort who had grown up under the shadow of the Vietnam War. By the time they were in high school, the compulsory draft had been eliminated and antimilitary feelings generally ran high in the United States.

Voluntary enlistment in the armed forces, however, remained an attractive alternative for minority youths from disadvantaged backgrounds whose mediocre school record might have led to employment problems. This was especially true for a generation that entered the work force during one of the major economic recessions in the United States since the Great Depression.

The appeal of military duty for these youths can also be linked to the educational and vocational benefits of the G.I. bill (Elder, 1986; Sellman, 1990). Educational assistance is extended to any veteran who served on active duty for more than 180 continuous days, any part of which occurred after January 31, 1955, and before January 1, 1977, and who was released under conditions other than dishonorable or who continues on active duty. An eligible veteran who has served a period of eighteen continuous months or more after January 31, 1955, is entitled to educational assistance for forty-five months. In addition, a veteran pursuing high school training after release from active duty may receive an educational assistance allowance without a charge against his or her basic entitlement. Also, a veteran who must pursue additional secondary training, such as refresher courses, or make up for deficiencies to qualify for admission to an appropriate educational institution may receive educational assistance without a charge against the basic entitlement.

Twenty-two youths among the delinquents in this birth cohort (some 30%) enlisted in the armed forces—the majority right out of high school. Two-thirds were 18 years old when they signed up; the others joined between ages 20 and 24. Two-thirds joined the U.S. Army, 14 percent joined the U.S. Air Force, 10 percent each joined the U.S. Navy and the U.S. Marines. Altogether, delinquent youths accounted for one-third of the voluntary enlistments into military service among members of this birth cohort. Enlistment rates among the individuals with records of juvenile offenses were more than twice as high as the national average (of 14.6%) for persons in their age group at that time (*Current Population Survey*, 1986).

The majority of the men (and one woman enlistee) served for three years or more. They rose from a pay grade of E-1 ($620 per month base pay and free room and board, health care, and commissary privileges) to a pay grade of E-5 ($890 per month base pay and attending privileges). All received a satisfactory performance rating and an honorable discharge, including the young marine who later died from AIDS.

There were also some adult casualties among the veterans: one out of five had criminal records by age 32—three for assault, two for theft, and two for driving under the influence of alcohol. One (with one of the lowest IQ scores among the veterans) had a record of wife abuse and delinquent child payments after discharge from the military and was eventually charged for attempted murder; he stabbed the boyfriend of his estranged wife.

But military service turned out to be a helpful moratorium for most delinquent youths and opened doors to educational and vocational opportunities that were utilized by two-thirds of these veterans during and after their enlistment period. Two among the army volunteers and one in the air force made the military a career and have served fifteen years in uniform. One became an army recruiter. Two-thirds of the men used their educational benefits to obtain technical training or a college education. Most often they chose junior college, but there were also some graduates of four-year colleges in this group. Those who used their educational benefits tended to have scores within the normal range of intelligence on PMA IQ tests at age 10 (between 90 and 115). What is most encouraging is the way in which the majority of the juvenile offenders used the military to open doors for future educational and vocational opportunities.

At age 31/32, some men fondly recalled the friends they had made in the military and the opportunities that opened up to them. Wrote a man who was a victim of child abuse, "I learned confidence on the job and how to be responsible." A security guard who served for three years in the air force remembered, "The best years of my life were my three years of service in Germany and all the friends I made." "The friends I made in the army have helped me most in life," wrote a former juvenile offender who had become a correctional officer for the state of Hawaii. The army recruiter considered his major mission on the job "to overcome the rejection by the public. I make people aware of what the army has to offer and the changes that have occurred over the years."

Marriage

Investigators in the Cambridge Study of Delinquent Development had noted that former delinquents who married were convicted of fewer crimes than was the case among those who remained single in their 20s (West, 1982). We found a similar trend among the former delinquents in the Kauai Longitudinal Study. By age 32, persistent offenders were more likely to be either single or divorced than were the men and women who refrained from criminal acts as adults.

The majority of respondents among the former delinquents who had committed no adult crimes by age 32 considered their spouses to be major sources of help in difficult times. Wrote a communication technician with a record of larceny as a teenager, "My wife has really kept me in line and has contributed to helping me deal with the big decisions in life. She has changed my life for the better and taught me things like being open-minded and looking at people from a more positive perspective." This sentiment was echoed by a fire equipment operator who had a juvenile record of shoplifting and malicious injury: "The most important thing that has happened to me in my life so far is getting married to a great wife. She taught me to stop and think things out before acting."

Several of the men who were rehabilitated juvenile offenders commented on the company and emotional support provided by their wives which had replaced the support of their former male associates. Wrote an electrician with a juvenile record of larceny and repeated traffic violations, "The best time of my life has been after marriage—it is very pleasant to have someone to come home to every night." "Talking to my wife" and "the positive attitude of my wife" were recurrent comments of delinquent males who were happily married and had committed no adult crimes.

The female delinquents who were settled in family life and who had no criminal arrest records as adults relied on their husbands as a major source of emotional support as well. One out of five among these women had had a first marriage (usually as a teenager) that ended in divorce, but each appeared happy with a second relationship. A library aide who had a teenage record as a runaway and shoplifter wrote, "The best years of my life are now. I am 32 years old and content in my marriage. I have a daughter, and now in the other half of my life I can teach and watch her grow."

A housewife with three children, who had a juvenile record of assault and battery, commented, "The understanding that my husband and I have shared helped the most. The most important thing that has happened to me so far is being married for ten years."

Some of the former delinquents stressed the importance of a faith or religious belief they shared with their spouses. A former runaway from a foster home who had been raped at age 16 and had subsequently become involved in sexual misconduct and narcotic offenses wrote, "My husband and I are both dedicated and baptized Jehovah's Witnesses. We attend four weekly Bible discussions. There we learn how to cope with various problems that confront us daily. I know now that marriage is not something to be taken lightly, but that it is a life-long commitment" (a considerable change in her attitude from the time she contracted her first marriage at age 15, which was annulled a week later because she found out she was not pregnant).

"Being born again" was an important experience for some married male delinquents as well. A truck driver with a record of juvenile thefts wrote, "Because I changed my whole life style for the better—personally and in my relationship to my wife—she and I can deal with all the stresses in life." "Believing in faith, the Lord, and my wife has made all the difference," commented a plantation worker with a juvenile record of malicious injury.

The quality of the relationship and the kind of person chosen as a marriage partner appeared more important for the former youthful delinquents than did the change from single to marital status per se. We also noted that most of the former offenders who now had stable marriages by age 31/32 had IQs (measured at 10) which fell in the normal range, while the persistent offenders with a high incidence of broken marriages tended to score in the "slow learner" range. And, not infrequently, it was a second marriage for both men and women in this group which had a restraining effect on them, rather than a hasty marriage contracted because of a teenage pregnancy.

Parenthood

More than half of the persistent male offenders among the former delinquents on Kauai (N: 10/18) had been sued by their wives for child support. More often than not their wages were eventually garnished by order of the court because the men were negligent in support. In contrast, delinquents who refrained from adult crime expressed a more positive and responsible attitude toward parenthood.

In response to our question, "What has been the most important thing that has happened in your life so far?" a factory mechanic exclaimed, "Being a father. Alyssa, my 10-month-old daughter, is my first and greatest accomplishment so far." "Seeing my kids grow up and the way they adjust to life makes me feel responsible," wrote a part-time plantation worker. "Understanding their ways of thinking and trying to put them in perspective with life is one of the most difficult things I had to learn about raising children," a fireman added. "Having your child lift you up when you are down has been the most satisfying experience as a father," wrote a warehouse manager. "Watching our kids grow up and learning from them and seeing a part of us in them" had been the most satisfying experience of a proud mother of three who had come a long way since her battered childhood and battering teens. "Teaching your children to do or be all they can be" was the challenge of a library aide who used to be an "incorrigible" runaway in her teens; and "Watching them grow up without being brats, like we were," was the joy of the mother of twins who had accumulated a police record of several offenses by age 15. Perhaps the army recruiter captured best a pride in parenthood which was shared by many: "The best period in my life is now. Why? Because I am a father and I know that the cycle of life is starting all over again."

In Sum

Most of the delinquent youths in this birth cohort did not go on to adult criminal careers. Three-fourths of the males and 90 percent of the females with records of juvenile offenses avoided arrest on reaching adulthood. This outcome was especially true for those with only one or two offenses before age 18.

The majority of the adult crimes in this cohort were committed by a small group of juvenile offenders with an average of four or more arrests before age 18. About half in this group had broken marriages by age 30 and were delinquent in child support payments, and included the men who had battered their wives and/or children. The vast majority of these persistent offenders had been in need of remedial education before they began their delinquent careers (by age 10), had been considered troublesome by their fifth-grade teachers and parents, and had grown up in homes where either the mother or father were absent for prolonged periods of time during adolescence.

In contrast, delinquent youths who did not go on to commit any adult crimes tended to score within the average range of intelligence in early and middle childhood, were not described as troublesome by their teachers or parents when they were in grade school, and during their teens had grown up in intact family units in which at least one of their elders (a parent, grandparent, or aunt) provided structure and stability in their lives. Military service, marriage to a stable partner, and parenthood proved to be positive turning points in the adult lives of these crime-resistant juvenile offenders—especially for the men.

John

John, one of the 77 males in the 1955 birth cohort who had an official delinquency record in adolescence, was also one of those who in the intervening years to adulthood had avoided further recorded offenses. His early history contains many of the characteristics predictive of delinquency and associated with the cohort members identified as delinquent in adolescence.

John was born to 30-year-old Caucasian-Pilipino parents who already had six other children. The oldest sibling, a severely brain-damaged and retarded child, had been born out of wedlock when his mother was only 14 years old. His mother experienced very long labor with John—"I had a hard time. I thought I would die. The doctor told me I could have had ten babies during that time." In spite of her difficulty, John's mother seemed happy and confident in the early months and the baby normal.

At the time of the one-year interview, John was considered to be a healthy, happy, fairly active baby, but with a definite temper. The mother was described by the public health nurse as "childlike, complaining, and unintelligent." She had had only a third-grade education, but the father had graduated from high school and taken additional college work in the armed services. Their standard of living was rated as low.

When the toddler was seen at 2 years, the pediatrician noted that he was well behaved and considered his physical development to be normal. The psychologist, however, suspected mental retardation along with parental rejection. The mother was considered "hostile and discontented," and John was described as a "disagreeable, insecure, stubborn, restless boy."

Between ages 6 and 8 years, John had been followed by the island's orthopedic clinic for Legg Perthes disease and had had hip surgery, necessitating a rather lengthy hospitalization. By age 10 he was a year behind his grade level in school and was receiving D's and F's. His classroom teacher believed that he could improve his reading comprehension with more outside reading. Psychological testing yielded a WISC (Wechsler Intelligence Scale for Children) Verbal IQ of 84, a Performance IQ of 97, and a Full Scale IQ of 89, scores that placed John in the slow learner range. He was described as "a shy, soft-spoken youngster, who is eager to please, but who becomes tense and uncomfortable when he feels he is unable to meet the demands of the situation." His classroom teachers noted that in the fifth grade John displayed "uncontrolled emotions and temper tantrums." He was frequently involved in playground fights at recess. In earlier grades, his unpredictable behavior had been considered his greatest difficulty by his teachers.

John's father was the informant for the 10-year parent interview. He reported that John's mother had had a nervous breakdown two years before, for which she was hospitalized. Describing her as "tense and easily upset," he said she did not try to handle John—"if she gets disturbed, she will leave the children and go into her room, and maybe cry." His father supervised their homework and activities and, in general, tried to make up for the mother's lack of involvement in child care, but he was often too busy. The father also provided most of the discipline—"it works better, my wife loses her temper"—consisting primarily of a loud voice or shaking, no spanking.

Describing John, his father said, "He keeps himself neat and clean. He presses his clothes each morning and polishes his shoes. But he never was able to hold still. He has temper tantrums, loses control, and gets vicious. It got worse after his illness with his leg. He'll throw anything handy—but usually misses his target. He will throw himself on the ground and kick and scream. The boy always had a bad temper, but being crippled made him worse because he couldn't do so many things, and because the boys on the playground would laugh if he fell."

Throughout his teens, John was still one year behind grade level, receiving C's and D's. His SCAT and STEP scores were below the twentieth percentile. Stresses that had occurred in the intervening years were related to ongoing failing grades in school and his parents' separation and father's remarriage. His identified delinquencies occurred in his early teen years (ages 14 and 15) and consisted of larceny (breaking and entering, but dropping stolen object when chased) and other neighborhood disturbances, such as shooting a pellet gun and harassing animals. These offenses were handled directly by the police and no referral was made to the court.

His interview at age 18, at the end of his senior year, suggested increased maturity. John reported that he liked sports and school and considered education important in finding jobs. He added, "I'm doing real good." He was working part-time as a mechanic and hoped to go to a junior college and take further mechanical training. He indicated that he got along well with his friends and liked those that "treat me good and make me feel happy."

His relationship with his father and stepmother had improved and seemed positive (his mother had died). "They treat me real good, and give me what I want, and let me do anything I feel I'm right in doing. They understand me." He described his stepmother as one who "treats me real good like a real mother—she talks to me about things." He said that his father was the main person who had influenced him "because he's the man of the family, and he tells everybody what to do and what is right."

Evaluating himself, John showed some insight into his behavior but also tended to gloss over some of his earlier difficulties: speaking of a car theft in his younger years, he focused on the fact that he had broken his arm in an accident, not on the theft itself. He did list as his weak point "I do wrong things at school and home" and said that what he most wanted to achieve in life was to "keep out of trouble and on the right track. I want to get more education and show my parents that I've grown up and know what's right." Describing himself as he neared the end of adolescence, John said, "In elementary school, I had a pretty hard time. From the time I entered high school, things were different. Teachers explained better and told you the facts. I see high school as a big thing. From high school on I grew up, and now I think I'm a man. I know now what's right and wrong. I'm happy. I think I will be away from here in ten years—I'll live in the states."

At age 32, however, John was back on Kauai, working in condominium maintenance. As he had earlier hoped, he had attended a junior college away from Hawaii, but had returned home after six months: "I got homesick. It was my first time away from the islands, and I had no local friends." Since that time, he had worked in a variety of jobs, primarily related to equipment maintenance. Like the majority of the juvenile offenders in our study, he had avoided adult crimes and was satisfied with his accomplishments. "I have no problems with anybody or anything. I just want to work and do my job as good as I can and please everybody." He reported occasional minor stresses related to misunderstanding with coworkers and said that he handled these by talking it over with his parents and girlfriend.

John had been living with his girlfriend for over five years and had three children by her. Her mother also lived with them. He described his girlfriend as "a nice lady, the quiet type. She keeps to herself and minds her own business. She tries to be friendly with those she can communicate with. Otherwise she keeps to herself." He admitted to some difficulties "just when she gets angry—then she's hard to talk to. Otherwise when she keeps cool, it's fine, and she's easy to talk with." Disagreements arose when he chose to spend time with friends, playing ball, hunting, and so on. His hopes for their relationship were continued improvement in communication and a house of their own. For his children he had "big hopes. I hope someday they can get into sports, do better in work as they go on in school, and get a better education and things like that."

His parents provided understanding and emotional support. "My stepmother is really kind. My father is really an understanding man. I can sit down and talk to them and solve all kinds of problems. I always go up there in the morning and evening, spend time with them, and check on them. They're getting old, and I'm the last one around that is still single and can check on them." He also expressed positive feelings toward his siblings and friends.

Sports and outdoor activities continued to be his major interests. Evaluating his strong and weak points, John said, "I'm someone that people can trust. I really can communicate with people. I'm really friendly, soft-hearted, and really understanding." His goal was to better himself, particularly on his job. Questioned about his worries, John said, "Well, what really worries me is my mom and dad and my children. I love them so much it makes me worried. And also my girlfriend too." Looking back, he described his hospital experience as the most critical in his life: "It really set me back for months. I missed a whole school year, but I thank them for everything they did for me. I enjoyed some of it and missed my friends there. There'll be a day when I want to go back and see them."

The major problem since high school? "The main one was when I came back from the mainland and had to start all over again. It was like starting a new life—make my pride get up again—start all over and find where I was. I was depressed in many ways, but I got help from my parents."

Asked how he felt about himself now, John said, "Well, I feel I'm doing really good since I'm out of high school. I'm going on the right track as life goes on. What really keeps me going too is my stepmom and dad and sons and my girlfriend too. I give them a lot of credit. They keep me up there."

Although John's earlier delinquencies were relatively minor and he now denied any problems and seemed optimistic about himself and his life, about six months after his 32-year interview a notice appeared in the local newspaper that a "misdemeanor marijuana charge" against John was "dismissed without prejudice." We wonder if he will he continue to beat the odds?

Ellen

Among the women in our cohort who had police records in adolescence was Ellen, the daughter of a Pilipino father and Hawaiian mother. Ellen's delinquencies were considered sufficiently minor that she was never referred to family court in her teens, although she had been followed by the probation officer in preadolescence. Nor was she ever arrested or convicted of any adult offenses. Like John, however, she displayed many of the characteristics we found associated with the delinquents in our cohort.

Ellen was the second of six children. Her birth weight was somewhat low (5 lbs., 9½ oz.), but the infant was apparently healthy. Her mother, an obese woman of over two hundred pounds, said, "I'm tickled," at the birth of her daughter and indicated that the baby was well accepted by both parents. Her father had been born in the Philippines, had only a third-grade education, and worked as a plantation laborer. Her mother had gone through twelfth grade on Kauai, but she was described by the nurse who interviewed her during pregnancy as a person who "tells many conflicting stories."

At the one-year examination, Ellen was getting along well, apparently receiving a good deal of attention. She was described as happy, healthy, and good-natured. Her mother, however, was considered by the visiting social worker to be "irresponsible, demanding, and someone who never tells the truth." On two occasions, during the second and third years of life, Ellen scored "low average" on the Cattell Infant Intelligence Scale and on the Vineland Social Maturity Scale. On both occasions, the child was also described as "bashful, hesitant, dependent, inhibited, passive, and quiet." Her mother appeared to be an easygoing woman who took things in stride, but was careless. There was a continued notation of the "many stories" she told.

By age 10, Ellen was in the fourth grade (having repeated the third grade), and was receiving C's and D's. Her PMA IQ was in the normal range (101). School records indicated that she was obese, slow moving, and listless. She tended to blame others when she got in trouble with her classmates, was irritable, and displayed lack of confidence. She was often truant, and the probation department who was involved in following her situation reported that her mother drank and gambled and neglected the children. The family home was described as disordered and filthy when the mother was not expecting visitors. The father bathed and cared for the children to the extent he was able. Ellen's "listlessness" was attributed to lack of sleep.

In spite of these negative observations by the classroom teacher and home visitors, the mother painted a fairly rosy picture. She described Ellen as having "a beautiful personality—she agrees with everything—she's always smiling and she tries to help others." She said that Ellen enjoyed reading and that she was rewarded for her good behavior by gifts of money. Her father was reported to spoil her. Her mother, however, also made reference to Ellen's difficulty in sitting still and her uncontrolled emotions: "She kicks and screams when she gets angry with her brothers." She also reported that Ellen's feelings were frequently hurt and that she cried easily. The plantation nurse, in turn, commented that the mother "is a great liar—we have a bad time with her." The school authorities sent a letter, in grade 5, to the parents suggesting the need for remedial help, but apparently there was no follow-through.

Ellen's delinquencies, consisting primarily of frequent truancies, occurred in the early high school years. She was sent to Honolulu to live with a brother but continued the truant patterns there. "I didn't go to school for a week, and my brother didn't know. When he found out, he actually threatened to kill me. They shipped me out back here." She received help from the school counselor throughout her high school years—particularly focusing on her relationship with her parents, or "when I can't handle a problem myself."

Ellen worked part-time during her last years in high school and during summers "to learn and get experience." She had a steady boyfriend, hoped to get married eventually, and planned to work "after the children were 4 years old." She reported that she got along well with her siblings and was particularly close to her older brother. She felt closer to her father, whom she described as "sweet and patient," than to her mother, who was "hot-blooded—as she doesn't trust me—she's afraid I'll embarrass her by getting pregnant." Ellen did not consider that either parent really understood her—"They don't try to understand—my mother never did try." Her parents frequently quarreled.

In describing herself at age 18, Ellen said, "I'm patient and understanding. I'm a semi-happy person—not really [happy], I have my ups and downs." She saw the future as a happier time than the present. Attempting to evaluate her strengths and weaknesses, she said, "The best part of me is I like school, and the worst is I'm not patient enough. But I'm not trying to change. I'm satisfied with the way I am."

By age 32, Ellen had been married for over eight years to a man twenty years her senior. She had four young adult stepchildren. She had not had schooling beyond high school but had worked in a variety of clerical jobs. When a job became stressful, she quit. The family's current income was adequate without her working.

Ellen's husband had been a plantation worker but was now on medical retirement, following major surgery four years earlier. Ellen described him as a "warm, loving, and good father—he's a mature person—he does not put too many demands on me—he's really understanding and open-minded. Our marriage started being superperfect since he's been home." In the early years of the marriage, she worried about his first wife: "she's given us an extremely hard time—she had the kids then, and wouldn't let him take them. She resented me as I took her place. She used the kids to get back at me."

She admitted to some disagreements with her husband about her two younger stepdaughters, who were now in their late teens: "He has his old-fashioned beliefs. I'm trying to make him see the modern. The girls deserve freedom and trust. He's too old-fashioned; the older one has to take the younger sister on dates. He's afraid to trust them—more, he's afraid to lose them. I look at them as my sisters—it works out better than being a stepmother. I know what I went through with my mom, but they talk to me." She described her stepchildren as "wonderful kids, easy to work with. Sometimes they have a hard time understanding where I'm coming from, but I made myself a sister; I played with them when they were younger. The eldest daughter accepted me from day one, and she helped the others understand what was going on with her father and me." As to their future, she said, "I don't have any hopes for them as I feel it's their life—it's up to them to decide. They make their own hopes and dreams." On the positive and negative aspects of parenting, Ellen said, "It's been good being able to give the kids something that I never had. My mother loved me, but she had her own thing going. What my mother never gave me, I'm trying to give the kids. . . . But the hard part was that I had to stop having what I wanted to have, go without a lot of things. I was married two years before we fought for custody of the kids. I was a spoiled brat. I had to change and adjust to being a stepmother."

At the time of the 32-year interview, Ellen's father was still alive, but her mother had died two years earlier. Ellen had frequent contact with her father, visiting him every weekend and calling him daily. She expressed concern that some of the other siblings took advantage of him. Reminiscing about her mother, she said, "She was a hard lady. She had problems with alcohol when I was young. She liked fun. She was happy-go-lucky," but "no matter where she was, if I needed her she was there. The difficult part was she was too demanding, she expected too much, put the responsibility on us. I was the oldest girl and had to watch the younger ones while she was off drinking and playing cards." She said that her mother had never interfered, "never stuck her nose in our marriage—she let me fight my own battles. They were both very accepting of the marriage." She saw her father as "superterrific, a hard-working man; he can't stay idle. Our relationship just started when Mother died. I felt what I'd had with her, I had to make up with him. My husband tells me he's needing me as Mother's gone. What I like about being married to my husband is he's older and helps me understand a lot of things. He's been through a lot, so he reminds me of it."

Ellen reported that she had a close relationship with her siblings, enjoyed her friends, and still liked outdoor activities, as well as reading and sewing. She considered her strong point to be "my attitude toward my marriage—the older man and the stepchildren. This is my strongest, most positive thing. I accept anybody and anything. I'm not prejudiced." She found it difficult to think of weaknesses: "I can't think of any now—I would just like to change my body. I'd like to have a major overhaul." The hardest problem Ellen had had to face since high school was her husband's suicide attempt following his surgery. "He felt he didn't belong any more. We both got hurt. We had psychological help, and the counselor said it was me—I was too pushy in the relationship—but they didn't really understand how different he was after his surgery from the man I had married. But now he's back to himself 98 percent. I'm not worried he'll do it again—it's all pretty much buried." Ellen said she handled stress by "blocking it off—not making it the most important thing in my life."

She considered her loss of her mother "just when I started to know her" as one of the most critical events in her life. "I guess the way I had felt about my mom and what she did, I don't want to put that on my kids. My mom just ignored me when I was young. She wasn't abusive. When she stopped drinking about two years before I was married, that was the turnabout in our relationship. We lived on opposite sides of the island, so I hardly saw her, and just as I really started to know her, she passed away. But there's a purpose in everything. I'm a very strong believer in that. There's a reason for it. I believe it strongly—like there's a purpose in my being here right now."

Summing up her perception of herself as she entered her 30s, Ellen said, "I'm a basic person—there's not much more to know. I'm me, and my life is just what I told you. I feel super. I like myself."

7

Mental Health Problems: Troubled Youths Grown Up

At age 10, 25 youngsters (14 boys, 11 girls) in this cohort needed long-term mental health care (of more than six months' duration). Their emotional problems had been identified through behavior checklists filled out independently by their parents and their teachers and confirmed by diagnostic tests and observations of clinical psychologists and child psychiatrists (Werner and Smith, 1977). Twenty (80%) of these children had conduct problems and displayed overt antisocial behavior. Among the other five were two diagnosed as adjustment reactions to childhood, and one each with a diagnosis of childhood neurosis, schizoid personality, and sociopathic personality.

By age 18, the number of individuals with serious mental health problems had grown to 70 youths (23 males, 47 females). Among them were teenagers who had been sent to the Hawaii State Mental Hospital or the local hospitals on Kauai for mental health reasons or who had been under treatment as outpatients of the Kauai Community Mental Health Center. Their diagnoses ranged from problems of sexual identity to neurotic symptoms, hysteria, severe depressions (including two suicide attempts), obsessive compulsive behavior, and paranoid, schizoid behavior. Half of the males and one-third of the females in this group also had records of juvenile offenses.

The changing sex ratio in mental disorders from childhood to adolescence which we found on Kauai is supported by national data from first admissions to public and private mental health hospitals, general hospitals, and outpatient clinics at that time (Gove, 1979). In childhood, boys tend to have higher rates of mental health problems than girls, but by late adolescence females tend to have higher rates than males. The pertinent literature on childhood and adolescence suggests that boys experience more stress than girls in the first decade of life and are more vulnerable than girls to the effects of biological insults or caregiving deficits in childhood (Rutter, 1985). This trend is reversed by the end of the second decade of life, with females reporting more stressful life events than males, especially when they are confronted with teenage pregnancies and early marriages (Werner and Smith, 1982).

We noted significant differences in exposure to stressful life events between youths with mental health problems in their teens and peers (of the same age and sex) without serious coping problems by age 18. Among both sexes, a higher proportion of individuals with mental health problems in adolescence had parents (especially mothers) who were alcoholic or psychotic and brothers or sisters who were developmentally disabled. A higher proportion of teenagers with mental health problems had experienced the arrival of a younger sibling before they were 2 years old and received "below normal" ratings on the 2-year developmental examination by the attending psychologists.

By age 10, the majority of the youths who developed mental health problems in their teens were already having problems in school. In adolescence, a higher proportion of these youngsters had conflict-ridden relationships with their peers and experienced prolonged parental absences due to desertion, separation, or divorce.

Predictors of Mental Health Problems

The Men

Among the data we had obtained in early childhood, a low standard of living at birth was the single most powerful early predictor of serious mental health problems for the males by age 18 (r = .21). A combination of low standard of living, moderate to high perinatal stress, high activity level, and distressing habits of the baby at year one with a low level of maternal education and low family stability in the first two years, was the most effective set of early predictors for the boys (R = .33).

For boys at age 10, the single most powerful predictor of serious mental health problems by age 18 was a recognized need for mental health services (of more than six months' duration) (r = .65). When we combined the diagnosis of need for long-term mental health services with the need for remedial education and the presence of a moderate to marked physical handicap at age 10, we obtained an R of .88.

The Women

For girls at age 2, a low socioeconomic status was the most powerful single predictor of serious mental health problems by age 18 (r = .31). A combination of low SES, the presence of a congenital defect, and a low rating of physical development by the pediatricians at age 2 was the most effective set of early predictors (R = .36).

For girls at age 10, the single most powerful predictor of serious mental health problems in late adolescence was a diagnosis of learning disability (r = .37). Multiple correlations, based on a combination of all 10-year data, rose to an R of .76. A recognized need for mental health services and the presence of a moderate to marked physical handicap by age 10, added to the diagnosis of learning disability, contributed most of the increased predictive power in the multiple regression equation.

For both sexes, a combination of serious learning and behavior problems with a moderate to marked physical handicap by age 10 was the most powerful set of predictors of serious mental health problems by age 18. The predictability of later mental health problems improved considerably from the early to the middle childhood years, an improvement reflecting the cumulative effects of biological predisposition and caregiving deficits during the first decade of life. Children who had grown up in chronic poverty were most vulnerable to this interaction.

Troubled Youths in Their Early 30s

We were able to obtain follow-up data at ages 31/32 for 81 percent (57/70) of the individuals with mental health problems in their teens (M: 23; F: 34). By the time they had reached their early 30s, more than half of the youths with mental health problems in adolescence had recovered. Nearly half of the men and two-thirds of the women in this group did not have any problems that necessitated the intervention of the courts, the Departments of Health and Mental Health, or the Department of Social Services of the state of Hawaii. The proportions of troubled youths who showed spontaneous recovery in adulthood in this rural Pacific Asian cohort are identical with those reported by Robins (1978) in her studies of Black and Caucasian teenagers in St. Louis and by Magnusson (1988) in his follow-up studies of a contemporary Swedish cohort.

There were some continuing casualties as well. About half of the troubled teenage boys and a third of the troubled teenage girls encountered problems in making the transition to adulthood. One-third of the men but only 8 percent of the women with mental health problems in their teens required public mental health services between ages 18 and 32. Among them were one male and two females who had previously been diagnosed as schizophrenic and three males who had problems with their sexual identity. One of the males in this group was dismissed from the air force after four months' service.

Nearly half of the men but only 5 percent of the women with mental health problems in their teens had criminal records by age 32. Among them were the majority of children who had been diagnosed as having conduct disorders by age 10. Twenty-two percent of the men with mental health problems in their teens had criminal court records *and* had been admitted to psychiatric care after age 18. Among them was an individual who had attempted murder, another who shot and killed a man in a domestic quarrel, and others who had been involved in serious narcotic offenses and repeated car thefts. These men had been referred to psychiatric care by the local courts.

Our findings are similar to those reported by Magnusson (1988) from his longitudinal study of a Swedish cohort born in 1955. He noted that during late adolescence about twice as many females as males require mental health services, but that fewer than every fifth female with psychiatric problems in her teens was still in psychiatric care during early adulthood. In his cohort, as in ours, about a third of the males with onset of psychiatric disorders in their teens remained in psychiatric care as young adults. Among Swedish males with previous mental health problems in their teens, about half of those with criminal records needed psychiatric care when they reached young adulthood. Our findings, albeit with different ethnic groups in a different geographical and cultural context, are identical and support his plea that effective research on psychiatric illness and criminality cannot be conducted in isolation from each other.

Most vulnerable in adulthood was the small group of teenagers who had both records of mental health problems and records of juvenile offenses by age 18 (see Tables 15 and 16 in Appendix I). Eleven of the twelve men in this group and six of the thirteen women had two or more coping problems by the time they reached their early 30s; these included broken marriages, criminal records, and/or psychiatric illnesses.

Troubled Youths and Their Low Risk Peers in Adulthood

How well did the troubled youths fare in adulthood in comparison with their low risk peers of the same age and sex who did not have a record of serious coping problems in their teens?

The Men

Only one out of five among the men with mental health problems in their teens had attended college, in contrast to more than half of the men without such problems. When confronted with difficulties in school, one out of three among the troubled youths had dropped out; very few (3%) of the men without mental health problems in their teens chose this route and closed the doors that a college education can open.

Men with mental health problems in their youth also had a more difficult time finding work to their liking. Two out of three had held four or more jobs since they left high school. By age 32, nearly one out of two (45.5%) held a semiskilled job—in contrast to only 8.3 percent of the men without mental health problems. Not one of the men with mental health problems in their youth held semi-professional or managerial positions by the time they had reached their early 30s, while nearly half of the men without mental health problems (40.7%) held such positions.

Fewer than half of the men with mental health problems in their youth were married (45.5%). Eighteen percent had marriages that had ended in divorce by age 32. Among those currently single, only half lived in long-term relationships. A significantly higher proportion of the men with than without mental health problems in their youth worried about their relationships with their spouses or mates in adulthood (27.3% vs. 9.6%).

In their early 30s, a significantly higher proportion of men with than without mental health problems in their youth relied on their friends for financial support (30% vs. 6.1%). A significantly lower proportion relied on their own determination and competence when faced with difficulties in life (27.3% vs. 52.8%). One out of four of the men with mental health problems in their teens reported stress-related health problems in adulthood, and about a third were ambivalent or unhappy about their present status in life.

The Women

Women with mental health problems in their teens had also obtained less schooling than their low risk peers. Nearly half had no additional training after they left high school. Only one out of three among the women with previous mental health problems but nearly two-thirds of the women without such problems had obtained some college education before they reached age 32.

Like their male counterparts, women with mental health problems in their teens tended to change jobs frequently. Three out of four had held three or more jobs since they left high school. In their early 30s, 40 percent of the women with previous mental health problems but only one out of ten of those without any previous problems were in semi- or unskilled jobs. Nearly half of the women with mental health problems in their youth were dissatisfied or had ambivalent feelings about their current jobs.

Three out of four among the women with previous mental health problems were married—proportions that were higher than for their male counterparts and for the women without mental health problems in their teens. They also had more children than their low risk peers. A third of the married women with mental health problems in their youth, however, were dissatisfied with their current marriages and their relationships with their offspring.

By age 32, half of the women with mental health problems in their teens still felt ambivalent about their status in life, and a third reported stress-related health problems. These women also had significantly higher mean scores on the Anger Scale of the EAS Temperament Survey for Adults than did the women without serious coping problems in their teens (see Table 7 in Appendix I).

New Admissions to Psychiatric Care after Age 18

Sixteen individuals in this birth cohort first received psychiatric care after our follow-up at age 18. Six (40%) were diagnosed as schizophrenics; two (13%) were diagnosed as suffering from severe depression; three (20%) had problems associated with marital maladjustment; three (20%) were diagnosed as adjustment reactions to adulthood, and two (13%) were diagnosed as having mental health problems associated with borderline mental retardation. One individual who attempted to murder the boyfriend of his estranged wife was referred for a sanity test (see Table 17 in Appendix I).

Men and women were about equally represented among the first admissions to psychiatric care at ages 18–19, 20–24, 25–30, and 30–32. Some 88 percent of the men but only 38 percent of the women in this group had been in need of remedial education by age 10 or had committed some juvenile offenses by age 18. A third of the males but none of the females among the first admissions to psychiatric care between ages 18 and 32 had a parent with a serious mental health problem and/or a criminal record by age 32.

We noted that four of the six individuals diagnosed as schizophrenics and one of the two individuals with affective disorders had been exposed to moderate to severe degrees of perinatal stress at birth. These rates are four to five times higher than for the cohort as a whole. Only 3 percent of all children born in 1955 had been exposed to severe perinatal complications, and 10 percent had experienced complications of moderate severity.

Although our sample is small, our findings agree with reports from larger studies with different ethnic groups on the U.S. mainland and in Denmark. Buka, Lipsitt, and Tsuang (1987) reported some preliminary results of a 20-year prospective investigation of perinatal complications and psychiatric outcomes. Their study cohort consists of 176 singleton births, diagnosed as either "severe toxemia" or "breech delivery," and 176 matched controls, all selected from the Providence, R.I., center of the National Collaborative Project (NCP). Preliminary analyses of their follow-up data at ages 18–24 suggests elevated rates of substance abuse, antisocial personality, and schizophrenia associated with the perinatal complications of breech birth or severe toxemia. Similar trends have been found by Katz (1990) and his collaborators in follow-up studies of Black youths who were part of the National Collaborative Project at the University of Pennsylvania in Philadelphia. Their samples include both mentally ill and homeless persons in their late 20s.

In Denmark, Mednick and his associates (1984) examined 204 offspring of schizophrenic mothers at the median age of 15 years. A higher proportion of these offspring who became mentally ill by their mid-20s had suffered from pregnancy and birth complications than did those who did not become psychotic. In both the Danish and the Kauai longitudinal studies, association between perinatal stress and deviant behavior in adulthood varied by gender.

Turning Points and Protective Factors

Psychotherapy

About a third of the men and women in this cohort who had been identified as having serious mental health problems received some form of mental health care in adolescence or young adulthood. This relatively small proportion was identical with the percentage of youngsters among child guidance referrals who received treatment one or two generations ago—before any widespread federal, state, or local concern for the mental health of America's youth (Robins, 1966; Levitt, 1971).

Among major sources of referral to state-supported mental health care for troubled youths were the courts and other community agencies (37.0%), private physicians and hospitals (22.2%), and family or friends (22.2%). There were relatively few self-referrals (14.8%). About half of the referred clients received mental health care in an inpatient setting, at local hospitals or in the state hospital in Honolulu; the other half were seen in outpatient clinics on Kauai or the other Hawaiian islands.

Of the third who received publicly funded mental health care, about half (44%) were judged to be "improved" at the time their treatment terminated. Mental health professionals tended to assign this label most often to men and women with the diagnoses of adjustment reactions to adolescence or adulthood and to individuals with marital problems, transitory depressions, and hysterical personality disorders. Among those judged "unchanged" or "undetermined" were individuals with major psychoses (schizophrenia, severe depression) and the "sociopathic" personalities. The fortunate few who had received counseling and were improved expressed less conflict, and greater self-insight and goal differentiation, in our interviews than did individuals whose condition had remained unchanged or worsened. They also had a more positive self-concept.

A young woman who had received help from mental-health professionals in her late teens and early 20s, and then went on to graduate with a law degree and become a manager of a legal department, wrote, "I am happy with myself now. I used to worry about achieving my goals and how others regarded me. I know now that I am a good thinker, articulate, rational, and committed, and that I have leadership qualities. I want to be the best attorney I can be." That refrain was echoed by another woman in this cohort who was once considered a "bright but neurotic youngster with obsessive-compulsive behavior characteristics." She sought counseling after a nervous breakdown precipitated by her decision to leave a graduate theological seminar. She felt then that she had let down her parents and friends. By age 31, she was a pension analyst, happily married, and expecting a baby. She wrote, "I have learned to get along with others and to make others feel good about themselves. My goal in life is to be happy and to love life to the fullest. I am married to an empathetic and loving husband who gives me constant support; the child within me brings forth much happiness, and I am also excelling in my career. I want to write a book someday about my experiences."

The men who had improved with the help of counseling were less defensive about their experience than men whose mental health problems persisted. Wrote a bartender in California who was the son of an alcoholic father who had abused him as a child, "In adolescence I found out that my father had an affair, so I got into self abuse, i.e., drugs and alcohol. What psychotherapy and a lot of reading has taught me is that I am responsible for myself, and that I can accept people the way they are. I can't change them unless they want to change, but I can be compassionate with them. I still worry sometimes about whether I will be successful, whether I will ever accept myself fully, and whether I can maintain a healthy relationship, but I am much more confident now."

Here, in contrast, were the views expressed by a young man of above average intelligence who had been in a severe depression since age 30. He had received state-funded mental health services, but his condition had not improved. His father had been chronically ill all his life, also disabled by severe depressions. The son had been exposed to severe perinatal stress. His mother had died when he was 4 years old, and he had lived with an aunt ever since. He had attended a four-year college but was unemployed and lived on food stamps from the Department of Social Services and Housing. When we interviewed him, he was unmarried and had no close friends.

Q: What has been the worst period of your life so far?
A: The last five years—the fear and threat of losing my life really got to me.
Q: What do you consider your strong points?
A: I am a very nice and caring individual, although I feel that this has been covered up by harsh situations, causing conflict to make it seem otherwise.

Q: What do you consider your weak points?
A: My situation in life. I have bad luck. It comes out at times. People take strong negative attitudes toward me, subtle, but hostile. I don't hate them, but I wish they could understand and help.
Q: What do you most want to accomplish in life?
A: A secure economic base where I can attain what I need in life. I can't even think of a family before I achieve this first objective.
Q: What kinds of things do you worry about most?
A: Running out of money, losing my aunt and my house. Being rejected for a job position, especially a decent one in which I can make a living. I also worry about someone wanting to scrutinize me and to nullify my efforts instead of assisting me. Sometimes they come in numbers, hiding behind others to cut your throat, putting you out in the cold. In other words, the people I know are full of shit. If I ever do something to avenge myself, I will be punished, but I don't see any of them being punished. THE WORLD IS INCORRECT.

Conversion to a Fundamentalist Religion

A significant minority among the individuals with mental health problems in our cohort (one out of five men, one out of three women) had converted to fundamentalist religions that assured them salvation, security, and a sense of mission. Prominent among them were the Jehovah's Witnesses and, to a lesser extent, the Church of Jesus Christ of Latter Day Saints.

Jehovah's Witnesses share a belief that the final battle between Good and Evil will occur in the very near future. The chief duty of faithful Witnesses is to warn nonmembers to join their New World Society to escape annihilation in this battle. Since Satan rules the world, the committed Witness will withdraw from society and take refuge in the fellowship of his congregation.

The Watchtower Bible Tract Society objects to higher education and psychiatry and, instead, empowers each of its members to be a minister and missionary to the world. Most Witnesses hold down secular jobs to support themselves and their families, but their main focuses are five regular meetings each week in the local Kingdom Hall and an average of eleven hours each month of door-to-door preaching. This schedule almost always mandates withdrawal from secular activities.

The simplicity of the life of most Witnesses is appealing. Many come from limited educational backgrounds. Among the men and women in our cohort who became converts and were active in the Watchtower Society, only one had attended a junior college. Her job as a bookkeeper in a local store was more skilled than those of the other Witnesses, who were housewives, waitresses, carpenters, and janitors. Two of the men worked full-time for the ministry, one as a bookbinder and one as a cabinetmaker. Both had been sent from Kauai to the world headquarters of the Jehovah's Witnesses in Brooklyn, New York, and considered their stays there the best periods of their lives.

Wrote the cabinetmaker, who was the son of a schizophrenic mother and who had been a slow and withdrawn child when he was seen in the local mental health clinic as a youngster, "I love Hawaii, the place where I was born and raised, and I think I always will, but the best part of my life has been my stay here at the world headquarters of the Watchtower Society. I have learned a lot, not only about my trade, but also about how to deal with people. I have many close friends here."

This view was echoed by a full-time minister back on Kauai, who was also a donut and pizza maker, cashier, and newspaper delivery man, "The best period of my life so far was between 1974 and 1983. I served as a volunteer at the Watchtower Bible Tract Society in Brooklyn, New York." To this young man, who was once placed in a class for the educable mentally retarded, the most important things in his life had been baptism as one of Jehovah's Witnesses and marriage. What had helped him most in dealing with difficulties and stresses in his life was "my Bible knowledge and my relationship with God." When we asked him what he most wanted to accomplish in his life, he cheerful replied, "To live forever on a Paradise Earth according to God's promises in the Bible." What he worried most about, however, was "how to pay the bills, keep the car running, and have food to eat."

His fellow volunteer, the cabinetmaker, was helped most in dealing with difficulties in life by "learning and applying Bible teachings. The hope that the Bible sets forth for the near future gives me peace of mind in spite of all the problems that face the world today." He, too, "hoped to live forever in a new system—God's Kingdom." For him, as for the other Watchtower members, the most important thing that happened in his life was "getting baptized as one of the Witnesses, as a symbol of my dedication of my life to Jehovah God."

The women Witnesses were equally devoted. Wrote one, who as a teenager had made several suicide attempts, "What helped me most in dealing with the difficulties in my life was prayer and acting upon the examples found in the Bible." She, too, wanted to "bring up her children and follow the Bible's examples as closely as possible. "She worried, though, that "with all the crime and violence in this world today, we won't be victims."

Perhaps the greatest transformation in this group had happened to a young woman who was raped at age 15 by a friend of her father's. Diagnosed as a "borderline psychotic" (severe depression and paranoia) at age 16, she became a drug addict by age 17. In her early 30s she was happily married and worked as a bookkeeper, but the main focus of her life was "the five weekly Bible discussion meetings that I attend with my husband. He and I are both dedicated and baptized Jehovah's Witnesses." For her, the most important thing that had happened in her life was "being a student of the Bible and living my life according to Bible standards."

Equally devoted to their faith were individuals who had had mental health problems in their youth and who had joined the ranks of the Latter Day Saints as young adults. The Mormon church is active in missionary work in Hawaii and has many features attractive to young seekers. Its members find a full and rich spiritual, social, and recreational life in its fellowship. Participation in the priesthood gives each Mormon male a sense of direct involvement in the church.

Mormons also know that their church is interested in their temporal welfare and will come to their aid if they should become ill or unemployed. The extensive church welfare program is one of the chief attractions of Mormonism. Latter Day Saints in good standing (who have contributed 10% of their gross income to the church, and another 2–3 percent to the upkeep of their local ward) can count on receiving substantial help in the form of food, clothing, cash, and help in finding a job. Needy Mormons may apply for assistance in case of sickness, unemployment, or other personal or family problems.

Mormons have a dedicated membership, a strong missionary impulse, and a tradition of encouraging large families and higher education. Among the members of this cohort who converted to the Mormon faith were individuals who were, on the average, better educated and more intelligent than those who became Jehovah's Witnesses. They also had more children than their peers (four or more by 32).

Their commitment to their new found faith reflected a strong missionary zeal. Wrote a security guard who had needed mental health care as a child, "What I want to accomplish most in my life is to fulfill my Heavenly Father's Plan." The most important thing that had happened in his life so far was "being married for Time and Eternity." What had helped him most in dealing with the difficulties in his life was "being a member of the Church of Jesus Christ of Latter Day Saints, and being able to rely on help from the bishop of the LDS Church."

"Knowing that we will be an eternal family" was the most positive aspect of motherhood for a Mormon convert woman, offspring of an alcoholic father and a severely depressed mother. She had seven children, ranging in age from 14 to 4, and enjoyed her work as a parent facilitator in the Department of Education. What she now wanted most was to get a college education and to help her children achieve all they could. She worried about "drugs, morality, and my children's values," but she valued the support of her religious affiliation and of an understanding husband. She, too, turned for help to the elders and bishop of her church and valued their interest in the material as well as spiritual welfare of their followers.

We could locate only a few studies that have dealt with the therapeutic aspects of fundamentalist religions in North America. The largest study was conducted on a representative cross-sectional sample of Black adults (18 years and older) in the continental United States (Neighbors, Jackson, Bowman, and Gunn, 1983). As poverty and personal problems increased among the Black respondents, so did the proportion of adult men and women who turned to prayer, religion, and their churches and ministers for support. Religiosity was also positively associated with mental health among both Black and Hispanic members (ages 13–77) of five Pentecostal churches in the South Bronx (Purdy, Simari, and Cowan, 1983). The parishioners had a strong sense of community and turned to their pastor as the primary helping person in times of mental distress.

A Canadian study of the emotional impact of fundamentalist religious participation in a Newfoundland coastal community came to similar conclusions (Ness and Wintrop, 1980). All fifty-one members of a Pentecostal church were interviewed with the Cornell Medical Index, and their religious behavior was observed over a twelve-month period. The more frequently individuals engaged in religious activities, the less likely they were to report symptoms of emotional distress.

A Supportive Spouse or Friend

By far the most frequently mentioned source of support in times of difficulties for individuals with mental health problems in this cohort was a supportive spouse or close friend. Nearly half of the men and two-thirds of the women with mental health problems in their youth reported that their spouses had helped them most in dealing with difficulties and stresses in their adult lives. Two-thirds of the men and half of the women also relied on the emotional support of close friends.

A marine mechanic who had been painfully shy in his teens and stuttered a lot in his youth wrote, "I am not too much into going out to night clubs or dancing. I like to stay home with my wife. She has given me a positive view of life. Now I have the confidence to give good advice to friends and family members."

A stock clerk who grew up with a rejecting father and turned into an aggressive, insecure teenager in need of psychotherapy added, "Talking things out with my girlfriend has made all the difference. She accepts me the way I am. The best period of my life is now, in my early 30s, when I have the good luck to meet her and start a family."

A welder who had been a troubled youth, but was happily married by age 32 and had two preschool children reported, "The most important thing that has happened to me so far in my life is my marriage. I learned how to give fifty-fifty and to talk my problems out with my wife."

Wrote a woman lawyer who had been diagnosed as having "adjustment reaction of adolescence" at age 18, when she was confused about her college plans and had broken up with someone she thought she would marry, "I met the right husband after college. We had good premarital counseling and have relied on our faith to guide us. I have learned in my marriage to respect and accept his point of view without requiring him to change into the person I think or want him to be, and he does the same with me."

"The best period of my life so far is right now," wrote a waitress who at 15 had been sexually abused by her adopted father and at 17 married an abusive husband. She received some counseling in the Battered Women's Center and got a divorce. She is happily married now to a man "with whom I can talk things over and whose company I can enjoy. I got to analyze my life, see things clearer. I like myself now."

Protective Factors in the Individual and Family Environment

Looking back at the lives of troubled youths who had recovered from their mental health problems by the time they reached their early 30s, we noted a number of characteristics within the individuals as well as in their family environments that contributed to positive changes in their life trajectories.

Such persons tended to be first-born or only children who had been considered cuddly and affectionate infants. Three out of four in this group were very active babies; all were within the normal range of physical development when they were examined by pediatricians by the end of their second year. None had suffered from any central nervous system impairment.

By age 10, these individuals had higher mean scores on a nonverbal measure of problem-solving ability (PMA Reasoning factor) than did youths with mental health problems who grew into a troubled adulthood (104 vs. 94). None had any physical handicaps, and few suffered from serious childhood illnesses. Both teachers and parents noted independently that a higher proportion of children in this group were shy and lacked self-confidence when they were in the elementary grades (43% vs. 24%). Delinquency rates among these youngsters were significantly lower than among youths with mental health problems whose troubles persisted into adulthood (21.5% vs. 56.0%).

Half of the youths whose mental health problems persisted into adulthood grew up in single-parent households in their teens, while youths who had recovered from their mental health problems by the time they reached their early 30s, grew up in homes where both parents were present. The majority had household chores to attend to, and their parents had curfew rules for them when they were adolescents. Overall, these youths had more positive relationships with members of their families in their teens than youngsters whose mental health problems persisted into early adulthood.

In Sum

A significant shift in life trajectories from risk to adaptation had taken place in about half of the individuals by age 32 who had been troubled by mental health problems in their teens. Positive changes in adulthood were more common among the women who had such problems in adolescence than among the men.

Only a minority of the troubled youths were still in need of mental health services in their early 30s, but a higher proportion of males than females with mental health problems in their teens had grown into adults who had difficulties finding and keeping a job, had marriages that ended in divorce, were delinquent in spouse and child support, and had criminal records by age 32.

Only a third of the individuals in need of mental health services had received some counseling or psychotherapy by the time they reached their early 30s. A significant minority found a sense of security and coherence in joining a fundamentalist religious group. The most significant turning point for the majority of the troubled youths, however, was meeting and marrying an accepting and supportive spouse.

Individuals who had been active and affectionate as infants and who had good problem-solving skills and few health problems as children were more likely to overcome mental health problems than individuals who elicited less positive responses from their caregivers and teachers. The presence of both parents in the family and the assumption of regular household responsibilities in adolescence were also associated with improvement in mental health status. Overall, the prognosis for youths who were shy and lacked confidence was considerably better than for youths who displayed antisocial behavior or for youths who had parents with serious mental health problems.

Ben

Ben, whose mental health problems had appeared in adolescence, continued to show residuals of his difficulties as an adult, although there had been few signs of impending problems in the first 10 years of his life.

Ben was the fourth child in a Japanese family that later included ten children. Birth was spontaneous and normal. The parents were happy with the baby, although the mother stated she had wanted a girl. The mother appeared relaxed at her postpartum interview. The father had taken a vacation for several weeks to help with the new infant.

Ben's development proceeded normally. At age one, he was described by his mother as a good baby, "the easiest of all," good-natured and fairly active. The public health nurse viewed him as "happy, alert, and healthy" and considered the mother "resourceful, responsible, self-confident, and reasonably relaxed."

At the 2-year exam, Ben's physical and mental development was rated as normal by both the examining pediatrician and the psychologist. He was described as an agreeable, cheerful, alert, and eager baby. The examiners also made positive comments about the mother, describing her as affectionate, kind, easygoing, and contented. Family stability was rated as high at that time.

By age 10, Ben was receiving above-average grades in most subjects, but his classroom teacher in the Catholic school he attended noted that he did not do his homework, and that he "could do better." His mother reported that he liked to read and be read to, and she herself belonged to several book clubs. She described him as "a very bright boy." Ben enjoyed Little League and 4-H activities and was an altar boy. Family activities included ball games and time at the beach. All the children helped with the work on the family farm. Some rivalry was noted between Ben and his older siblings, "as Ben is smarter." Although the mother saw no real problems, she noted that Ben persisted in coming home late. At such times, scolding or deprivation of privileges were used as a means of discipline—with an occasional spanking.

When he reached mid-adolescence, the picture had changed. Although Ben's achievement test scores were average and above, his grades in high school were now largely D's and F's. His teachers reported him to be a "discipline problem—antisocial and truant, unable to communicate with adults." He was referred to the school social worker and eventually to the family court because of a car theft and a number of petty larcenies. The probation officer found that he was unable to talk with Ben in the presence of his father and noted that his relationship with his father was "based on fear of punishment, not respect." The father, embarrassed by his son's behavior, believed that Ben was "emotionally disturbed and disoriented." He strongly disapproved of Ben's friends.

After another burglary offense, Ben was referred to the Division of Mental Health Services. The psychiatrist described him as "quiet and uncommunicative, but not hostile." He also noted, "Ben has an extremely poor relationship with his father, who exerts a great deal of pressure on him and is sometimes unreasonable. The relationship is characterized by resentment, rejection, and frustration. The boy's poor self-image contributes to poor performance in school and in home." There was "no evidence that he was psychotic or required intensive psychiatric treatment," but continued supervision by the family court and counseling with the probation officer were recommended. The goals for counseling were to "increase his self-esteem, and rid the father of the feeling that Ben was abnormal—to create some level of understanding between father and son."

Ben, interviewed at the end of his senior year, reported that he was not doing well in school and that he was dissatisfied with his courses ("I don't have enough choices of classes"). He enjoyed athletics and music. He had been "looking forward to going to college, but it's too late already, so I guess I'll join the service." His father was encouraging him to join the service "to broaden his mind and get a free education."

Discussing his family and what they did together, he said, "Just eat.

We don't get along too well. I get along with my brothers and sister, but not with my parents. They don't like my smoking cigarettes and drinking. They don't want me to stay out late and go to the pool halls. They think I associate with low-type people—they don't like my friends. They don't understand why I stay out late, and why I hang around with the kind of friends I do. . . . My mother is OK—she's a warm person. She tries to straighten me out as much as possible, but I'm hardheaded. My father brought me up too strict. I stayed out late, and he picked me up and gave me a licking until I was 15 years old. I don't feel close to my parents. They still make the rules, but I don't listen. They say, 'Don't stay out too late, don't smoke till you can support yourself.' We argue a lot and then I finally just walk away." He acknowledged, "I don't feel I'm going to be what they want me to be. I'm going to be what I want me to be, as after all, I'm going to be doing the stuff."

Not quite 18, Ben indicated that he was still on probation and would be until he came of age. He was no longer seeing his probation officer regularly and expressed ambivalence about his experience with him. "I was just confused when I stole the car. I guess I was trying to get even with my parents. I didn't know what they did. I guess they were trying to help me, but I just didn't see it that way. When I first saw the probation officer, I didn't like him. Then when we got along, I went for counseling once every two to three weeks for about six months. Then I finally stopped going, because I didn't get along too well. No one made me go back—there was no checkup. I was just dropped." Ben admitted to using marijuana "once in a while—can't see anything wrong with marijuana. Some drugs I can see why they don't make it legal and some I cannot. Drinking is OK—it's just that you have to have money. Money has influenced me a lot."

Evaluating himself at age 18, Ben at first had difficulty expressing himself: "I don't know my strong and weak points." Then, after some hesitation: "Me, I try to think things out, I try at least. But sometimes I don't think things out, and it doesn't work out too good. Right now I don't know what I'm going to do when I grow up and graduate. . . . Pretty soon I'll have to live on my own. I worry that I'm going to have to live on my own, and if I can succeed in life or not, and how well I get along with other people." His goals included being a musician and enjoying life. His thoughts on how to accomplish the latter: "I take it as it comes I guess."

By age 32, Ben had left Hawaii and his family and had been living on the mainland for over five years. His work career had included a stint in the army as well as clerical and restaurant jobs. His present job was as a bartender, and he reported being "mostly satisfied" with his work, but noted interpersonal difficulties and poor pay as stressful aspects of the job. His criminal record since age 18 included several drunken-driving arrests and a narcotics offense.

Ben's plans for college had not materialized, although he had attended a junior college for a while. This had not been a particularly satisfying experience: "I like one-on-one learning. There's not enough of that in conventional schools. I stopped going." Similarly, he had found no real satisfaction in his relationships with women, and twice his girlfriends had become pregnant. "My relationships with girls have been so-so. I have no present relationship. Learning to relate is hard for me." He handled these stresses by terminating the relationship. Ben's earlier pattern of walking away from difficulties apparently had become a well-established coping style.

He continued to be dissatisfied with his relationship with his parents—less so with his mother than his father. The stresses he perceived in these relationships included "child abuse and inconsistency in discipline. They did not instill responsibility in me; they said, 'Do as I say, not as I do.'" He had been helped some by "psychotherapy and a lot of reading in self-help books." In spite of some shared interests, Ben was also dissatisfied with his relationships with his siblings. Although he reported having only a few friends, these relationships were more satisfying to him.

The high degree of self-insight noted at age 18 was apparent at age 32 as well. Evaluating himself, Ben considered his "lack of self-esteem and lack of social skills" and his "need for approval, his impatience, and spendthrift habits" as his weak points. What he most wanted to accomplish was "to be happy, financially successful, and raise loving, competent kids." Sadly, however, his worries at age 32 showed little change from those of 14 years earlier: "Will I be successful? Will I ever accept myself? Can I maintain a healthy relationship?"

In retrospect, Ben considered his childhood "totally carefree," the best period of his life, and his adolescence as the worst period. "I found out my father had an affair, so I got into self-abuse, drugs and alcohol." He saw leaving Hawaii and his family as the most important thing that had happened to him so far.

Ben's mental health problems, first seen in his mid-teens, continued to be a part of his life as he entered his 30s. While he had learned some more acceptable ways of handling stresses and clearly made strides in some areas of his life, his lack of self-esteem and his concern about maintaining healthy interpersonal relationships suggested that Ben was still trapped in his battle against the odds.

Amy

In contrast, the story of Amy, one of the women in our cohort who had had serious mental health problems in her teens, shows the growth of a remarkable young woman who had matured against the odds.

Amy's parents were of Pilipino-Hawaiian-Portuguese descent. Her mother had not completed high school; her father was unable to read. The 28-year-old mother had been married previously, had six children from her first marriage, and at the time of Amy's birth was not looking forward to the arrival of her seventh child. She had married Amy's father after a short acquaintance and had experienced many problems with him and her new in-laws. Frequent quarrels were the norm; the parents had left each other on several occasions; and the mother, nervous and tired, was anticipating a "breakdown" with this pregnancy. The public health nurse considered her to be under high stress and noted her poor capacity to cope. The early background was indeed a preview of things to come.

Amy was described as a normal baby at birth. She was not nursed, as the mother considered this a waste of time. When she was one, her pediatrician considered her physical development to be normal. She was described as somewhat shy and had difficulty separating from her mother. She vomited when left with her grandmother for babysitting and cried until the mother returned. Although the public health nurse saw the baby as alert and healthy, her mother described her as fretful. Observers rated the mother herself restless and discontented, giving up easily. At the time of her 2-year examination, Amy was considered physically normal, but shy and judged to be of average intelligence on the Cattell Infant Intelligence Scale.

The 10-year follow-up found little change in the parents' situation. The father had his steady work as a truck driver for a plantation. The mother did not work outside the home but continued to manifest signs of significant disturbance. Drinking exacerbated her problems, and the family frequently quarreled. She often talked of "ending up in Mahelona" (the local psychiatric hospital). The family shared few activities together other than occasional church attendance. They lived in chronic poverty and provided little educational stimulation and even less emotional support for Amy.

Amy's mother reported, however, that Amy enjoyed school and studying, that she was "always reading books," and that she was intelligent and curious, the "smartest" of her ten children. According to her report, Amy tried hard in school and was very helpful and dependable. Her outside activities consisted of attending Sunday school and 4-H. Although her mother considered Amy easy to manage, she noted that the girl cried easily, protested about too much responsibility, and was jealous of her father's rapport with her siblings, often repeating, "Daddy doesn't love me."

The mother's evaluation of Amy's schoolwork was somewhat at odds with the school report, which noted her as below average in her achievement. Her classroom teacher described her as "timid and rather withdrawn; she cries easily, but tries to do her best." She was referred for individual psychological evaluation and received a WISC Verbal IQ of 101, a Performance IQ 111, and a Full Scale IQ of 107. The psychologist wrote, "Amy is a poised, mature young lady whose speech and language usage is above average. She sighed often and gave the impression of being generally bored with her family, home, and school. Test results indicate that she is functioning within the normal range of intelligence. Perhaps a lack of, or too little, stimulation within the home and school environment accounts for her underachievement and observed boredom."

During her early adolescent years, Amy and her parents became well known to mental health services in the community, both public and private. Within a two-year period, Amy had made three suicide attempts, for which she had been briefly hospitalized, and her mother, fulfilling her earlier prophesies, had "ended up in Mahelona," where she was treated for a hypomanic disorder and alcoholism. Attempts were made to provide both family and individual psychotherapy, but the destructive forces within the family continuously sabotaged these efforts. At one point, the Department of Social Services and Housing attempted to locate another home for Amy, but this plan, too, was unsuccessful. Agency reports were discouraging. The Department of Social Services, in closing its case, said, "Such service as possible has been given, but to no avail." Amy's relationships with her parents were at best dismal and at worst highly destructive and chaotic throughout her adolescence.

Probably the most positive relationship in Amy's life during this period was the sustained one she had with her Big Sister. Big Sisters was particularly active during this period on Kauai. Fortunately, Amy's Big Sister persisted in spite of many roadblocks, including Amy herself, who at times distanced herself from her. Looking back at this relationship at age 18, Amy said, "She was a lot of help. I kept away for a while though, as she got too involved with my family, and I was just trying to protect her . . . and the doctors helped me, but when my family found out I had an appointment with a psychiatrist, they blew their top. They were afraid of what I'd say. Everyone who's tried to help me gets involved with my family, and I don't want them to get involved. I always had to stop seeing them because of my parents' pressure. My parents gave me heat, so I kept away from them so they wouldn't get involved. I needed my Big Sister badly, but at the end I was trying to keep her from getting involved."

School was another positive aspect in Amy's life during her teens. Although her grades and test scores were only average and she was reported to have "nervous tendencies," she found school to be very satisfying. She received top (1) behavioral ratings in all areas—industry, initiative, responsibility, concern, and leadership—and enjoyed many extracurricular activities. "I liked all of it. I got to be a part of it all. It took my mind off things at home. I liked my teachers and my friends—I could talk to them. It was hard, but I did OK. I didn't fail anything." During high school, she had an active social life, with her spare time spent with friends rather than with family. Although she dated several boys, she had no special romantic attachments.

Amy was interviewed shortly after her graduation from high school. At that time, she planned to take a two-year course in secretarial work at a community college. She had originally planned to attend a four-year college, but with the primary goal of independence from her family had selected the shorter course. She hoped for marriage at a later date but viewed her career and independence as most important at this time. She was working part-time in a gift store, as she had since her freshman year in high school. Her earnings had helped her parents and had helped to pay for her future schooling.

Describing her family situation at age 18, Amy said, "We do nothing together except for an occasional party. But I usually don't go. There is lots of drinking so I stay home. Getting along with my parents during high school years, it was really rough. To me, my mother is emotionally sick—and the doctor has said it—because she's sick, she can't help what she's doing. She is a problem drinker. She picks on us and on my father. I don't feel any closeness to them. I don't stay mad at my father though. The fights are worse, but afterwards, the feeling goes away, and I don't stay mad. I stay mad at my mother longer. My father will come and say "sorry"—I guess that's why. My parents don't understand me, not at all. They are both explosive. They seem to be more happy fighting than keeping quiet. I just want to be different, I want to be the opposite—be everything they are not."

Asked about her health, Amy said that she had "mental fatigue" during adolescence. She added that she often experienced depression and that she just stayed home and cried—"I have those emotional sicknesses. I'm not so healthy. I want to shut out what bothers me, and just keep to myself." She saw her strong point as standing up for what she believed in, and her weakness as giving in to her family too much—"I should use more force. They take advantage of me. I just talk and cry, and to them that's nothing. . . . I want a chance to be happy and for my family to be happy and not have a sad family life like we've had. I just want to get away from home. I guess I have to give myself some credit as I've often wanted to rebel and run away, but I just held back as I felt it wasn't right." Asked what she considered had contributed most to making her the kind of person she was, she said, "My childhood I guess. Like now, I can remember only the bad side of it. I was the one with the most problems. But you learn from your mistakes too." Nevertheless, she expressed some optimism about the future—"Now that I'm out of school and have a job, I'm feeling better because I'm away from home more. I'm not involved in the big problems. I just hear about them later."

Interviewed at age 32, Amy presented a picture very different from that of her teen years. She had been employed as a secretary at one of the major island companies for over five years and looked forward to continuing to work her way up. She found considerable satisfaction in her work, in her ability "to meet everyday pressures," and in the "rewards you get from satisfaction with the amount of work you do." Earlier job experiences had not been quite as satisfying—"I'd cry to myself as I couldn't speak out. Then I made up my mind I was going to think positive." She had worked for a year after high school—her family had been "totally against" her obtaining further schooling—but she had wanted it so badly that she forged her father's signature on her community college application. She received financial help from a junior college on the island of Oahu, had some assistance from the Department of Social Services, and worked nights.

Amy had lived with her husband for several years before marriage and had now been married for about five years. They had one child. She had planned to "start a new life away from Kauai" but had returned to her island home after her marriage. "It made me stronger to face up to it. I realize my parents will never change, and we have a better relationship now." Her relationship with her husband also improved over the years.

"We have a stable marriage now, but we didn't get married for over five years, as I said, 'No marriage—we have too many problems!' I remember telling you [in her 18-year interview] that I don't believe in living together before marriage, but we did after all. We argued about lots of small things. He used to spend a lot of time with his friends. In the beginning, it was every day. I felt his friends came first. Then I gave up arguing about it, and now he just goes with them once a week."

Amy's concern for her daughter is largely related to "trying to not make the same mistakes as I think our parents made. Hardly any affection was shown to us. I show affection, and try not to do as they did. When I was young, my parents' arguments upset me so that I tried to kill myself. I don't argue in front of my child. I want to do the right thing, show her what is right and wrong; it's hard. I want to build a basic solid environment for her. I'll let her be what she wants to be, but I'm going to stress education."

By age 32, Amy had made considerable strides in coming to terms with her parents and her past relationship with them. She reported that she saw them fairly often, that "we've gotten closer because I'm more open now. With all the problems I had, I thought I'd be a wreck—maybe even an alcoholic as that's what I grew up with. But I made up my mind to do better. I told my mother so when I came home. I got it off my chest. Though they've stopped drinking, my mother is still basically the same—she's arrogant, but she's sick, unstable. She had several more hospitalizations at Mahelona. I hated her—I actually hated her and blamed her for all the misery. Even today, they still yell at each other. They have short fuses, but it's mostly my mother. My father is not as mean as people think. He was strict, but more understanding than my mom. I thought I could handle it all—even the suicidal part. I thought maybe they'd listen to me. But today, if an argument starts up, I just leave."

Amy was able to talk freely about herself, her earlier traumas, her relationships and hopes. Her life in her early 30s centered around her work and her husband and child. Friends were important to her, but she had little time for them. Where earlier she had enjoyed gardening and athletics, her weekend activity was now primarily child-centered—"Now I'd call myself a boring person." Her chief goal was for the couple to own their own home.

Evaluating herself at age 32 she said, "I can express myself more now than I could. I'm still sensitive, but not as much. I'm stronger now. I can handle more pressures and responsibilities. But I think too much. My mind is going, even when I'm sleeping. I can't stop thinking." She considered the major problem she had to face since leaving high school: "Growing up! Life as a whole. Keeping up with it. It all happened so fast to me." The most critical event in her life to date? "Being a parent. That's the first step. Now I know how it was for my parents. I can see how hard it is. I can say they were failures, but it was not really easy for them. I just have one child, and they had so many." "I'm not really religious, but I know God, and I pray some, and that and church used to help the pain go away." She credited her husband and her coworkers as helping her in dealing with stress. But it was Amy herself who had taken control of her own destiny in her 20s, adjusted her expectations to be compatible with reality, and achieved a serenity that enabled her to accept the present and look forward to the future.

And how did she feel about herself in her early 30s? "Sometimes I like myself. But not all the time. I don't like it that I'm still scared sometimes."

8

Stressful Events in Childhood and Youth and Adult Adaptation

A number of studies have shown that stressful life events in adulthood can play a significant role in the genesis of health problems and psychological disorders (Antonovsky, 1979, 1987; Dohrenwend and Dohrenwend, 1974), but there is a paucity of empirical data on the long-term effects of adverse experiences in childhood and youth. The available evidence is based mainly on retrospective accounts of individuals who have come to the attention of mental health professionals or of child advocates rather than on prospective studies that include appropriate control groups (Garmezy, 1983).

The few researchers who have examined the long-term effects of childhood stressors by using data from longitudinal studies have usually focused on associations between single stressful childhood events and psychological disturbances in adulthood—for example, loss of the mother (Brown, Harris, and Bifulco, 1986), parental divorce (Hetherington, Stanley-Hagan, and Anderson, 1989; Wallerstein and Blakeslee, 1989), parental mental illness (Anthony, 1987; Bleuler, 1978), or the birth of a younger sibling (Moore, 1975). The intercorrelations among a number of concurrent stressors in children's lives and possible common antecedents (such as preexisting psychiatric problems in parents and subsequent marital breakups) are often overlooked in such investigations (Robins, 1983).

In a state-of-the-art review entitled "Stress, Coping and Development:

Some Issues and Some Questions," Rutter (1983) has argued for a more discriminating analysis of the effects of the various types of life events considered stressful—such as happenings that reflect some form of loss or disappointment and those that involve disturbed interpersonal relationships. There is need to explore both the direct and the indirect ways in which adverse life events may influence early developmental processes as well as later functioning. Early adverse events may alter a person's sensitivities to stress or modify styles of coping; these effects may then predispose that person toward disorders in adult life when he or she faces subsequent stress. A stress amplification process can be anticipated if these early events are extremely traumatic or affect multiple domains in the life of the youngster and/or are of long duration (Aldwin and Stokols, 1988).

The data available on the men and women in this longitudinal study permit us to trace some of the direct and indirect links between stressful life events they had experienced in childhood and adolescence, and multiple coping problems in adulthood. They also enable us to examine, at each stage of the developmental cycle, the patterns of intercorrelations among early adverse experiences which best discriminated among 32-year-old individuals with and without broken marriages, criminal records, or public records of psychiatric disorders.

The sources of stress in our analysis include chronic conditions of the families and economic environments in which the men and women in this cohort had spent their childhoods and youth (parental psychopathology; poverty), chronic demands made on the individual because of an illness or handicap or the disability of a sibling, serious disruptions of the family unit (departures or deaths of family members, foster home placement, parental divorce), and chronic discord (parental conflict, conflict between the youngster and parents or peers).

Information on such stressful life events had been obtained independently at several stages of this longitudinal study: in interviews with the children's caregivers in the postpartum period and at year one (by public health nurses), during the 2-year developmental examinations (by psychologists), during home visits at 10 years (by social workers), and in interviews with the youths themselves at 18 years (by psychologists). At each of these follow-up stages, we also had corroborating data from health and social service records which contained information on chronic sources of stress to which the men and women in this cohort had been exposed in childhood and adolescence (see Chapter 2).

Criteria for Adult Adaptation

Ratings of the quality of adult adaptation were based on both the individuals' self-evaluations (in the clinical interviews and biographical questionnaires) and on their records in the community at age 31/32. A detailed account of the scoring system can be found in Appendix II. The ratings were made independently of any knowledge of the information on stressful life events which had been obtained at previous follow-up stages in childhood and adolescence. A developmental psychologist and a graduate student in child development independently read transcripts of the adult interviews and the questionnaire data and agency records that contained information on the current status of the men and women who participated in the 31/32 year follow-up.

The following criteria in six categories were used to define successful coping in early adulthood:

School/work: Individual is employed and/or is enrolled in school. Is (very) satisfied with work and/or school achievement.

Relationship with spouse/mate: Individual is married or in long-term committed relationship, is (very) satisfied with partner and reports little or no conflict. No record of desertion, divorce, or spouse abuse appears in court files.

Relationship with children: Individual evaluates children (very) positively, is (very) satisfied with parental role. No record of child abuse or delinquent child support payments appears in court files.

Relationship with parents and siblings: Individual evaluates father, mother, and siblings positively, reports little or no conflict with them.

Relationship with peers: Individual has several close friends who provide emotional support when needed, is (very) satisfied with their relationships. No record of assault, battery, rape, or other criminal offenses appears in court files.

Self-assessment: Individual is (very) happy or mostly satisfied with present state of life, reports no dependency on alcohol or drugs, has no psychosomatic illnesses. No record of psychiatric disorders appears in mental health register.

Some 50 percent of the individuals (M: 239; F: 239) in this birth cohort on whom we have follow-up data in adulthood and who were still alive by age 30 (478 out of 505) satisfied our criteria for "successful adult adaptation." One out of three (M: 68; F: 56) cohort members had developed minor problems in the transition to adulthood. Many of these were marital problems that led to divorce in 15 percent of the marriages. Approximately one out of six members (M: 43; F: 34) had developed serious coping problems in early adulthood that included at least two of the following conditions: a criminal record, a record of mental health problems, a marriage irrevocably broken, and/or a poor self-evaluation —a finding similar to that reported by Magnusson (1988) in his follow-up study of the young adults of an urban Swedish cohort born in 1955.

Men and women were nearly equally presented among the adults with serious coping problems in their early 30s. Among individuals with minor coping problems were more men than women. Among those without coping problems were more women than men.

Direct Links between Early Stressors and Adult Coping Problems[1]

Figures 2 and 3 show some of the stressful life events in childhood and adolescence which linked directly to coping problems in the early 30s: being born into and raised in poverty; having a sibling less than two years younger; the prolonged absence of mother and father because of separation or divorce during the individual's childhood and adolescence; and school failure, marriage, or financial problems in the teen years. These stressors had significant (though modest) associations with the coping problems of both men and women in their early 30s.

The number of stressful life events in childhood (involving mostly loss or separation from a caregiver) associated with adult coping problems was larger among men than among women. The number of stressful life events in adolescence (involving mostly disturbed interpersonal relationships) associated with adult coping problems was larger among women than among men.

Our results for our cohort in their early 30s are in agreement with our previous findings for 18-year-olds that indicated that boys were more vulnerable to the effects of adverse experiences in the first decade of life and girls more vulnerable in the second decade (Werner and Smith, 1982). A reverse shift appears to be under way in the third decade of life: a larger number of stressful life events encountered between ages of 18 and 30 differentiated between men with and without coping problems than between women with and without a successful adult adaptation at 31/32 (see Tables 18 and 19 in Appendix I).

1. The reader is referred to Figures A1 and A2 in Appendix I for the results of path analyses that trace both the direct and indirect links between early stressors and adult coping problems.

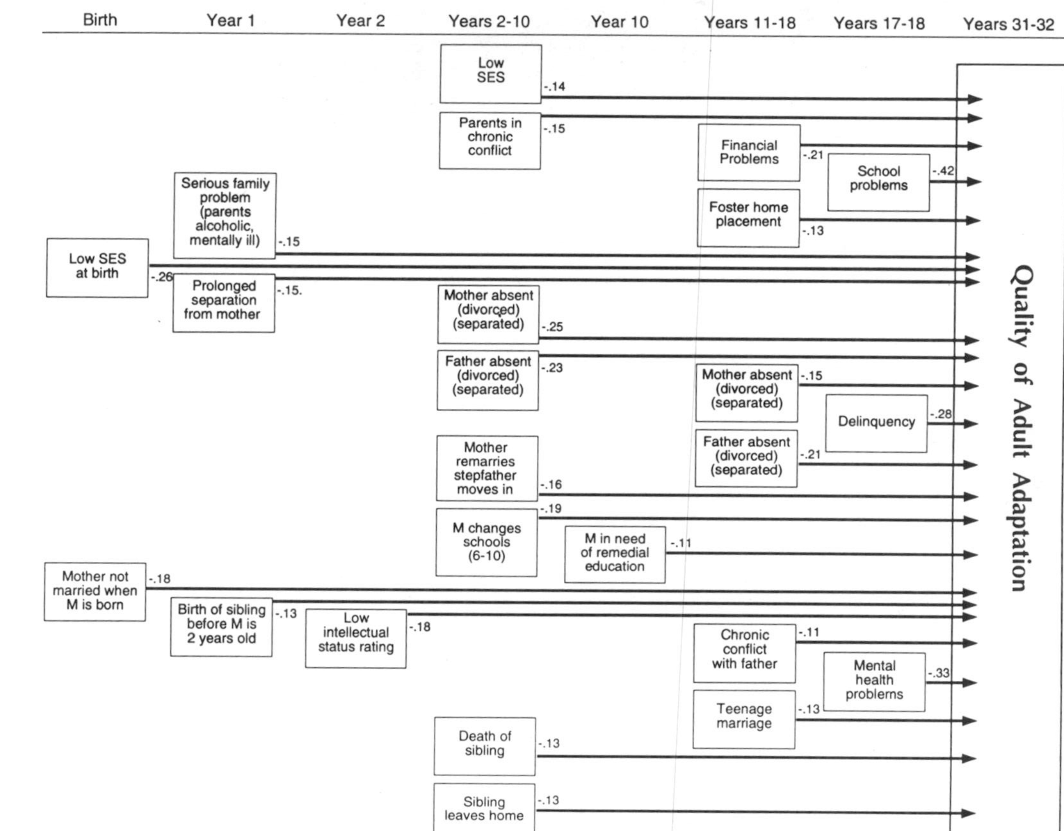

Figure 2. Correlation coefficients linking stressful life events in childhood and adolescence to quality of adult adaptation: males

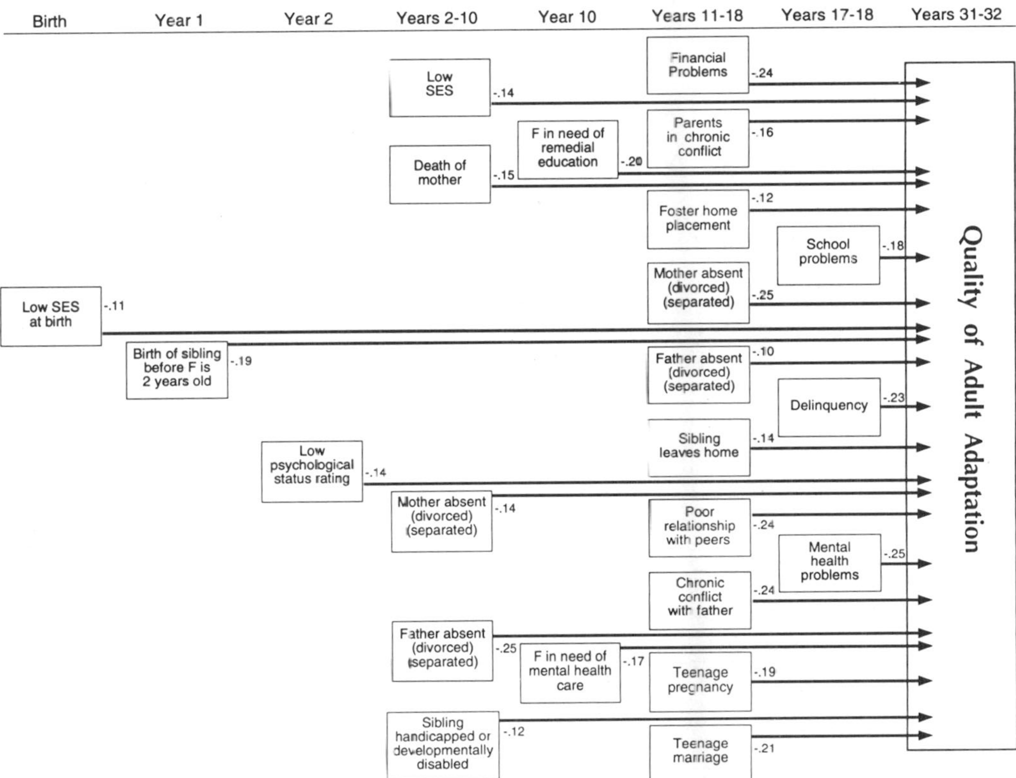

Figure 3. Correlation coefficients linking stressful life events in childhood and adolescence to quality of adult adaptation: females

Patterns of Early Stressors Linked to Poor Adult Adaptation

So far, we have presented associations between single stressors in childhood and adolescence and quality of adult adaptation. An examination of patterns of life events, however, may enable us to predict outcomes better than does the consideration of any single adverse event. Discriminant function analysis allows us to examine the pattern of weights of sets of stressors which predict membership in a given group (i.e., good/poor adult adaptation). It can be used with qualitative as well as quantitative variables (Gilbert, 1968; Norusis, 1983).

We performed several discriminant function analyses—by gender and developmental stages. We tested the effectiveness of the discriminant functions by checking how well we could predict membership in a good or poor outcome group at age 32 for the men and women in this cohort from patterns of stressful life events that occurred between birth and age 2, ages 2 and 10, and ages 11 and 18 (see Table 20 in Appendix I).

The Men

There was a steady and significant increase in the percentage of men whose classification as "coping" or "noncoping" could be correctly predicted as we added the stressors that had occurred at later developmental stages to the earlier ones. When we utilized only the information on stressful life events between birth and age 2, we correctly identified 59.4 percent of the males with serious coping problems at age 32, and 71.6 percent of the males without coping problems. The inclusion of stressors in middle childhood and adolescence increased the percentage of correct predictions to 87.5 percent of the men with serious coping problems in adulthood and to 95.5 percent of the men without such coping problems (canonical correlation = .82; $p < .0001$).[2]

When we examine the patterns of standardized correlation coefficients which discriminated between men with and without two or more serious coping problems at age 32, we see that some stressful life events tend to contribute more weight to the discriminant function than others. Among

2. SHAZAM, a logit regression model, is as useful as discriminant function analysis when the dependent variable is a binary variable and when the independent variables are categorical. SHAZAM correctly identified 96.8 percent of the men with serious coping problems in their early 30s and 98.5 percent of the men without such problems.

variables making the greatest (negative) contribution in infancy were: a mother who was not married at the time of her son's birth, prolonged disruptions in family life, and prolonged separations from the primary caregiver in year one, as well as the birth of a younger sibling and a below normal physical status rating by the pediatrician at age 2. In middle childhood the prolonged absence of the father, a change in schools between age 6 and 10, and a recognized need for remedial education and mental health care by age 10 contributed relatively large weights. For boys between ages 11 and 18, the absence of the mother and remarriage of a parent carried strong negative weights, as did conflict with the father, school failure associated with mental health problems, and a teenage marriage.

The Women

When we entered only stressful life events that had occurred between birth and age 2 in our discriminant function analyses, we correctly identified 63 percent of the women who developed serious coping problems by age 32, and 69 percent of the females without coping problems. The percentage correctly identified steadily increased with the addition of stressful life events in middle childhood and adolescence. When we utilized all the information available from birth to 18, the percentage correctly identified rose to 73 percent of the women with serious coping problems and 93 percent of the females without problems in their early 30s (canonical correlation = .70; $p < .005$).[3]

The pattern of the standardized canonical coefficients that discriminated between women with and without two or more serious coping problems at age 31/32 was different from the men. No single stressful life event in infancy contributed much to this function—except for a below average psychological status rating of the toddler at age 2. When a girl was between ages 2 and 10, the death of the mother, the prolonged absence of the father, and chronic conflict between the parents made a greater (negative) contribution to the discriminant function. The largest weights were contributed by stressful life events in adolescence, that is, financial problems, teenage pregnancy, teenage marriage, and poor relationships (conflict) with peers.

3. The proportions correctly identified by SHAZAM were 65.4 percent and 97.9 percent respectively.

Patterns of Stressors Linked to Divorce

About 15 percent of the marriages among the members of the 1955 birth cohort had ended in divorce by age 32. We were interested to see how well a combination of stressful life events before entry into the first marriage could predict the likelihood of divorce (see Table 21 in Appendix I).

The Men

There was a significant increase in the proportion of males correctly identified, as we added stressors that had occurred at later developmental stages to the adverse events of early childhood. When we entered only the stressful life events that had occurred between birth and age 2 in the discriminant function, we correctly identified 51.2 percent of the men with a divorce record by age 32, and 70.1 percent of the males who had stable marriages or long-term relationships. When we added all the stressful life events recorded between birth and age 18, we were able to correctly identify 74.4 percent of the men with divorce records by age 32, and 83.3 percent of the men whose marriages or long-term relationships were intact (canonical correlation = .65).[4]

When we added the stressful life events that had occurred in the period between ages 18 and 30 into the discriminant function, we were able to correctly identify 84 percent of the men with and 97 percent of the males without a failed marriage by age 32 (canonical correlation = .84, $p <$ .0001). The discriminant function based only on the stressful life events reported by the men in young adulthood (ages 18–30) correctly identified about the same proportion of males without a divorce record (97.8%) but only 58.3 percent of the men with a failed marriage by age 32 (canonical correlation = .53).

Among the stressful life events experienced by the men from birth to age 18 which contributed most to this discriminant function were adverse life experiences that pointed to a loss or separation from a caregiver. Among stressors contributing the greatest weight to this function in infancy were the prolonged disruption of family life (because of major illness of the caregiver) and the birth of a younger sibling before the boy reached age 2. Among adverse experiences in childhood which carried

4. The proportions correctly identified by SHAZAM were 71.8 percent and 86.4 percent respectively.

the greatest weights were the death of the mother, the prolonged absence of the father, the departure of a sibling caregiver from the household, and educational difficulties requiring remedial education by age 10.

Among adverse experiences in adolescence which contributed the most weight to this function were the prolonged absence of a mother figure because of separation or divorce, chronic conflict between parents, the remarriage of the parent and the entry of a stepparent into the household, and failure in school. Among stressful events between ages 18 and 30, the death of the mother and the breakup of a long-term relationship (outside of marriage) contributed most to the discriminant function that separated men with divorce records by age 32 from males in stable committed relationships.

The Women

There was a significant increase in the proportion of females correctly classified as we added stressors that had occurred at later developmental stages to the earlier ones. When we entered only the stressful life events that had occurred in infancy and early childhood, we correctly identified 65.6 percent of the women with divorce records by age 32 and 69 percent of the women without such records who were in stable marriages and/or committed long-term relationships.

When we added all the stressful life events between birth and 18 years into the discriminant function, we reached a significant canonical correlation (= .64, $p < .05$). The combination of all the stressors occurring in the first 18 years of life increased the proportion of women correctly identified to 67.7 percent of the females with divorce records and to 89.6 percent of the females without divorce records by age 32.[5]

When we added the stressful life events that had occurred in the period between ages 18 and 30 to the discriminant function, we were able to correctly identify 82.1 percent of the women with divorce records by age 32 and 97.9 percent of the females without broken marriages (canonical correlation = .81, $p < .0001$). The discriminant function based only on the stressful life events reported by the women between ages 18 and 30 correctly identified about the same percentage of females without divorce records (93.2%) but *only* 62.9 percent of the women with divorce records by age 32 (canonical correlation = .61).

5. The proportions correctly identified by SHAZAM were 61.3 percent and 92.7 percent respectively.

Most of the stressful life events that contributed to the discriminant function that separated women with a failed marriage by age 32 from women who were in stable relationships reflected discord and disturbed interpersonal relations in the girls' families. Among stressors contributing the greatest (negative) weights in infancy were a mother who was not married at the time of the birth of her daughter and a low intellectual and psychological status rating given to the toddler by psychologist at age 2. Stressors between ages 2 and 10 which contributed the greatest weight to this discriminant function were an alcoholic or mentally ill mother, the death of the mother before the daughter was 10, the prolonged absence of the father, chronic conflict in the family, and educational difficulties by age 10.

Most of the variables with the greatest discriminatory power for the women were stressors of adolescence, that is, the prolonged absence of the mother because of separation or divorce, a father who was alcoholic or mentally ill, conflicts with parents (especially the father) and peers, teenage pregnancy, teenage marriage, and financial problems during the teen years.

Among the adverse life experiences between ages 18 and 30, parental divorce or marital separation and the breakup of a long-term relationship (outside of marriage) contributed the greatest negative weights to the discriminant function that separated women with broken marriages from women in stable, committed relationships in their early 30s.

Patterns of Early Stressors Linked to Criminal Behavior

Twenty-six males and 5 females from the 1955 birth cohort had criminal records by age 32. Because of the small number of women and the large number of recorded stressful life events, we performed discriminant function analyses only for the men on whom we had complete follow-up data from birth to age 32 (see Table 22 in Appendix I).

In contrast to the results of other analyses, we obtained significant canonical correlations at each developmental stage, with coefficients ranging from .57 (birth to age 2) to .90 (birth to age 18). When we entered only the stressful life events recorded for the males in infancy, we correctly identified 52.6 percent of the men who were to have criminal records by age 32, and 88 percent of the men without such records.

When we added the childhood stressors to the stressful life events reported in infancy, the proportion correctly identified rose to 68.4 percent of the men with criminal records by age 32 and to 92.4 percent of the men without such records. When we entered all stressful life events recorded in the first 18 years of the men's lives, we correctly identified all men with criminal records by age 32 and 98.5 percent of the males without such records who had made successful transitions into adulthood. (SHAZAM, a logit regression model, correctly identified all men in both categories.)[6]

Among the variables making the greatest (negative) contribution to this function were a number of adverse experiences in infancy which included being reared by a mother who was not married at the time of the boy's birth, prolonged disruptions of family life (unemployment of the major breadwinner, parental illness, and major moves), and the birth of a sibling before the boy was age 2. A below-normal rating in physical development contributed most (negative) weight in early childhood.

Adverse experiences that contributed more weight in middle childhood were the prolonged absence of the mother, the departure of a sibling caregiver from the household, and change of schools in the first four grades (between ages 6 and 10). The permanent absence of the mother and foster home placement between ages 11 and 18 contributed an even greater weight to this function, as did the remarriage of the custodial parent after a divorce. Other stressors in adolescence that significantly contributed to this function were conflict in relationship with the father and a teenage marriage. A delinquency record carried less (negative) weight in the discriminant function than did a record of school failure and mental health problems in adolescence.

6. For the women, the number of stressful life events significantly associated with a criminal record by age 32 was larger than for the men. Among major childhood stressors were long-term absence of the mother, long-term absence of the father, remarriage of the mother and entry of a stepfather into the household, and death of a sibling before the girl was 10. Among major stressors in adolescence significantly associated with a criminal record for females in adulthood were foster home placement, conflict with the father, failure in school, mental health problems, a teenage marriage, and a delinquency record.

Patterns of Stressors Linked to Adult Psychiatric Disorders

We identified 12 men and 13 women in this cohort who had public records of psychiatric disorders (including affective or schizophrenic psychoses) and who had sought and/or received treatment from public agencies in the state of Hawaii in early adulthood (between ages 18 and 32). (A caveat is in order: we do not know whether other persons had sought private mental health care and did not report this fact in our interviews or questionnaires. Hence our numbers are quite small and representative only of individuals with mental health problems who come from the lower end of the socioeconomic ladder.)

When we combined all stressful life events occurring between birth and age 18 into a discriminant function analysis, we were able to correctly classify 96.3 percent of the individuals without coping problems at age 32 and 66.7 percent of the individuals with public records of psychiatric care (canonical correlation = .70, $p < .0001$).

Stressful life events that made a major contribution to this discriminant function were prolonged separation from the mother without stable or adequate childcare in year one, prolonged absence of the father between ages 2 and 10, remarriage of the mother and the entry of a stepfather into the household, foster home placement between ages 11 and 18, and mental health problems (already recognized) in adolescence (see Table 23 in Appendix I).

Early Economic and Biological Risk Factors Linked to Adult Health Problems

Economic Status

There were significant social class differences in the adult health status of individuals who had experienced moderate-severe perinatal stress or whose physical development was below normal in early childhood. Thirty percent of the men and women who had been reared in poverty *and* had experienced moderate to severe perinatal stress reported serious health problems by age 32, in contrast to only 10 percent of the individuals who had suffered moderate to severe perinatal complications but who had grown up in middle class homes. One out of five among the individuals who had been considered below normal in physical development during the pediatric examination at age 2 and who grew up in poverty reported serious health problems in their early 30s, but none of the individuals who had received a similar rating at age 2 and who had grown up in middle class homes reported any serious health problems. Among those with a moderate to severe physical handicaps at age 10 who had grown up in poverty, the proportion of self-reported serious health problems at age 32 was 38.5 percent; among individuals with the same degree of handicap who had grown up in more affluent homes the proportion of self-reported health problems was 16.7 percent—less than half.

Gender Differences

Males who had been exposed to moderate to severe perinatal stress or who had received a "below normal" physical status rating by pediatricians at age 2 or who had a moderate to severe physical handicap by age 10 more often reported serious health problems in adulthood than did females exposed to the same health risks in childhood. This was especially true for individuals who had been "below normal" in physical development as toddlers: 25 percent of the males but only 5.9 percent of the females in this group reported having serious health problems in their early 30s.

Among the 28 cohort members who had died by age 30, males from poor and unstable homes who had suffered moderate to severe degrees of perinatal stress, who had had abnormal cord and placental conditions, or who had been delivered by Ceserian section were overrepresented—as were males whose mothers had suffered serious psychological trauma and physical abuse during pregnancy. Death rates of females with moderate to severe degrees of perinatal stress did not differ significantly from peers of the same age and sex without such conditions.

In Sum

The results of our analyses of links between adverse experiences in childhood and youth and coping problems in early adulthood can be summed up as follows.

(1) A core of adverse experiences during the formative years linked directly (albeit to a modest degree) to problems in adult coping for both

men and women in this birth cohort. None of the events was under the control of the youngster. Such sources of stress included chronic poverty and the disruption of the family unit, that is, the long-term absence of a parent (due to separation, desertion, or divorce) and the introduction of a stepparent into the family unit during middle childhood and adolescence. The most common childhood stressor with long-term consequences in this birth cohort, however, was the birth of a younger sibling before the second birthday of the index child.

Our results with a Pacific Asian cohort born in 1955 on Kauai complement those of Elder and his associates (Elder, 1974; Elder, Liker, and Cross, 1984; Elder, Van Nguyen, and Caspi, 1985), who traced the long-term effects of economic deprivation on two cohorts of Caucasian youngsters who grew up in Berkeley and Oakland during the Great Depression. They also complement the findings by Wallerstein and her colleagues from a longitudinal study of children and adolescents from a largely white middle class population of divorced families in northern California. We find, as she does, that some psychological effects of parental divorce extend into adulthood, at least for a minority of the most troubled youngsters (Wallerstein, 1985; Wallerstein and Blakeslee, 1989). The same appears to hold for the introduction of a stepparent into the family (Hetherington, Stanley-Hagan, and Anderson, 1989).

Less frequently explored, but of considerable interest in view of the numbers of children who have been exposed to this childhood stressor (some one out of four in this cohort), are the long-term effects of the closely spaced birth of a younger sibling on adult adaptation. Hobcraft, McDonald, and Rutstein (1985) found across thirty-four developing countries an increased risk of childhood mortality and morbidity for children followed by a closely spaced birth. The older child in such a pair may be more vulnerable because of the premature termination of breastfeeding and the redirection of maternal attention to the younger child.

Dunn and her colleagues (Dunn and Kendrick, 1980; Dunn, Kendrick, and Mac Namee, 1981) found a short-term increase in behavioral problems for 2- to 3-year-old English children after the birth of a sibling and less playful interactions of the mothers with the older child, as well as more evidence of negative verbal interactions, including confrontations and prohibitions. Moore (1975), in a small-scale longitudinal study, found that some 15 percent of London children with a closely spaced younger sibling developed problem behaviors and disturbed mother-child relationships. The long-term effects of this childhood stressor clearly deserve more attention—perhaps with available archival longitudinal data.

Given the relatively late age of childbearing among contemporary American families, the incidence of closely spaced births may well increase.

(2) Stressful life events in childhood tended to be more often significantly associated with coping problems in adulthood among the males of this cohort. Stressful life events in adolescence tended to be more often associated with coping problems in adulthood among the females in this cohort. Males, in turn, reported more stressful life events in the third decade of life than did females, and such events discriminated more often between men with and without coping problems than they did among the women of the same age.

Our results for our cohort at age 32 complement our earlier findings from our 18-year follow-up, which indicated that boys were more vulnerable to the effects of adverse experiences in the first decade of life and that girls were more vulnerable in the second decade (Werner and Smith, 1982). Rutter (1983) has reported similar findings in a review of European studies of stress, coping, and development. However, we now have additional data that point to another shift toward greater male vulnerability in the third decade of life—in spite of the fact that the women in this cohort were confronted with more transitions in their life trajectories, that is, entry into the world of work, marriage, and motherhood. Further research across the life span is needed to show whether there are other periods in adulthood (i.e., midlife) when there is increased vulnerability for women, or whether their greater resilience as a gender stabilizes by the early 30s and continues into old age.

(3) Stressful experiences involving loss or separation from a caregiver or loved one in infancy and childhood tended to be more often significantly associated with coping problems in adulthood among the males in this cohort. Stressful life events involving discord or disturbed interpersonal relationships in adolescence tended to be more often significantly associated with coping problems in adulthood among the females, especially when we examined the childhood antecedents of their failed marriages.

Differences in sex role socialization may account for some of the differential impact of these sources of stress on the men and women in this cohort. Girls who are traditionally socialized to be more conciliatory and compliant than boys may be especially vulnerable when confronted with stressful life events that generate conflict (with parents or peers). Boys who are expected to earn their masculine identity by assertiveness and a "take charge" attitude may be especially vulnerable to life events they cannot control or influence—deaths, departures, separations from loved ones.

Our results indicate the need to expand the search for significant attachments and hence significant separation experiences beyond mothers and mother surrogates to fathers, siblings, grandparents, childhood friends, and adolescent peers. The results of our analyses of the links between stressful childhood events and adult adaptation suggest that the negative effects of early loss or prolonged separation from a parent may be aggravated by separation from a sibling caregiver (who departs the household or dies), a friend in the elementary grades (who moves to another school), or the breakup of a long-term relationship in late adolescence.

(4) In both the first and second decades of life, stressful life events tended to be associated with concurrent behavioral problems or school failures; these, in turn, correlated significantly with later coping problems in adulthood. This association was especially apparent when we examined the childhood antecedents of adult criminal behaviors and psychiatric disorders.

Our findings are quite similar to those reported by Farrington (1987) from the Cambridge Study of Delinquent Development and by Douglas and Mann (1979) from the National Survey—both longitudinal studies with Caucasian samples in Great Britain. Douglas and Mann found, as we did, that family adversities experienced in childhood (such as parental divorce) were statistically associated with psychiatric problems in adult life. A more detailed analysis of their data, however, showed that this link was almost entirely a function of the prior associations of adversity in childhood with behavioral disorders in childhood. This deviant behavior in childhood persisted into adult life (Rutter, 1983).

(5) We found it useful to examine the intercorrelations between stressful life events and behavioral and/or learning problems at each stage of the developmental cycle (early and middle childhood, adolescence and young adulthood), and then to combine stressful life events chronologically, adding stressors that occurred in later developmental stages to earlier ones. Our results enabled us to see more clearly that coping problems in adulthood cannot be explained *solely* by correlations with recent or concurrent stressful life events—though individuals without coping problems reported significantly fewer concurrent stressful life events in their transition to adult life. Likewise, we could not account for coping problems in adulthood solely by looking at associations with early adverse events in infancy and childhood, though the majority of the individuals who were coping satisfactorily in adulthood had not experienced such early adversities.

Our successive analyses showed consistently that the addition of new stressors in middle childhood, adolescence, and young adulthood to the stressful events experienced in infancy significantly increased the proportion of individuals with coping problems at age 32 who were correctly identified—whether these were men and women with failed marriages or men with criminal records or individuals with mental health problems or adults with a combination of two or more such coping problems. Thus we surmise that boys and girls exposed to adversities in early childhood are not predestined to grow into adults with failed marriages, criminal records, or psychiatric disorders. At each developmental stage, there is an opportunity for protective factors (personal competencies and sources of support) to counterbalance the negative weight exerted by adverse experiences. We turn now to a consideration of the long-term effects of such protective factors in the lives of the men and women in this birth cohort.

9

Protective Factors and Adult Adaptation

We now take a look at the relationship across time between individual dispositions and sources of support that contributed to resiliency and/or recovery among the high risk children and youths in this cohort.

The variables we present in this chapter discriminated significantly between high risk boys and girls with good and poor outcomes in adulthood (see Tables 24 and 25 in Appendix I). In Figures 4 and 5, we show the correlations that link protective factors in infancy, childhood, adolescence, and young adulthood to global ratings of the quality of adult adaptation for high risk individuals.[1]

Protective Factors within the Individual

Among infant characteristics that acted as protective buffers for both high risk boy and girl babies was the absence of distressing sleeping and eating habits. Being perceived as "affectionate and cuddly" was a protective factor for infant girls, being perceived as "very active" was a protective factor for infant boys.

During the developmental examination at age 2, independent observers (pediatricians and psychologists) recorded a significantly higher proportion of positive adjectives for high risk children who grew into adults without any major coping problems in their early 30s. Most of

1. The reader is referred to Figures A3 and A4 in Appendix I for the results of path analyses that trace *both* the *direct* and *indirect* links between stressful life events and protective factors in childhood and adolescence and quality of adaptation in adulthood.

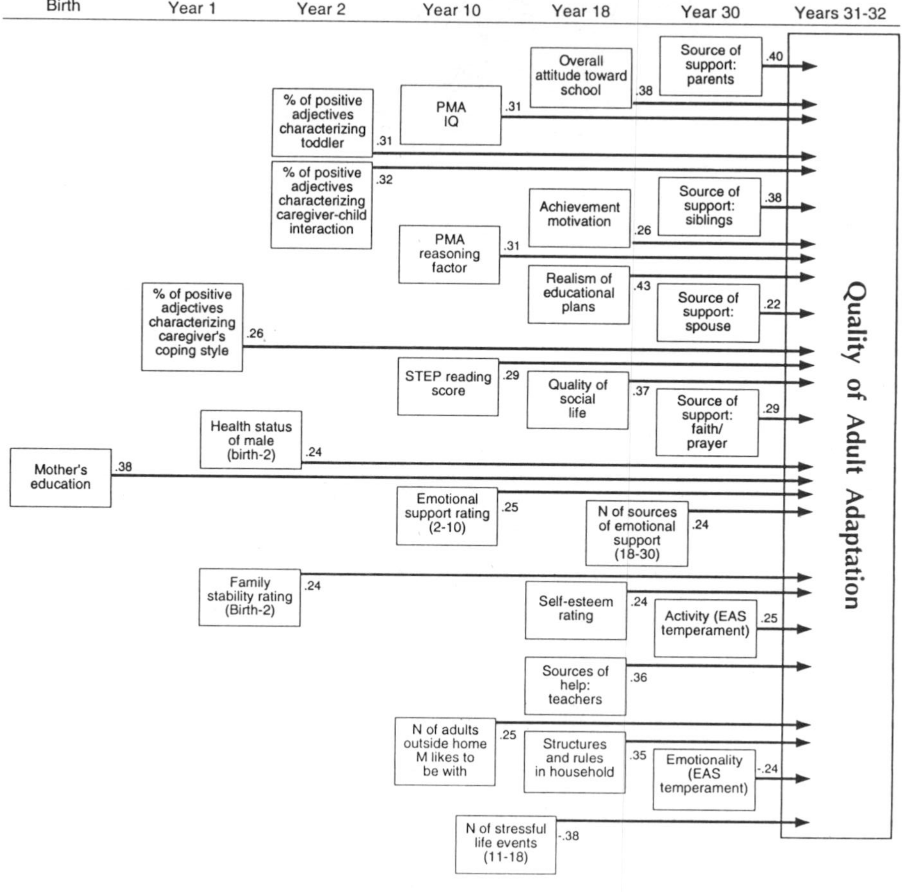

Figure 4. Correlation coefficients linking protective factors to quality of adult adaptation: high risk males

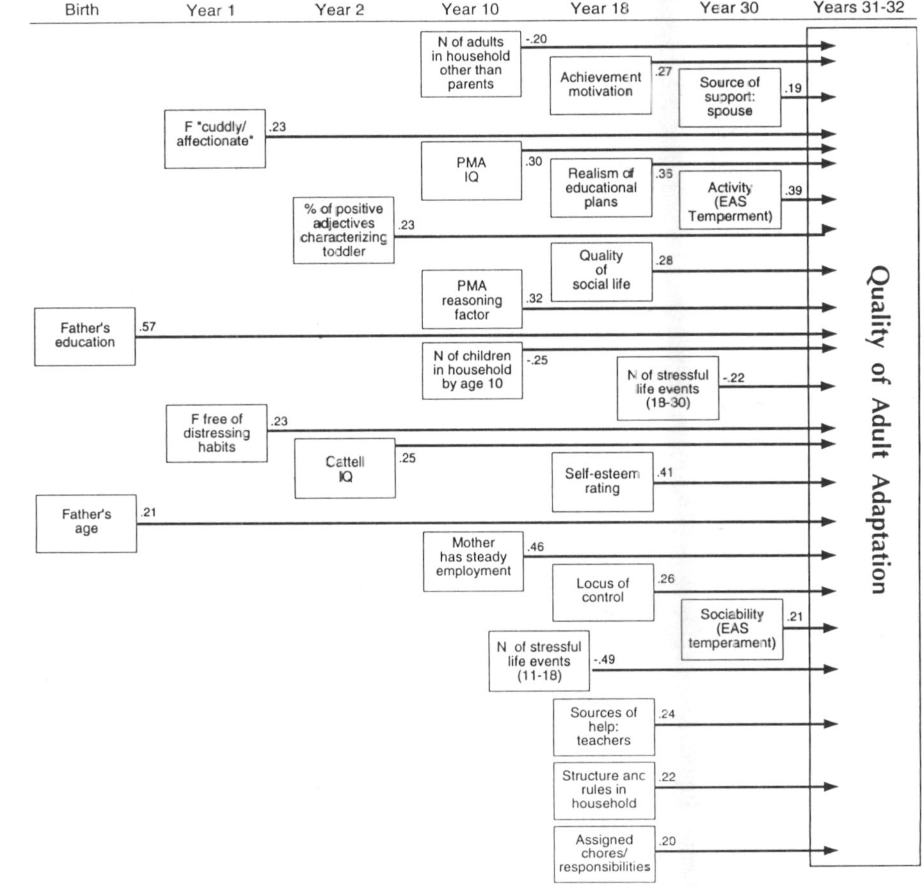

Figure 5. Correlation coefficients linking protective factors to quality of adult adaptation: high risk females

these adjectives denoted a positive social orientation. Observers described a high proportion of these toddlers as "agreeable," "cheerful," "friendly," "relaxed," "responsive," "self-confident," and "sociable" (in contrast to their high risk peers who later developed problems and who were significantly more often characterized as "anxious," "bashful," "disagreeable," "fearful," "suspicious," "withdrawn," or, at best, "ambivalent" with strangers).

In independent assessments of the children's behavior at age 10, teachers checked significantly fewer behavior problems for high risk boys who made a successful adult adaptation at age 31/32; parents checked significantly fewer behavior problems for high risk girls who coped successfully in adulthood. In the assessments of the quality of their social lives at age 17/18, these same boys and girls received significantly higher ratings for popularity with their peers than did high risk youths who as adults developed coping problems.

The EAS Temperament Survey for Adults also revealed significant differences between individuals who had made a successful transition into adulthood and their high risk peers of the same age and sex who had developed problems at age 31/32. High risk men and women without coping problems in adulthood rated themselves significantly lower on Distress/Emotionality (the tendency to become upset easily and intensely) than did high risk individuals who had developed problems in their early 30s. The women who had made a successful transition to work, marriage, and parenthood rated themselves significantly higher on the Sociability dimension (i.e., the tendency to prefer the presence of others to solitary activities) and significantly lower on the Anger Scale.

Among the high risk individuals who succeeded against the odds, there was a significant association between PMA IQ, a (nonverbal) measure of problem-solving skills at age 10 (PMA Reasoning factor), and successful adaptation in adulthood. By grade 4, they also had significantly higher scores on the STEP Reading achievement test than did their high risk peers who developed coping problems in adulthood. This difference was especially pronounced for the boys.

In their senior year in high school, these same individuals evaluated their school experience more positively and had higher expectations for future educational accomplishments than did the high risk youths who developed coping problems in adulthood. Their educational and vocational plans were more realistic as well. Interviewers gave them a significantly higher self-esteem rating at age 17/18 than they did for men and women who subsequently developed problems in the transition to work, marriage, and parenthood.

A significantly higher proportion of high risk women who succeeded against the odds had regular household chores and domestic responsibilities during adolescence. The successful high risk men rated themselves higher on the EAS Temperament Survey Activity Scale (tempo, vigor) than did high risk men who developed coping problems by age 31/32.

A potent protective factor among high risk individuals who grew into successful adulthood was a faith that life made sense, that the odds could be overcome. This faith was tied to active involvement in church activities, whether Buddhist, Catholic, mainstream Protestant, or fundamentalist. The high risk men and women who made successful transitions into adulthood also had a more internal locus of control: At age 18 and again at age 31/32, they expressed a strong belief that they could control their fates by their own actions.

Protective Factors within the Family

One of the most powerful variables positively associated with the successful adult adaptation of high risk children was the educational level of the opposite-sex parent: mother's educational level for boys, father's educational level for girls.

For high risk boys, the coping style of the primary caregiver in the first year of life was significantly associated with quality of adult adaptation in their early 30s. Mothers of high risk sons who succeeded against the odds, as contrasted with mothers of sons with adult coping problems, were significantly more often characterized by observers in the home as "intelligent," "self-confident," and "self-controlled"; but they also indulged their boy babies more than did mothers of high risk sons who developed problems in the transition to adulthood.

Psychologists and pediatricians also noted significant differences in the coping styles of the caregivers of high risk children during the developmental examination at age 2. Caregivers whose sons and daughters developed into adults without coping problems were more accepting of and responsive to the toddlers approaches than were the caregivers whose children later developed problems, and were more often characterized as "affectionate," "kind," "temperate," and as taking things "in stride."

For high risk boys and girls, there was also a significant association between the presence of rules and structure in the household in adolescence and a successful adaptation in adulthood. The model of a mother who was gainfully and steadily employed was a significant protective factor for high risk girls who grew into competent, confident, and caring adults.

Protective Factors in the Community

The number of caring adults outside the family with whom the child liked to associate was a significant protective factor for both high risk boys and girls who made a successful transition into adulthood. Among these surrogate parents were grandparents, uncles, aunts, neighbors, parents of boy- or girlfriends, youth leaders, and members of church groups.

During adolescence, a caring teacher was an important protective factor for boys and girls who succeeded against the odds. This teacher served not only as an academic instructor but also as a confidant and an important role model with whom a student could identify. During young adulthood, spouses served a similar role for high risk men and women; high risk men who succeeded against the odds also relied on the emotional support of kith and kin, preferring informal over formal sources of emotional support.

"Second Chance" Opportunities at Major Life Transitions

Finally, opportunities at major life transitions turned the trajectories of a significant proportion of high risk men and women on the path to recovery. Among the life events considered critical turning points for high risk members of this birth cohort who grew into competent, confident, and caring adults were: marriage or entry into a long-term committed relationship (more so for women than for men), the birth of a child (for both men and women), joining the work force and establishing a career (for both men and women), going to college (more so for women than men), graduating from high school or joining the armed forces to gain additional educational and vocational skills (more so for men than for women), and becoming an active member of a church group (for both men and women).

In contrast, men and women with coping problems in their 30s tended to point to life events that closed rather than opened doors. Among the most important life events mentioned in this group were: divorce or breakup of a long-term relationship (for both men and women), death of a parent (for the women), and moving away from home (for the men).

Predictors of Satisfaction with Work at Age 31/32

Let us now turn to an examination of protective factors in the work lives of men and women who successfully surmounted adversities in childhood and youth and who were working well in a job and/or a chosen field of study in early adulthood. The dependent variable is the individual's ratings of satisfaction with work or school achievement at age 31/32 (see Scoring System for Ratings of Adult Adaptation in Appendix II). The scores ranged from 4 (most satisfied) to 10 (most dissatisfied).

The Men

High risk men, who liked their jobs or the schooling that went with a successful career in adulthood tended to be sons of older fathers (r = .31). Their parents had characterized them as very active babies (r = .28) who were good-natured and even tempered (r = .23).

They tended to have had fewer stressful life experiences in the first two years of life than did high risk males who were dissatisfied with their work and post high school educational experiences (r = −.24). A psychologist's rating of family stability (r = .38) and the proportion of positive caregiver interactions with the boy at age 2 noted by independent observers at the developmental examinations (r = .42) were among the most powerful predictors of work satisfaction in adulthood for these high risk males. Psychologists' ratings of the emotional support provided by family members at age 10 also correlated positively with work satisfaction at age 31/32 for the high risk men (r = .28), as did a boy's favorable attitude toward school in his senior year in high school (r = .21).

The Women

High risk females who were satisfied with their work and post high school education by age 31/32 tended to have had fewer distressing eating and sleeping habits in infancy (r = .29). They also rated themselves lower on the Distress/Emotionality Scale of the EAS Temperament Survey for Adults (r = −.26).

The best predictor in middle childhood for these women was the midpercentile score on the STEP Reading test at grade 4 (r = .45). Other significant predictors for the women were the PMA IQ (r = .28) and the PMA Reasoning factor (r = .25)—a nonverbal measure of problem-solving ability. There was also a (modest) positive correlation between maternal employment during the childhood years (ages 2–10) and the work satisfaction and success of their daughters in adulthood (r = .22). But the most powerful predictors were ratings of achievement motivation (r = .53) and self-esteem (r = .44) made by independent interviewers at age 17/18 when the young women were about to graduate from high school.

Prediction of Satisfaction with Interpersonal Relationships at age 31/32

We turn now to an examination of the protective factors in childhood and adolescence which had positive associations with satisfactory interpersonal relationships in early adulthood for high risk men and women. The dependent variable is the individual's rating of satisfaction with relationships with parents, spouse or mate, children, and friends at age 31/32 (see Scoring System in Appendix II). The scores on these ratings ranged from 7 (most satisfied) to 20 (most dissatisfied).

The Men

High risk males who were satisfied with their interpersonal relationships at age 31/32 had displayed fewer behavior problems at home at age 10 than had men who had unsatisfactory relationships with their families and friends by age 31/32 ($r = -.41$). They were also exposed to more caring adults (other than their parents) ($r = .52$) and experienced fewer stressful events in childhood ($r = -.25$). The two most powerful predictors of satisfying relationships in adulthood for the men were a strong internal locus of control at age 17/18 ($r = .42$) and popularity with peers in high school ($r = .40$).

At age 31/32, the successful adults rated themselves significantly lower on the Distress/Emotionality Scale than did their high risk peers who had trouble getting along with parents, mates, or children ($r = -.46$). They also had significantly lower scores on the Anger ($r = -.40$) and Fear ($r = -.46$) scales of the EAS Temperament Survey for Adults.

High risk males with satisfactory interpersonal relationships by age 31/32 relied on a greater number of sources of emotional support than did males who had trouble making lasting and caring commitments. Support by a spouse ($r = .32$), by parents or parents-in-law ($r = .31$), and by mental health professionals ($r = .27$) were positively correlated with satisfactory interpersonal relationships for these men.

The Women

For the high risk females, the educational level of the father was the most powerful predictor of satisfactory interpersonal relationships by age 31/32 ($r = .51$). The proportion of positive adjectives used by observers in the home to characterize the mothers' caregiving styles with their infant daughters also had a significant (though modest) association with the women's satisfaction with their interpersonal relationships in their early 30s ($r = .22$).

High risk females who had established satisfactory interpersonal relationships with parents, partners, and children in their early 30s had had better problem-solving skills at age 10 than had women with unsatisfactory interpersonal relationships in adulthood ($r = .23$). They also tended to have mothers who were gainfully employed ($r = .29$) and were assigned more responsible/household chores in adolescence ($r = .23$). At age 31/32, these women tended to rate themselves lower on the Activity Scale of the EAS Temperament Survey for Adults than did their troubled peers who were dissatisfied with the quality of their interpersonal relationships ($r = -.28$)

Prediction of Satisfaction with Self at Age 31/32

We close this section with an examination of variables that predicted a positive self-evaluation in adulthood for the high risk individuals in this birth cohort. The dependent variable is the individual's rating of satisfaction with his or her state of life at age 31/32 (see Scoring System in Appendix II), with scores ranging from 3 (most satisfied) to 10 (most dissatisfied).

The Men

For the high risk males, poor health status in infancy ($r = -.28$) and number of behavior problems checked by teachers ($r = -.28$) and parents ($r = -.24$) at age 10 correlated negatively with a positive self-evaluation in adulthood. The best predictor for a positive self-evaluation at age 31/32, however, was the number of sources of emotional support the men could draw on ($r = .39$), especially the support of a spouse or mate ($r = .48$).

The Women

For the high risk females, there was a (modest) positive correlation between the father's educational level and the daughter's self-evaluation in adulthood ($r = .31$). There were also significant associations between the proportion of positive adjectives checked by independent observers to characterize the behavior of the toddler ($r = .38$), the quality of the caregiver's interaction with the child at age 2 (r = .33), and the woman's satisfaction with her life at age 31/32.

At age 10, both the PMA IQ (r = .35) and the STEP Reading score (r = .31) were significant predictors of a positive self-evaluation at age 31/32 for the women. The two most powerful predictors, however, were two measures obtained in the senior year in high school: the Nowicki Locus of Control score (r = .48) and Self-Esteem score (r = .39).

Discriminant Function Analyses

So far, we have looked at links between single protective factors in childhood and youth and the quality of adult adaptation in high risk boys and girls who grew up under adverse life circumstances. We now present a set of predictors that maximally differentiated between high risk individuals with successful adult adaptation and high risk men and women with one or more coping problems in their early 30s (see Table 26 in Appendix I).

We performed several discriminant function analyses—by gender and by developmental stages. We looked first at the predictive power of protective factors that had buffered life's adversities at each separate developmental stage, that is, early and middle childhood, adolescence, and young adulthood. We then combined the most discriminating protective factors chronologically, first entering those that had operated between birth and age 2, then adding significant buffers between ages 2 and 10, and continuing with the addition of protective factors in adolescence and young adulthood which had discriminated between good and poor outcomes at ages 31/32.

The High Risk Men

There was a significant increase in the percentage of men for whom we could make correct predictions when we added protective factors that had operated at later developmental stages to earlier buffers. When we utilized only the information on protective factors in the child and his caregiving environment which was available between birth and age 2, we correctly identified 87.5 percent of the high risk males who made a successful adult adaptation at ages 31/32 and 71.4 percent of the high risk males with one or more coping problems in their early 30s. The inclusion of protective factors that operated in middle childhood, late adolescence, and young adulthood increased the percentage correctly identified to 94.4 percent of the high risk males without coping problems at ages 31/32 and to 96.8 percent of the high risk males with one or more coping problems in their early 30s (canonical correlation = .89; $p < .02$).[2]

When we examined the pattern of standardized canonical coefficients which discriminated between the high risk men who made successful adult adaptations and those who had records of divorce, crime, mental health problems, and/or a poor self-evaluation, we noted that some protective factors tended to contribute more weight to the discriminant functions than did others. Among variables making a significant contribution in infancy were the mother's educational level, the infant's activity level, his good natured disposition, and absence of distressing habits. The proportion of positive responses elicited by the child from caregivers (at home) and strangers (during the developmental examination at age 2) also contributed significantly to this function. Higher scores on the PMA IQ and smaller family size at age 10 were significantly associated with a positive outcome at age 31/32 for the high risk males, as was the number of caring adults outside of the family with whom the boy liked to associate.

Among protective factors that contributed positively in adolescence to the likelihood of successful adult adaptation for the high risk men were high achievement motivation, realistic educational and vocational plans, teachers who served as mentors, and structure and rules in the household. Among the most potent protective factors for high risk men in young adulthood were the number of sources of help (spouse, parents, siblings, neighbors), as well as low levels of Distress/Emotionality on the EAS Temperament Survey for Adults.

The High Risk Women

When we entered only the protective factors that operated in early childhood in the discriminant function analyses for the high risk women, we correctly identified 88.2 percent of the females who made successful adaptations in adulthood, and 90.5 percent of the females who developed one or more coping problems by their early 30s. The addition of protective factors that operated at later stages in their lives (i.e., middle childhood, late adolescence) increased the percentage correctly identified to 100 percent of the females without coping problems and to 94 percent of

2. The proportions correctly identified by SHAZAM, the logit regression model, were 94.1 percent and 93.7 percent respectively.

the females with coping problems at age 31/32 (canonical correlation = .84; $p < .02$).[3]

Among variables that contributed significantly to the discriminant function of the women were not only the age and educational level of the father but also an affectionate disposition and the absence of distressing eating and sleeping habits in the baby girl. Like their male counterparts, high risk women who made a successful adult adaptation tended to elicit a higher proportion of positive responses from their caregivers as well as from strangers when they were 2 years old. Higher scores on the PMA IQ and smaller family size at age 10 were significantly correlated with successful adult adaptation for high risk women as well. A mother who was gainfully and steadily employed was a significant buffer for the high risk girls in middle childhood.

Realistic educational and vocational plans by age 17/18 contributed a significant weight to the discriminant function, as did a positive self-concept. The most powerful discriminators at age 31/32 were the number of sources of emotional support. Like their male counterparts, high risk women who made a successful transition into adulthood tended to rate themselves lower on Distress/Emotionality on the EAS Temperament Survey for Adults than did those who were less successful.

Individual Dispositions versus Outside Sources of Support

Protective factors within the individual (such as an "easy" temperament, good reasoning skills, self-esteem, and internal locus of control) consistently tended to make a greater impact on the quality of adult coping among the high risk females than among the high risk males. Outside sources of support tended to make a greater difference in the lives of the high risk men than of the high risk women.

In infancy, the educational level of the mother, the proportion of positive maternal interactions observed during the developmental examination at age 2, and a rating of family stability (from birth to age 2), predicted successful adult adaptation better for high risk males than for high risk females. Behavior characteristics of the one-year-old infant and

3. The proportion correctly classified by the logit regression analyses reached 100 percent in both groups.

the 2-year-old toddler predicted successful adult adaptation better for high risk females than for high risk males.

In *childhood*, the emotional support provided by the family (between ages 2 and 10), the number of children in the family, and the number of adults outside the household with whom the youngster liked to associate were more potent predictors of successful adult adaptation for the high risk boys than for the high risk girls. For the high risk girls, the best predictors of a successful adaptation in early adulthood were the PMA IQ, the PMA factor R (a nonverbal measure of problem-solving skills), and the model of a steadily employed mother.

In *late adolescence*, the availability of a teacher as mentor or role model and the assignment of regular household chores and responsibilities were better predictors of successful adult adaptation for high risk men than for high risk women. A high self-esteem rating and realistic educational and vocational plans were better discriminators for high risk women than for high risk men who later coped successfully with the demands of adult life.

In *early adulthood*, the number of sources of emotional support available in times of stress were better predictors of successful adaptation at age 31/32 for the high risk males than for the high risk females. Temperamental characteristics, such as activity level and (absence of) emotionality and distress, were better predictors of the quality of adult adaptation than the number of outside sources of support available to the high risk women.

In Sum

Most of the childhood predictors of successful adaptation in adulthood for high risk men and women exposed to childhood poverty, parental psychopathology, and perinatal stress had also emerged as powerful discriminators between good and poor outcomes in late adolescence (Werner, 1990; Werner and Smith, 1982). Among them were temperamental characteristics of the individual which elicited positive responses from their caregivers, problem-solving skills in middle childhood, the number of children in the family (four or fewer), the presence of alternate caregivers (other than the parents), and structure and rules in the household during adolescence.

For high risk girls, a strong internal locus of control and high self-esteem had been important buffers in adolescence; another protective factor was the role model of a competent mother who had held a steady job and who had delegated household chores and responsibilities to her daughter during the teen years. For high risk boys, it was the presence of a male mentor or role model and the advantage of having been a first-born son.

Our present analysis, with subsequent follow-up data, points to additional moderators of the relationship between childhood adversity and adult adaptation. Among the protective factors that discriminated between high risk individuals with and without coping problems in early adulthood were the educational level of the parents (especially the opposite-sex parent), the availability of caring adults outside the home, and supportive teachers in school who acted as role models and assisted the youths with realistic educational and vocational plans. Other potent buffers of adversity in early adulthood were the emotional support provided by spouses, kith, and kin, the power of faith and prayer, and the opening up of opportunities that increased the individual's competence and confidence. Equally powerful in adulthood as predictors of successful adaptation were temperamental characteristics that have a strong genetic base: activity level, sociability, and emotionality. Protective factors within the individual tended to make a greater impact on the quality of adult adaptation of high risk women; outside sources of support tended to make a greater impact on the overall adaptation of high risk men.

Are our findings, though consistent, limited to the life experiences of a particular cohort of men and women on a small Pacific island? We do not think so. A crucial test of any research is whether comparable studies have reported similar findings. We are encouraged by the fact that our results are in broad agreement with reports from other investigators who have followed high risk individuals from childhood or adolescence into adulthood.

Our findings, together with the research reviewed in the first chapter, suggest that a number of potent protective factors or buffers have a more generalized effect on the life course of vulnerable children than do specific risk factors or stressful life events. They appear in the life histories of individuals from various ethnic groups and socioeconomic backgrounds who grew up in different regions of the United States (the Far West, the Midwest, and the Northeast), and in various countries in Europe (Denmark, England, the Federal Republic of Germany, Sweden, and Switzerland). They also seem to transcend cohort effects.

Despite the heterogeneity of risk conditions studied (poverty, parental psychopathology, caregiving deficits, delinquencies, teenage motherhood, to name but a few), one can discern a common core of individual dispositions and sources of support which contributes to resiliency and/or recovery in adulthood among individuals reared under adverse circumstances. This core includes temperamental characteristics that elicit positive social responses from parents, peers, and teachers; efficacy, planfulness, and self-esteem; competent caregivers and supportive adults (other than parents) who foster trust and a sense of coherence or faith; and "second chance" opportunities in society at large (at school, at work, in church, in the military) which enable high risk youths to acquire competence and confidence.

Some of the moderators of the relationship between childhood adversity and adult adaptation, such as scholastic aptitude (IQ) and school achievement, are also predictors of good adaptation in low risk conditions, at least in societies that stress literacy and formal schooling. The importance of these resources, however, increases in the context of high risk conditions, that is, when a child grows up in chronic poverty or in a multiproblem family (Masten, 1990).

For example, Elder (1974) found, as we did a generation later, that achievement motivation was correlated more highly with ability among economically deprived youths than it was among the more affluent. Long and Vaillant (1984) reported along the same lines that for men who had grown up in multiproblem families childhood IQ showed a stronger relationship to upward social mobility and successful adaptation in midlife than it did for men from more stable homes. More recently, Masten (1990) has shown that cognitive functioning was an important moderator of the relationship between adversity and quality of adaptation in a sample of Minneapolis school children who had been exposed to a variety of stressful life events. We found the same links between cognitive competence and successful adaptation for the multiracial children who had grown up under adverse circumstances on Kauai—in middle childhood, in late adolescence, and in early adulthood. Scholastic competence is a potent buffer in adversity for high risk women as well as for high risk men, especially at a time when women are expected to fill the multiple roles of wage earner, wife, and mother.

10

Summing Up

"Hope" is the thing with feathers—
That perches in the soul—
And sings the tune without the words—
And never stops—at all—
Emily Dickinson (1861)

The Kauai Longitudinal Study began at a time when the systematic examination of the development of children exposed to potent biological and psychosocial risk factors was a rarity. In the mid 1950s, when the men and women in this cohort were born, investigators attempted to reconstruct the events that led to school failure, criminal behavior, and mental health problems by studying the history of individuals in whom such problems had already surfaced. This retrospective approach can create the impression that a poor outcome is inevitable if a child is exposed to poverty, perinatal trauma, or parental psychopathology, since it examines only the lives of the casualties, not the survivors.

By the mid 1980s, when the children of Kauai reached adulthood, perspectives had changed. A handful of prospective longitudinal studies in the United States and Europe have now followed infants and young children exposed to pre-, peri-, and postnatal risk factors over extended periods of time; these have consistently demonstrated that there are large individual differences among high risk children in response to chronic adversity in their lives. Our study provided us with a rare opportunity to examine the interplay between protective factors in the individual, the immediate family, and the broader social context which contribute to resiliency in childhood and adolescence and to the process of recovery in young adulthood.

We trust that our findings are of relevance to professionals who care for and about our nation's children and to policy makers who have to make choices about when and how to intervene to prevent the occurrence of delinquent behavior, mental health problems, and teenage pregnancies or how to lessen their cost to the individual and society in later life.

Here we review first the life course of this cohort from birth to their early 30s and then summarize what we have learned about the long-term consequences of stressful life events in childhood and adolescence and about the process by which a chain of protective factors was forged which afforded vulnerable individuals an escape from childhood adversity. We then consider the implications of our findings for future research and social action that might benefit youngsters exposed to biological or social conditions that are hazardous to their development and psychological well-being.

The Children of the Garden Island

The social and historical context of the Kauai Longitudinal Study and the research design were presented in Chapters 1 and 2. The 505 individuals whom we followed from the prenatal period until they reached their early 30s grew up in a small island community in the youngest state of the union. They belonged to the post–World War II baby-boom generation whose childhood and adolescence was overshadowed by the war in Vietnam, the War on Poverty, and the Civil Rights Movement. Sons and daughters of immigrant plantation workers, they entered the work force during a serious economic recession in the United States; but by the time they reached their early 30s, the island economy had staged a recovery, based mainly on an expanding tourist industry.

Like the participants in other longitudinal studies, the men and women in our study shared a unique ethnic heritage and a unique historical experience in a unique geographical setting. When we compare our findings with the results of other prospective studies of high risk children and youths from different generations, however, we are encouraged by the fact that the protective factors and processes that acted as buffers against chronic sources of stress among the children of Kauai were also found among children and adolescents living in the American heartland and on the shores of the Atlantic as well as the Pacific Ocean. We suspect that cohort effects may influence the definition and prevalence of what one considers a developmental risk more than the process by which individuals manage to cope with their vulnerabilities.

About half of the children in this cohort grew up in poverty and were reared by parents who had not graduated from high school. Some 10 percent were exposed to moderate prenatal or perinatal stress, that is, complications during pregnancy, labor, or delivery. Three percent suffered severe perinatal trauma. One out of every six children in this cohort who survived infancy had physical or intellectual handicaps of perinatal or neonatal origin which were diagnosed between birth and age 2 and which required long-term specialized medical, educational, or custodial care.

About one out of every five children in our study group developed serious learning or behavior problems in the first decade of life which required more than six months of remedial work. By the time the children were 10 years old, twice as many children needed some form of remedial education (usually for problems associated with reading) as were in need of medical care. By the age of 18, 15 percent of the youth had delinquency records, and 10 percent had mental health problems requiring either in- or outpatient care.

As we followed these children from birth to the threshold of adulthood, we noted two trends: the impact of reproductive stress diminished with time, and the developmental outcome of virtually every biological risk condition was dependent on the quality of the rearing environment. We did find some correlations between moderate to severe degrees of perinatal trauma and major physical handicaps of the central nervous system and the muscular-skeletal and sensory systems. Perinatal trauma was also correlated with mental retardation, serious learning disabilities, and chronic mental health problems, such as schizophrenia, which arose in late adolescence or early adulthood.

Overall, rearing conditions were more powerful determinants of outcome, however, than was perinatal trauma. Prenatal and perinatal complications were consistently related to impairment of physical and psychological development in childhood and adolescence only when they were combined with chronic poverty, parental psychopathology, or persistently poor rearing conditions, unless there was serious damage to the central nervous system (Werner and Smith, 1977).

The High Risk Children as Adults

We designated about one-third of the surviving boys and girls in this cohort as high risk children because they were born into poverty (their parents were semi- or unskilled plantation workers) and they had experienced moderate to severe degrees of perinatal stress, or they lived in a family environment troubled by discord, divorce, parental alcoholism, or mental illness. Two-thirds of these children (who encountered four or more of such risk factors by age 2) did indeed develop serious learning or behavior problems by age 10 or had delinquency records, mental health problems, or pregnancies by the time they were 18 years old. Clearly the odds were against them.

Yet one out of three of these high risk children (some 10 percent of the cohort) grew into competent young adults who loved well, worked well, played well, and expected well. None developed serious learning or behavior problems in childhood or adolescence. As far as we could tell from interviews and from their records in the community, they succeeded in school, managed home and social life well, and expressed a strong desire to take advantage of whatever opportunities came their way when they finished high school.

Three clusters of protective factors differentiated this resilient group from the other high risk youths who developed serious and persistent problems in childhood and adolescence: (1) at least average intelligence and dispositional attributes that elicited positive responses from family members and strangers, such as robustness, vigor, and an active, sociable temperament; (2) affectional ties with parent substitutes such as grandparents and older siblings, which encouraged trust, autonomy, and initiative; and (3) an external support system (in church, youth groups, or school) which rewarded competence and provided them with a sense of coherence (Werner and Smith, 1982, 1989).

The major lessons we learned from our most recent follow-up during the age 30 transition period are described in detail in Chapters 3–7. With few exceptions, the resilient children grew into competent, confident, and caring adults whose educational and vocational accomplishments were equal to or exceeded those of the low risk children in the cohort who had grown up in more affluent, secure, and stable environments. Personal competence and determination, support from a spouse or mate, and reliance on faith and prayer were the shared qualities that characterized the resilient individuals in their early 30s.

As a group, they worked and loved in contexts far different from the traumatic domestic scenes that had characterized their childhoods. Career consolidation was the primary goal for both the resilient men and women at this stage of their lives. Those who were married (a majority of the women, but only a minority of the men) had strong commitments to intimacy and sharing with their partners. Those who had children (more women than men) had a strong sense of generativity which enabled them to be caring parents who respected the individuality and encouraged the autonomy of their offspring.

These competent adults, however, felt a persistent need to detach themselves from parents and siblings whose domestic and emotional problems still threatened to engulf them. The balancing act between forming new attachments to loved ones of their choice and the loosening of old family ties that evoked painful memories had exacted a toll in their adult lives. Some men in this group were reluctant to make a definite long-term commitment to a mate; some of the women exhausted themselves in trying to meet the demands of marriage, motherhood, and a career. The price they paid varied from stress-related health problems to a certain aloofness in their interpersonal relationships. They tended to keep their own counsel, but there was little bitterness and much compassion in their reflections on their childhood adversities.

One of the most striking findings of our follow-up in adulthood was that most high risk youths with serious coping problems in adolescence had staged a recovery of sorts by the time they reached their early 30s. This was true for the majority of the troubled teens, but more so for high risk females with problems in adolescence than for high risk males.

On the whole, the situations of the teenage mothers had improved significantly over time. In almost all respects, except for marital stability, they were better off than when we had seen them in their late teens and mid-20s. Sixty percent had obtained additional schooling and 90 percent were gainfully employed. On the average, they had fewer children than their families of origin—about the same number as anticipated by the women in this cohort who started childbearing later. In their early 30s, they expressed a stronger belief in their ability to control their own fates than they had at 18 or at 26.

The paths that had led to improvement for the majority of the teenage mothers on rural Kauai were similar to those reported by Furstenberg and his associates (1987) for a much larger sample of Black adolescent mothers who grew up in metropolitan Baltimore. The development of the women's personal resources, their competence and motivation, the support of kith and kin, and stable marriages all contributed to positive changes in their life trajectories from high risk pregnancy to successful adult adaptation. Other data from several national surveys seem to confirm these findings from Caucasian as well as Black samples. Educational achievement, fertility control, and marriage have proved to be alternative but complementary routes to effective management of teen childbearing (Furstenberg, Brooks-Gunn, and Chase-Landsdale, 1989).

Likewise, most of the delinquent youths in this birth cohort did not go on to an adult criminal career. Only one-fourth of the males and only 10 percent of the females with records of juvenile offenses also had criminal records by age 32. The majority of the adult crimes in this cohort were committed by a small group of individuals with an average of four or more juvenile arrests before age 18. About half in this group also had broken marriages by age 32, had battered their wives, and were delinquent in child support payments. The vast majority of these chronic offenders had been in need of remedial education by age 10, before they began their delinquent careers, and had been considered troublesome by their teachers in the classroom and by their parents at home. Both parents and teachers had noted at that time that they were "aggressive," "bullying," and "frequent liars." Most of the individuals in this group grew up in families in which either the mother or the father was absent for prolonged periods of time during adolescence because of desertion, separation, or divorce.

Our findings on Kauai, with a Pacific Asian sample, are very similar to those reported by Wolfgang, Thornberry, and Figlio (1987) from two cohorts of Black and Caucasian males born in Philadelphia in 1945 and 1958, and by Farrington (1989) from a cohort of London males born in the mid 1950s. All three studies found that, on the average, the earlier an offender started, the more juvenile and criminal offenses he accumulated. Wolfgang and his associates (1987) have argued persuasively that the juvenile justice system must be flexible so that it can react strongly to this small group of chronic offenders and react softly to the much larger group of nonserious offenders.

The majority of the delinquent youths on Kauai who did not go on to commit any adult crimes had scored within the average range of intelligence in early and middle childhood, were not described as troublesome by their grade school teachers, and had grown up in intact families during their teens. One of their elders (a parent, grandparent, uncle, or aunt) provided structure and stability in their lives. Military service, marriage to a stable partner, and parenthood proved to be positive turning points in the adult lives of these crime-resistant juvenile offenders.

By the time they were in their early thirties, a significant shift in life trajectories from risk to adaptation had also taken place in about half of the individuals who had been troubled by mental health problems in their teens—a finding similar to that reported by Magnusson (1988) for a contemporary urban Swedish cohort. Positive changes were more often noted among the women who had such problems in adolescence than among the men.

Only a minority of the troubled youths were still in need of mental health services by the time they reached their early 30s; but a higher proportion of males than females with mental health problems in their teens had grown into adults who had difficulties finding and keeping a job, who had marriages that ended in divorce, who were delinquent in spouse and child support, and who had criminal records.

Only a third of the individuals in need of mental health services during childhood or adolescence had actually received some counseling or psychotherapy—a proportion similar to that reported by Tuma (1989) for nationwide trends in the utilization of mental health services for young people. A significant minority had found a sense of meaning and security in their lives through active involvement in a religious group. The most salient turning points on the road to recovery for most of these troubled individuals, however, were meeting a caring friend and marrying an accepting and supportive spouse.

Men and women who had been more active and affectionate as infants and who had had fewer health problems and better problem-solving skills as children were more likely to overcome serious mental health problems in their teens than individuals who had elicited less positive responses from family members, teachers, and peers. The presence of both parents and the assumption of responsible chores in the household during adolescence were also associated with improvement in mental health status.

Overall, the prognosis for youths who were shy and lacked confidence was considerably better than for youths who displayed antisocial behavior, or for youths who had parents with chronic mental health problems and who had been exposed to serious perinatal trauma. Similar findings have been reported from studies with other ethnic groups on the U.S. mainland and in Europe (Buka, Lipsitt and Tsuang, 1987; Mednick et al., 1984; Patterson, DeBaryshe, and Ramsey, 1989).

Our follow-up of the high risk youths in this cohort leaves us with a sense of hope about the process of recovery which is possible during early adulthood—when many young people seize the opportunity to leave troubled homes and take on the responsibilities of work, marriage, and parenthood. As members of a generation that came of age during hard times in the United States, these 30-year-olds can look with pride on their accomplishments.

Approximately one out of six (18%) in this cohort, however, became troubled adults who had serious coping problems that included at least two of the following conditions: a broken marriage, a criminal record, chronic mental health problems, and a poor self-concept. Two-thirds of the individuals with serious coping problems by age 31/32 had been high risk youth who had been exposed to poverty and family disorganization since early childhood and who subsequently developed records of school failure, repeated delinquencies, and/or mental health problems. Our cohort study of Asian Americans on rural Kauai and Magnusson's (1988) study of urban Swedish males are consistent in their findings that individuals who are characterized by several problem areas at an early age are more stable in their patterns of maladjustment up into adulthood than are persons who have problems in a single area. They need our attention the most!

Pathways between Early Stressors and Adult Adaptation at 31/32

One of the objectives of our follow-up was to document the effects of stressful life events in childhood and adolescence on the adult lives of the men and women in this birth cohort. We hoped to be able to discriminate between childhood stressors that have long-term effects (and that should be assigned priority status in intervention programs) and other stressors whose effects turn out to be more transient. The results of our analyses are presented in Chapter 8 and in the path diagrams in Figures A1 and A2 in Appendix I.

For men, both discriminant function and latent variable path analyses showed modest but *direct* links between *disruptions of the family unit*, involving loss or separation from a caregiver or loved one in early and middle childhood, and coping problems in adulthood. Among the manifest variables that comprised the latent variable in that category were: being born to a mother who was not married at the time of the birth of her son, the birth of a younger sibling before the index child was age 2, separation from mother or father because of desertion or divorce between ages 2 and 10, the death or departure of a sibling from the household before age 10, and the remarriage of the mother before the boy was 10.[1]

For women, there was a modest, but *direct*, link between *chronic discord* with parents and peers in childhood and adolescence and coping

1. Latent variables (LV) in path analyses are higher order constructs that are the observed common factor shared by observable or manifest variables (Lohmöller, 1984). The latent variable loading patterns for the stressful life events are given in Table 27 in Appendix I.

problems at age 31/32. Among the manifest variables that comprised the latent variable in that category were: chronic conflict between the biological parents or conflict with a stepfather between ages 2 and 10; being reared by an alcoholic or mentally ill mother between ages 2 and 10; the presence of an alcoholic or mentally ill father between ages 11 and 18, chronic conflict between the parents in adolescence, and conflict with the mother, conflict with the father, and conflict with peers during the teen years.

Poverty at birth was associated to a moderate degree with disruptions in the family unit and with illnesses or handicaps for both sexes in infancy. *Poverty in childhood* and adolescence, however, had only modest *direct* associations with deviant outcomes at ages 10 and 18 for either sex. Such outcomes were more strongly associated with disrupted or disturbed family relationships, regardless of social class.

For both boys and girls, *disruptions of the family unit* in the first year of life were linked to a significant (but modest) degree to deviant outcomes at age 2 (i.e., below average intellectual and psychological functioning).

For both sexes, *chronic discord* between ages 2 and 10 was significantly linked to a need for remedial education and/or mental health care at age 10. For the females, such deviant outcomes at age 10 also had a significant link with adult coping problems. Chronic discord between ages 11 and 18 was also significantly linked to deviant outcomes at age 18, such as delinquency, mental health problems, and school failure for both sexes. For the males, such deviant outcomes at age 18 had a significant association with serious coping problems in adulthood as well.

Our findings from the Kauai Longitudinal Study complement the results of a handful of prospective studies of the consequences of childhood stress which extend into adolescence (Compas, 1987a). They suggest only a modest support for a stressful life events → deviant behavior path and a stronger support for a deviant behavior → stressful life events path.

Our analyses have shown, however, a differential vulnerability of boys and girls to some stressful life events in childhood and adolescence whose effects carry over into adulthood. Boys appear to be more vulnerable to separation from and loss of caregivers in early and middle childhood; girls appear to be more vulnerable when confronted with chronic discord and disturbed interpersonal relationships in adolescence. Even though the impact of stressful life events in childhood and adolescence on adult coping is modest and can be substantially buffered by protective factors in the individual and by a support system, we should be cognizant of the fact that some frequently encountered transitions in the family lives of American children, such as the closely spaced birth of a sibling and the divorce and remarriage of their parents, can create vulnerabilities that may resurface long after adolescent sons and daughters have come of age and confront the adult roles of spouse and parent.

This vulnerability was most apparent in the men and women in our study whose marriages ended in divorce by age 32. Among the most potent stressors in the lives of these young adults (that differentiated between them and their same-sex peers who had established stable relationships in their early 30s) was the experience of parental divorce and/or remarriage. While there has been an abundance of research on the immediate and short-term consequences of the events surrounding these marital transitions (for a child's perspective, see the review by Hetherington, Stanley-Hagan, and Anderson, 1989), there has been a paucity of long-term studies that have looked at the adult lives of the offspring of divorced parents.

We share a common concern with Wallerstein and Blakeslee (1989), who have now published their findings on young adults (in their 20s) who experienced the breakup of their families during childhood or adolescence. They find in a clinical sample what we find in an entire birth cohort: The psychological effects of parental divorce extend into adulthood and can interfere with the establishment of a strong bond of commitment and intimacy for a significant minority of men and women. Because parental divorce is currently the most prevalent risk factor for children in our society, its long-term consequences for the children need more attention.

Links between Protective Factors and Successful Adult Adaptation in High Risk Children and Youths

A major objective of our follow-up into adulthood was to document how a chain of protective factors, linked across time, afforded vulnerable children and teenagers an escape from adversity and contributed to positive outcomes in their adult lives. The results of our analyses are presented in Chapter 9 and in the path diagrams in Figures A3 and A4 in Appendix I. The protective factors we summarize here discriminated significantly between high risk men and women with good and poor outcomes in adulthood (as defined in Chapter 8). Either they had no significant discriminating effects among their low risk peers of the same age and gender (for example the number of caring adults outside the home with whom the child associated), or their effects were magnified in the presence of poverty and family disorganization (for example the activity level and sociability of the infant became a powerful protector).

The protective factors that correlated significantly with successful adult adaptation among both men and women grouped themselves into several constructs—called "latent variables" in our path analyses.[2] Some were characteristics of the individual which elicited positive responses from persons in their caregiving environments (such as an "easy" infant temperament characterized by high activity, sociability, and freedom from distressing habits); autonomy and social competence as a toddler; scholastic competence in middle childhood, including age-appropriate reading skills; the absence of behavior problems in the classroom and at home by age 10; high self-esteem, an internal locus of control, and realistic educational and vocational goals by age 18; and a low level of distress and emotionality by age 31/32.

The other variables that appeared as protective buffers in the lives of high risk children were parental competence and caregiving style (especially that of the mother) and a variety of sources of support in the family, neighborhood, school, and community which the individual attracted during early and middle childhood, late adolescence, and young adulthood. Among gatekeepers that fostered trust, autonomy, and initiative were grandparents, older siblings, caring adults in the neighborhood, teachers that acted as role models and counselors, ministers and youth workers, close friends, spouses or mates; and the support derived from faith and prayer.

When we examined the links between protective factors within the individual and outside sources of support or stress, we noted a certain continuity that appeared in the life course of the high risk men and women who successfully overcame a variety of childhood adversities. Their individual dispositions led them to select or construct environments that, in turn, reinforced and sustained their active, outgoing dispositions and rewarded their competencies. In spite of occasional deviations during transitional periods such as adolescence, their life trajectories re-

2. The latent variable loading patterns for the protective factors are given in Table 28 in Appendix I.

vealed cumulative interactional continuity. These continuities have also been demonstrated in other cohorts of high risk individuals followed into adulthood, for instance, in the life course of shy and ill-tempered Caucasian children in the Berkeley Guidance Study (Caspi, Elder, and Bem, 1988) and in the life trajectories of the Black teenage mothers followed by Furstenberg and his associates (1987).

There was, for example, a significant positive link between an "easy" infant temperament and the sources of support available to the individual in early and middle childhood. Active and sociable babies, without distressing sleeping and feeding habits, tended to elicit more positive responses from their mothers at age one and from alternate caregivers by age 2. In middle childhood, such children tended to rely on a wider network of caring adults both within and outside the family circle.

Positive parental interactions with the infant and toddler were, in turn, associated with greater autonomy and social maturity at age 2 and with greater scholastic competence at age 10. "Difficult" temperament traits in infancy, in contrast, were moderately linked with behavior problems in the classroom and at home at age 10, which, in turn, generated fewer sources of emotional support during adolescence.

Scholastic competence at 10, however, was positively linked with the number of sources of help that the teenager attracted, including support from teachers and peers as well as from family members. Scholastic competence at 10 was also positively linked with a sense of self-efficacy (self-esteem, internal locus of control) at age 18. A greater sense of self-efficacy at age 18 was, in turn, linked to less distress and emotionality for the high risk men at age 31/32 and generated a greater number of sources of emotional support for the high risk women in early adulthood, including support from a spouse or mate.

For the women, a sociable temperament in infancy and young adulthood showed a stronger link with positive outcomes by age 31/32 than for the men. Mothers who had graduated from high school and who were steadily employed by the time their children were 2 years old appeared to be more powerful positive buffers in adversity for their daughters than for their sons. The absence of behavior problems in middle childhood, and high self-esteem, efficacy, and an internal locus of control at age 18, also were more strongly linked to successful adult adaptation for the women than for the men.

For the men, scholastic competence at 10, including at least average intelligence and problem-solving and reading skills, was more strongly associated with a successful transition into adult responsibilities than for the women. The strongest positive buffers for the men, however, were the sources of emotional support on which they could rely after they left home, including the support of a spouse or mate, siblings and elders, as well as faith and prayer.

Parental competence, as manifested in the educational level of the opposite-sex parent (fathers for women, mothers for men) also proved to be a significant protective factor in the lives of the men and women on Kauai who grew up in childhood poverty. The majority of the immigrant parents in our birth cohort had only eight years or less of formal education, but each additional grade completed strengthened the link between parental and child competence—especially graduation from high school. Better-educated parents had more positive interactions with their children in the first and second years of life and provided more emotional support for their offspring during early and middle childhood—even when the family lived in poverty. Parental education was also positively linked to the infant's health and physical status by age 2.

There were also significant positive links between parental educational level and the child's scholastic competence at 10; one path was direct, the other was mediated through the infant's health and physical status. Better-educated parents had children with better problem-solving and reading skills, but they also had healthier children with fewer handicaps and absences from school due to repeated serious illnesses.

While parental competence and the sources of support available in the childhood home were modestly linked to the quality of adult adaptation, they made less of a direct impact in adulthood than the individuals' competencies, degree of self-esteem and self-efficacy, and temperamental dispositions. Many resilient high risk youths left the adverse conditions of their childhood homes (and their island community) after high school and sought environments they found more compatible. In short, they picked their own niches (Scarr and McCartney, 1983).

As they moved into adulthood, they encountered opportunities that turned the life trajectories of a significant proportion of high risk men and women who had struggled with personal problems in their teens on the path to recovery and maturity. Among the life events that these men and women considered critical turning points were: the birth of a first child, marriage or entry into a long-term committed relationship, joining the work force and establishing themselves in a career or job, seeking additional education in a (community) college, joining the armed forces to gain educational and vocational skills, and becoming an active member of a church or religious community.

Implications

What lessons have we learned from following the lives of the children on the "Garden Island" that might be of relevance to those who care for other children, of other races, in different places, at different times?

The most precious lesson that we choose to learn from this study is hope, a hope reinforced by reports from a handful of other long-term studies into adulthood which have identified some of the protective buffers and mechanisms that operated in the lives of vulnerable children and youths who succeeded against the odds. In a variety of risk conditions studied—economic hardships (by Elder and Vaillant); parental psychopathology (by Anthony and Bleuler); foster home placement (by Rutter and Quinton); teenage motherhood (by Furstenberg and associates)—there appeared a common core of individual dispositions, sources of support, and pathways that led to positive outcomes in adulthood.

Our findings and those by other American and European investigators with a life-span perspective suggest that these buffers make a more profound impact on the life course of children who grow up under adverse conditions than do specific risk factors or stressful life events. They appear to transcend ethnic, social class, geographical, and historical boundaries. Most of all, they offer us a more optimistic outlook than the perspective that can be gleaned from the literature on the negative consequences of perinatal trauma, caregiving deficits, and chronic poverty. They provide us with a corrective lens—an awareness of the self-righting tendencies that move children toward normal adult development under all but the most persistent adverse circumstances.

Implications for Developmental Research and Theory

Our findings fit into the framework of a number of complementary developmental models. The three perspectives we found most useful in interpreting our data are the structural-behavioral model of development by Horowitz (1987), the theory of genotype → environment effects by Scarr and McCartney (1983), and the concept of the "developmental niche" proposed by Super and Harkness (1986).

As the Horowitz (1987) model would suggest, we noted a range from relative resiliency to vulnerability in the face of adverse environmental conditions, a range that changed at different points of the life cycle—for example at the onset of adolescence or in the transition to adulthood. Some children drew consistently on constitutional resources that allowed them to overcome adverse experiences relatively unscathed. Others went through a period of reorganization after a troubled adolescence which changed their place on the continuum from vulnerability to resiliency. Some individuals who grew up in relatively affluent and supportive home environments in childhood and adolescence became more vulnerable when faced with an accumulation of stressful life events in adulthood. The transactions across time between constitutional characteristics of the individual and aspects of the caregiving environment that were supportive or stressful determined the quality of adult adaptation in different domains—at work, in interpersonal relationships, and in the person's overall satisfaction with life.

Our findings also lend some empirical support to Scarr and McCartney's (1983) theory of the way people make their own environments. They propose three types of genotype → environment effects on human development: a passive kind, through environments provided by biologically related parents; an evocative kind, through responses elicited by the individual from others; and an active kind, through the selection of different environments. In line with their propositions, we noted that over time there was a shift from passive to active genotype → environment effects, as the youths and young adults in our study left stressful home environments and sought extrafamilial environments (at school, work, in the military) which they found more compatible and stimulating. Genotype → environment effects of the evocative sort tended to persist throughout the various life stages we studied, as individuals elicited differential responses from other people (parents, teachers, peers) based on their physical characteristics, temperament, and intelligence.

The handful of investigators who, like ourselves, have taken a long-term view on risk and resiliency have all focused on children who live in societies where poverty is an exception rather than the rule, where parents have options to pursue different child-rearing philosophies and techniques, where children are expected to spend some ten to twelve years in compulsory schooling to become literate, and where much of their socialization is undertaken by a succession of unrelated strangers who prepare them for entry into a competitive economy that prizes assertiveness and mobility and values human control over social and physical environments.

We suggest that future research on risk and resilience needs to look more systematically at other developmental niches that characterize the interface of child and culture. The physical and social settings in which children live, the customs of child care and sex-role socialization, and parental beliefs concerning the nature and needs of children vary greatly in those parts of the world where five out of every six children born today will live—in Asia, Africa, Latin America, and the Middle East. So do the mortality rates of boys and girls, and the risk factors that challenge the resiliency and increase the vulnerability of the survivors (Werner, 1986).

Our search should focus on individual dispositions, sources of support, and protective mechanisms that operate effectively in a variety of high risk contexts. If we encourage and nurture these dispositions and competencies in our children as best we can, we have a basic survival kit for meeting adversities that tax the human spirit. We also need to examine the price exacted from individuals who succeed against great odds, for some protective attributes may promote positive adaptation in one context and have negative effects in another (Masten, 1990). The costs and benefits for men and women will vary with the sex-role expectations and the prevailing values of a given culture.

Implications for Social Action

Rutter (1987) reminds us that if we want to help vulnerable youngsters we need to focus on the protective processes that bring about changes in life trajectories from risk to adaptation. He includes among them (1) those that reduce the risk impact; (2) those that reduce the likelihood of negative chain reactions; (3) those that promote self-esteem and self-efficacy; and (4) those that open up opportunities. We have seen these processes at work among the resilient children in our study and among those youths who recovered from serious coping problems in young adulthood. They represent the essence of any effective intervention program, whether by professionals or volunteers.

We noted, for example, that structure and rules in the household reduced the likelihood that youths committed juvenile offenses, even when they lived in delinquency-prone environments, and that children of parents with chronic psychopathology could detach themselves from the discord in their households by spending time with caring adults outside the family circle. Both processes altered their exposure to the potent risk condition in their homes. In other cases, the negative chain reactions following the intermittent hospitalizations of psychotic or alcoholic parents or parental divorce were buffered by the presence of grandparents or older siblings who acted as substitute parents and provided continuity in care.

The promotion of self-esteem and self-efficacy in a young person is probably the key ingredient in any effective intervention process. We saw, for example, how effective reading skills by grade 4 were one of the most potent predictors of successful adult adaptation among the high risk children in our study. More than half of the school failures detected at age 10 were due to deficiencies in that skill. Some children profited substantially from short-term remedial work in the first three grades by teachers' aides and peer tutors at a critical period when achievement motivation is stabilized.

Self-esteem and self-efficacy were derived not only from academic competence. Most of the resilient children in our high risk sample were not unusually talented, but they took great pleasure in interests and hobbies that brought them solace when things fell apart in their home lives. They also engaged in activities that allowed them to be part of a cooperative enterprise, such as being cheerleader for the home team or raising an animal for the 4-H Club.

Self-esteem and self-efficacy also grew when youngsters took on responsible positions commensurate with abilities, whether part-time paid work or managing the household when a parent was incapacitated or, most often, caring for younger siblings. At some point in their young lives, usually in middle childhood and adolescence, the youngsters who grew into resilient adults were required to carry out some socially desirable task to prevent others in their family, neighborhood, or community from experiencing distress or discomfort. Such acts of required helpfulness (Rachman, 1979) can also become a crucial element of intervention programs that involve high risk youths in part-time community service—either paid, or for academic credit (for examples, see Danzig and Scanton, 1986).

Most of all, self-esteem and self-efficacy were promoted through supportive relationships. The resilient youngsters in our study all had at least one person in their lives who accepted them unconditionally, regardless of temperamental idiosyncracies, physical attractiveness, or intelligence. Most established such a close bond early in their lives, if not with a parent, then with another family member. Some of the high risk youths who had problems in their teens but who staged a recovery in young adulthood gained a more positive self-concept in the context of an intimate relationship with a spouse or mate. The experiences from intergenerational mentoring programs also suggest that a close one-to-one relationship with an unrelated elder can foster self-esteem in a troubled child or youth. An essential aspect of the encounter is that the youth feels special to the other person (Freedman, 1989).

One of the most important lessons we learned from our adult follow-up was that the opening up of opportunities led to major turning points in the lives of high risk individuals as they entered their 20s and early 30s. Our findings for age 31/32 indicate that earlier events in the lives of high risk children and youths are not the only ones to affect their later adjustment to the world of work, marriage, and parenthood. We agree with the conclusions by Furstenberg and his associates (1987) that from a policy perspective the opportunities for recovery that occur during adulthood have barely been tapped.

Our study identifies several routes out of poverty and despair in the later life of the Asian American youths on Kauai. Some of these pathways have also been traced by Furstenberg and his associates (1987) for Black teenage mothers in Baltimore. Such roads were also taken by Caucasian youths of the Great Depression generation (Elder, 1974; Long and Vaillant, 1984). Among the most potent forces for positive change for high risk youths on Kauai in adulthood were: education at community colleges, educational and vocational skills acquired during service in the armed forces, and active involvement in a church or religious community.

Attendance at community colleges and enlistment in the armed forces were also associated with geographical moves for many of the high risk youths. Both settings provided them with an opportunity to obtain educational and vocational skills that were instrumental in moving them out of a context of poverty into skilled trades and middle class status.

Community colleges and courses on army, navy, and air force bases, as well as on board ship for some of the young sailors, also offered remedial work that allowed high school dropouts to take the General Education Development Test. This opportunity was most welcome to the teenage mothers who, in their 20s, learned that high school graduation was necessary for career advancement. Some of the teenage mothers in this cohort used welfare support to complete high school and even college before they returned to the job market with technical or professional skills—a tendency also observed by Furstenberg and his associates (1987) among Black teenage mothers in Baltimore.

Military service turned out to be a constructive option for most of the delinquent youths in our cohort. The majority utilized the educational benefits they earned both during and after the enlistment period. Military service also provided them with opportunities for personal growth in a structured setting and a chance to take on responsibilities that enhanced their self-esteem. Elder (1986) and Long and Vaillant (1984) have noted that military service performed a similar function for earlier generations of youths during World War II and the Korean War.

Involvement in church activities and a strong faith provided meaning to the adult lives of many high risk youths as well. Such a faith was tied to identification with fundamentalist religious groups for a significant minority who had been troubled by mental health problems in their teens. Participation in their communal activities provided structure for their lives and assured them salvation, security, and a sense of mission in an alien world.

For the majority of the men and women in this cohort, however, faith was not tied to a specific formal religious affiliation but rather to confidence in some center of value. Their faith enabled them to perceive the traumatic experiences of their childhood or youth constructively, even if these events had caused pain and suffering. It did not seem to matter whether they were nominally Buddhist, Catholic, mainstream Protestant, or members of a minority religious group such as the Church of the Latter Day Saints—the resilient individuals used their faith to maintain a positive vision of a meaningful life and to negotiate successfully an abundance of emotionally hazardous experiences. Those who have studied child survivors of the Holocaust and of contemporary wars have noted that this sense of meaning persists even in children scattered as orphans and refugees to the four corners of the earth (Antonovsky, 1979; Ayala-Canales, 1984; Moskovitz, 1983).

The central component in the lives of the resilient individuals in this study which contributed to their effective coping in adulthood appeared to be a confidence that the odds can be surmounted. Some of the luckier ones developed such hopefulness early in their lives, in contact with caring adults. Many of their troubled peers had a second chance at developing a sense of self-esteem and self-efficacy in adulthood, sometimes even by virtue of apparent chance encounters with persons who opened up opportunities and gave meaning to their lives (see also Bandura, 1982).

We need to keep in mind that our research on individual resilience and protective factors has focused on children and youths who pulled themselves up by their own bootstraps, with informal support from kith and kin, not children who were recipients of intervention services. Yet there are some lessons these young people can teach us about the need for setting priorities, about critical time periods for prevention and intervention, and about the need for a continuum of care and caring that should include volunteers as well as professionals.

Our examination of the long-term effects of childhood adversity and of protective factors and processes in the lives of high risk youths has shown that some of the most critical determinants of adult outcomes are present in the first decade of life. It is also apparent that there are large individual differences among high risk children in their responses to both negative and positive circumstances in their caregiving environments. The very fact of individual variation among youngsters who live in adverse conditions suggests the need for greater assistance to some than to others.

Our findings alert us to the need for setting priorities, to choices we must make in our investment of resources and time. Intervention programs need to focus on children and youths who appear most vulnerable because they lack some of the essential personal resources or social bonds that buffer chronic adversity or stress. Among them are the increasing numbers of preterm survivors of neonatal intensive care, the offspring of parents with severe psychopathology (chronic substance abuse, affective disorders, and schizophrenia), children reared by isolated single parents with no roots in a community, and preadolescents with conduct disorders who have poor reading skills. From a longitudinal perspective, these youngsters appear most at risk of developing serious coping problems in adulthood—especially if they are boys.

Assessment and diagnosis, the initial part of any intervention program—whether preventive or ameliorative—need to focus not only on the risk factors in the lives of these children but also on the protective factors. These include competencies and sources of informal support that already exist in the extended family, the neighborhood, and the community at large and that can be utilized to enlarge a child's repertoire of problem-solving skills and self-esteem and self-efficacy.

Our own research, as well as that of our American and European colleagues who have followed resilient children into adulthood, has repeatedly shown that, if a parent is incapacitated or unavailable, other persons in a youngster's life can play such an enabling role, whether they are grandparents, older siblings, caring neighbors, family day-care providers, teachers, ministers, youth workers in 4-H or the YMCA/YWCA, Big Brothers and Big Sisters, or elder mentors. Such informal and personal ties to kith, kin, and community are preferred by most children and families to impersonal contacts with formal bureaucracies. These ties need to be encouraged and strengthened, not weakened or displaced, by legislative action and social programs.

A cooperative effort by concerned volunteers and competent professionals could generate a continuum of care which cuts across narrow disciplinary boundaries. It would involve health-care providers who give advice on family planning and deliver follow-up care for children with disabilities, preschool teachers for high risk infants and toddlers, peer tutors for children who have reading problems in the primary grades, counselors who assist high school youths with realistic educational and vocational plans, retired individuals who become mentors for potential school dropouts or jail-bound juvenile offenders, foster grandparents who work with teenage mothers and their infants, community college instructors who encourage young adults motivated to return to school to upgrade their skills, and civic and religious leaders who provide a sense of moral values. A number of such exemplary intergenerational programs already exist which involve no great expenditures of money but commitments in time and caring. But, if these programs are to multiply across the country, we need a change in America's individualistic "habits of heart" (Bellah et al., 1985).

The life stories of the resilient youngsters now grown into adulthood teach us that competence, confidence, and caring can flourish, even under adverse circumstances, if children encounter persons who provide them with the secure basis for the development of trust, autonomy, and initiative. From odds successfully overcome springs hope—a gift each of us can share with a child—at home, in the classroom, on the playground, or in the neighborhood.

Appendixes

Table 1. Kauai Longitudinal Study: 1955 birth cohort

Total N of live births in cohort	837
S's with pediatric and psychological exams at age 2	734
S's with 2- and 10-year exams	698
S's with follow-up data at 18	614
S's with follow-up data at 31/32	505
Deaths between birth and age 2	12
Deaths between ages 2 and 10	3
Deaths between ages 10 and 18	2
Deaths between ages 18 and 32	11

Source: Werner, Bierman, and French (1971); Werner and Smith (1977).

Table 2. Adults with records in the courts and mental health register of the state of Hawaii who had problems by age 18

Number of problems by 18	Criminal courts %	Family courts %	Mental health register %
Males	(N: 26)	(N: 30)	(N: 12)
None	13.5	40.0	16.7
One	42.3	40.0	16.7
Two	26.9	13.3	50.0
Three	15.4	3.3	16.7
Four	3.0	3.3	0.0
Females	(N: 5)	(N: 23)	(N: 13)
None	40.0	47.8	38.5
One	20.0	13.0	23.1
Two	20.0	26.1	15.4
Three	0.0	13.0	15.4
Four	20.0	0.0	7.7

Table 3. Teenagers with problems who had records in the courts and mental health register of the state of Hawaii by age 32

Number of problems by 18	Criminal courts %	Family courts %	Mental health register %
Males			
None (N: 184)	1.6	6.5	1.1
One (N: 102)	10.8	11.8	2.0
Two (N: 45)	15.6	8.9	13.3
Three (N: 8)	50.0	12.5	25.0
Four (N: 3)	33.3	33.3	0.0
Females			
One (N: 240)	0.8	4.6	2.1
Two (N: 63)	1.6	4.8	4.8
Three (N: 14)	0.0	21.4	14.3
Four (N: 5)	20.0	0.0	20.0

Table 4. Interview results: males at age 31/32

	Low risk	High risk		
Topics	No problems at 18 (N: 126) %	Resilient at 18 (N: 27) %	Delinquent by 18 (N: 50) %	Mental health problems by 18 (N: 23) %
Education				
Schooling beyond high school:				
Technical training	21.3	26.1	62.1**	40.0
Junior college	16.7	26.1	27.6	10.0
Four-year college	53.7	43.5	13.8**	20.0*
Graduate or professional school	13.9	11.8	0.0*	0.0
No schooling beyond high school	10.2	13.0	10.3	10.0
Satisfaction with school achievement:				
Did very well	55.7	40.0	29.2**	44.4
Did adequately	35.1	50.0	70.8**	55.6
Did not do well	9.3	10.0	0.0	0.0
Work				
Current employment status:				
Professional	15.7	21.7	0.0	9.1
Semiprofessional, managerial	40.7	17.4	13.3**	0.0**
Skilled trade	31.5	43.5	56.7	45.5
Semi- or unskilled job	8.3	13.0	30.0**	45.5**
Unemployed	3.7	4.3	0.0	0.0
Job satisfaction:				
Satisfied	74.6	81.0	72.4	77.8
Ambivalent	25.2	19.0	20.7	22.2
Dissatisfied	0.0	0.0	6.9	0.0
Marriage				
Marital status:				
Married	50.9	39.1	40.0	36.4
Divorced (not remarried)	13.9	8.7	13.3	9.1
Single, in long-term relationship	11.1	21.7	23.3	18.2
Single, without long-term relationship	21.3	21.7	13.3	27.3
Remarried (after divorce)	2.8	8.7	10.0	9.1
Marital satisfaction:				
Mostly satisfied	87.8	88.2	70.4*	66.7*
Somewhat dissatisfied	11.0	5.9	18.5	22.2
Mostly dissatisfied	1.2	5.9	11.1	11.1
Conflict resolution:				
Discuss and arrive at joint resolution	32.5	64.7**	47.6	14.3
Decision made by one partner, other goes along	14.5	11.8	4.8	0.0
No conflict resolution	7.2	11.8	14.3	28.6

Table 4. Interview results: males at age 31/32 (continued)

Topics	Low risk	High risk		
	No problems at 18 (N: 126) %	Resilient at 18 (N: 27) %	Delinquent by 18 (N: 50) %	Mental health problems by 18 (N: 23) %
Children	54.6	43.5	73.3*	63.6
Positive aspects of parenting:				
Self-development	4.8	66.7**	0.0	0.0
Social aspects	0.0	0.0	5.3	0.0
Strengthening marriage	1.6	0.0	0.0	0.0
Opportunity to care for other	17.7	66.7**	21.1	28.6
Pleasure of seeing child grow	59.7	33.3	42.1	42.9
Satisfaction with present relationship with children:				
Mostly satisfied	84.5	100.0	89.5	85.7
Somewhat dissatisfied	13.8	0.0	10.5	14.3
Mostly dissatisfied	1.7	0.0	0.0	0.0
Parents/siblings				
Relationship with mother:				
Mostly satisfied	86.2	75.0	72.7	66.7*
Somewhat dissatisfied	12.8	15.0	27.3	22.2
Mostly dissatisfied	1.1	10.0	0.0	11.1
Relationship with father:				
Mostly satisfied	81.1	52.6**	69.6	80.0
Somewhat dissatisfied	16.7	31.6	26.1	10.0
Mostly dissatisfied	2.7	15.8	4.3	10.0
Relationship with siblings:				
Mostly satisfied	75.0	100.0	52.4**	70.0
Somewhat dissatisfied	23.9	0.0	33.3	20.0
Mostly dissatisfied	1.1	0.0	14.3	10.0
Positive aspects of relationship with siblings:				
Financial support	21.4	4.8	12.0	10.0
Emotional support	55.1	47.6	56.0	20.0
Shared interests, activities	39.8	14.3*	56.0	60.0
Shared values	36.7	14.3*	12.0*	20.0
Provider of child care	9.2	0.0	12.0	10.0
Can't think of anything positive	9.2	19.0	20.0	20.0
Friends				
Relationship with friends:				
Mostly satisfied	86.2	66.7	81.8	90.0
Somewhat dissatisfied	13.8	33.3	18.2	10.0
Positive aspects of relationship with friends:				
Financial support	6.1	0.0	16.0	30.0*
Emotional support	73.7	59.1	64.0	50.0
Shared interests, activities	97.0	77.3**	88.0	90.0
Shared values	56.6	13.6**	32.0*	40.0

Table 4. Interview results: males at age 31/32 (continued)

	Low risk	High risk		
Topics	No problems at 18 (N: 126) %	Resilient at 18 (N: 27) %	Delinquent by 18 (N: 50) %	Mental health problems by 18 (N: 23) %
Provider of child care	8.1	4.5	8.0	20.0
Can't think of anything positive	1.0	4.5	4.0	0.0
Self				
Preferred recreation:				
Watching TV	6.0	0.0	0.0	10.0
Reading	14.0	4.5	0.0*	0.0
Sports, outdoor activities	93.0	86.4	88.0	80.0
Social activities	9.0	4.5	4.0	10.0
Hobbies	23.0	50.0*	28.0	20.0
Travel	7.0	4.5	8.0	0.0
Goals in life:				
Self-development	39.8	34.8	16.7*	36.4
Close relationship with friends/ family	12.0	8.7	10.0	9.1
Happy marriage	17.6	26.1	20.0	9.1
Children	22.2	26.1	36.7	27.3
Career or job success	25.0	39.1	20.0	0.0*
Helping mankind	9.3	13.0	3.3	0.0
Major worries:				
Finances	34.6	31.8	43.3	36.4
Spouse, mate	9.6	18.2	26.7*	27.3*
Children	20.2	18.2	33.3	18.2
Work	17.3	18.2	36.7*	27.3
Friends	3.8	4.5	0.0	0.0
Social issues	8.7	4.5	3.3	9.1
Health problems:	7.5	54.5**	10.3	27.3*
Feeling about self at 31/32:				
Happy	21.5	33.3	26.7	9.1
Mostly satisfied	48.6	33.3	43.3	54.5
Ambivalent	28.0	23.8	26.7	36.4
Mostly dissatisfied, unhappy	1.9	9.5	3.3	0.0
Major sources of help:				
Own determination, competence	52.8	73.9*	50.0	27.3
Spouse, mate	59.3	39.1	46.7	63.6
Parents	53.7	17.4**	33.3*	18.2*
Siblings	30.6	4.3**	20.0	0.0*
Other family members	24.1	13.0	16.7	27.3
Friends	53.7	17.4**	60.0	54.5
Neighbors	6.5	0.0	3.3	0.0
Teachers, mentors	9.3	8.7	6.7	9.1
Co-workers	27.8	4.3**	23.3	27.3

Table 4. Interview results: males at age 31/32 (continued)

	Low risk	High risk		
Topics	No problems at 18 (N: 126) %	Resilient at 18 (N: 27) %	Delinquent by 18 (N: 50) %	Mental health problems by 18 (N: 23) %
Boss	3.0	4.3	13.3	9.1
Minister	7.4	0.0	3.3	9.1
Mental health professional	4.6	0.0	3.3	9.1
Self-help organization	2.8	0.0	10.0	18.2*
Faith, prayer	9.3	17.4	10.0	9.1

*High risk group differs significantly from low risk peers of same gender: $p < .05$.
**High risk group differs significantly from low risk peers of same gender: $p < .01$.

Table 5. Interview results: females at age 31/32

	Low risk	High risk			
Topics	No problems at 18 (N: 137) %	Resilient at 18 (N: 36) %	Teenage mothers (N: 26) %	Delinquent by 18 (N: 22) %	Mental health problems by 18 (N: 34) %
Education					
Schooling beyond high school:					
Technical training	23.8	11.8	13.6	6.7*	4.3*
Junior college	19.2	44.1**	18.2	33.3	21.7
Four year college	43.8	38.2	9.1**	0.0**	13.0**
Graduate or professional school	16.9	2.9*	4.5	0.0*	13.0
No schooling beyond high school	8.5	23.5*	40.9**	40.0**	43.5**
Satisfaction with school achievement:					
Did very well	53.7	59.3	47.1	33.3	50.0
Did adequately	39.8	40.7	47.1	66.7	43.8
Did not do well	6.5	0.0	5.9	0.0	6.3
Work					
Current employment status:					
Professional	20.9	6.1	4.5*	0.0*	8.7
Semiprofessional, managerial	14.7	39.4**	27.3	14.3	13.0
Skilled trade	45.7	30.3	36.4	42.9	26.1
Semi- or unskilled job	9.3	9.1	27.3*	7.1	39.1**
Unemployed	9.3	15.2	9.1	35.7*	13.0

Table 5. Interview results: females at age 31/32 (continued)

	Low risk	High risk			
Topics	No problems at 18 (N: 137) %	Resilient at 18 (N: 36) %	Teenage mothers (N: 26) %	Delinquent by 18 (N: 22) %	Mental health problems by 18 (N: 34) %
Job satisfaction:					
Satisfied	80.6	69.7	81.0	71.4	56.5
Ambivalent	16.9	24.2	19.0	21.4	39.1*
Dissatisfied	2.4	6.1	0.0	7.1	4.3
Marriage					
Marital status:					
Married	66.9	67.6	54.5	60.0	78.3
Divorced (not remarried)	9.2	5.9	40.9**	13.3	13.0
Single, in long-term relationship	9.2	2.9	4.5	6.7	0.0
Single, without long-term relationship	12.3	8.8	0.0	13.3	8.7
Remarried (after divorce)	2.3	14.7*	0.0	6.9	0.0
Marital satisfaction:					
Mostly satisfied	86.1	71.0	45.0**	53.8**	66.7*
Somewhat dissatisfied	13.0	22.6	45.0	38.5	28.6
Mostly dissatisfied	0.9	6.5	10.0	7.7	4.8
Conflict resolution:					
Discuss and arrive at joint resolution	57.6	48.3	47.4	54.5	63.2
Decision made by one partner, other goes along	17.4	24.1	10.5	18.2	15.8
No conflict resolution	5.4	20.7*	5.3	0.0	0.0
Children	58.9	76.5*	95.5**	80.0*	77.3*
Positive aspects of parenting:					
Self-development	4.0	16.0*	0.0	0.0	0.0
Social aspects	5.3	8.0	0.0	0.0	0.0
Opportunity to care for other	34.7	20.0	30.0	36.4	20.0
Pleasure of seeing child grow	53.3	64.0	50.0	63.6	40.0
Satisfaction with present relationship with children:					
Mostly satisfied	88.7	80.0	78.9	72.7*	66.7*
Somewhat dissatisfied	11.3	20.0	15.8	18.2	33.3
Mostly dissatisfied	0.0	0.0	5.3	9.1	0.0

Table 5. Interview results: females at age 31/32 (continued)

	Low risk	High risk			
Topics	No problems at 18 (N: 137) %	Resilient at 18 (N: 36) %	Teenage mothers (N: 26) %	Delinquent by 18 (N: 22) %	Mental health problems by 18 (N: 34) %
Parents/siblings					
Relationship with mother:					
Mostly satisfied	82.2	62.5*	90.0	69.2	68.4
Somewhat dissatisfied	15.0	31.2	10.0	30.8	21.1
Mostly dissatisfied	2.8	6.3	0.0	0.0	10.5
Relationship with father:					
Mostly satisfied	70.3	73.3	73.7	66.7	61.1
Somewhat dissatisfied	24.8	20.0	21.1	33.3	38.9
Mostly dissatisfied	5.0	6.7	5.3	0.0	0.0
Relationship with siblings:					
Mostly satisfied	82.0	60.0	77.8	61.5	73.3
Somewhat dissatisfied	16.0	40.0	22.2	30.8	20.0
Mostly dissatisfied	2.0	0.0	0.0	7.7	6.7
Positive aspects of relationship with siblings:					
Financial support	19.1	9.1	19.0	7.1	25.0
Emotional support	78.2	69.7	57.1*	35.7**	50.0*
Shared interests, activities	69.1	30.3**	71.4	42.9*	50.0
Shared values	47.3	9.1**	33.3	28.6	35.0
Provider of child care	14.5	6.1	28.6	21.4	10.0
Can't think of anything positive	6.4	9.1	9.5	21.4*	5.0
Friends					
Relationship with friends:					
Mostly satisfied	84.2	80.0	100.0*	84.6	86.7
Somewhat dissatisfied	15.8	20.0	0.0	15.4	13.3
Positive aspects of relationship with friends:					
Financial support	1.8	3.1	4.8	7.1	5.0
Emotional support	87.5	59.4**	61.9**	42.9**	60.0**
Shared interests, activities	94.6	78.1**	85.7	85.7	90.0

Table 5. Interview results: females at age 31/32 (continued)

	Low risk	High risk			
Topics	No problems at 18 (N: 137) %	Resilient at 18 (N: 36) %	Teenage mothers (N: 26) %	Delinquent by 18 (N: 22) %	Mental health problems by 18 (N: 34) %
Shared values	56.3	15.6**	57.1	42.9	50.0
Provider of child care	11.6	3.1	19.0	7.1	25.0
Self					
Preferred recreation:					
Watching TV	6.3	6.1	0.0	0.0	0.0
Reading	36.6	33.3	23.8	14.3	30.0
Sports, outdoor activities	71.4	81.8	52.4	78.6	55.0
Social activities	9.8	15.2	9.5	7.1	20.0
Hobbies	55.4	42.4	42.9	42.9	35.0
Travel	6.3	12.1	4.8	0.0	0.0
Goals in life:					
Self-development	36.9	38.2	27.3	13.3*	17.4*
Close relationship with friends/family	11.5	2.9	4.5	0.0	0.0
Happy marriage	22.3	17.6	4.5*	0.0*	4.3*
Children	38.5	14.7*	18.2*	13.3*	30.4
Career or job success	32.2	64.7**	27.3	26.7	13.0
Helping mankind	6.2	5.9	0.0	0.0	0.0
Major worries:					
Finances	38.6	44.1	42.9	46.7	54.5
Spouse, mate	14.2	14.7	19.0	33.3*	22.7
Children	39.4	35.3	38.1	40.0	54.5
Work	14.2	5.9	19.0	13.3	22.7
Friends	0.8	0.0	0.0	6.7	0.0
Social issues	9.4	8.8	4.8	6.7	4.5
Health problems:	13.2	41.2**	13.6	20.0	34.8**
Feeling about self at 31/32:					
Happy	31.5	52.9*	45.5*	33.3	34.8
Mostly satisfied	53.5	26.5	9.1	26.7	17.4
Ambivalent	12.6	14.7	45.5**	40.0*	47.8**
Mostly dissatisfied, unhappy	2.4	5.9	0.0	0.0	0.0
Major sources of help:					
Own determination, competence	63.1	61.8	50.0	33.3*	52.2
Spouse, mate	64.6	50.0	50.0	53.3	65.2
Parents	53.8	14.7**	36.4	13.3**	34.8
Siblings	43.8	11.8**	40.9	33.3	30.4
Other family members	28.5	17.6	18.2	26.7	30.4
Friends	66.2	29.4**	54.5	26.7**	52.2
Neighbors	9.2	0.0	4.5	6.7	4.3

Table 5. Interview results: females at age 31/32 (continued)

	Low risk	High risk			
Topics	No problems at 18 (N: 137) %	Resilient at 18 (N: 36) %	Teenage mothers (N: 26) %	Delinquent by 18 (N: 22) %	Mental health problems by 18 (N: 34) %
Teachers, mentors	10.8	2.9	9.1	0.0	13.0
Co-workers	32.3	8.8**	22.7	0.0**	30.4
Boss	14.6	2.9*	9.1	0.0	17.4
Minister	14.6	5.9	4.5	13.3	13.0
Mental health professional	13.1	5.9	4.5	6.7	8.7
Self-help organization	2.3	2.9	9.1	6.7	4.3
Faith, prayer	33.1	41.2	9.1*	6.7**	17.4

*High risk group differs significantly from low risk peers of same gender: $p < .05$.
**High risk group differs significantly from low risk peers of same gender: $p < .01$.

Table 6. Means and standard deviations on Rotter's Locus of Control Scale and the EAS Temperament Survey for Adults: males at age 31/32

	Low risk		High risk					
	No problems at 18 (N: 126)		Resilient at 18 (N: 27)		Delinquent by 18 (N: 50)		Mental health problems by 18 (N: 23)	
	Mean	SD	Mean	SD	Mean	SD	Mean	SD
Rotter's Locus of Control Scale	4.8	2.8	4.6	1.9	4.9	2.6	4.9	2.6
EAS Temperament Survey for Adults								
Distress	2.2	0.7	2.1	0.7	2.4	0.9	2.5	1.0
Fear	2.2	0.6	2.0	0.5	2.2	0.7	2.2	1.0
Anger	2.4	0.6	2.4	0.6	2.8	0.8*	2.3	0.7
Activity	3.1	0.6	3.2	0.7	3.3	0.8	3.2	0.6
Sociability	3.3	0.6	3.2	0.9	3.2	0.7	3.1	0.4

*High risk group differs significantly from low risk peers of same gender: $p < .05$.

Table 7. Means and standard deviations on Rotter's Locus of Control Scale and the EAS Temperament Survey for Adults: females at age 31/32

	Low risk		High risk							
	No problems at 18 (N: 137)		Resilient at 18 (N: 36)		Teenage mothers (N: 26)		Delinquent by 18 (N: 22)		Mental health problems by 18 (N: 34)	
	Mean	SD	Mean	SD	Mean	SD	Mean	SD	Mean	SD
Rotter's Locus of Control Scale	5.1	2.7	4.8	2.6	3.3	2.7**	5.1	2.5	4.0	2.0*
EAS Temperament Survey for Adults										
Distress	2.3	0.7	2.3	0.8	2.2	0.9	2.7	1.0*	2.5	0.9
Fear	2.4	0.6	2.5	0.9	2.6	0.8	3.1	0.8*	2.6	0.7
Anger	2.4	0.7	2.4	0.8	2.3	0.7	3.1	0.8*	2.7	0.8*
Activity	3.2	0.7	3.1	0.8	3.5	0.7	3.5	0.7	3.5	0.9
Sociability	3.5	0.7	3.6	0.7	3.9	0.7*	3.5	0.6	3.7	0.7

*High risk group differs significantly from low risk peers of same gender: $p < .05$.
**High risk group differs significantly from low risk peers of same gender: $p < .01$.

Table 8. Significant differences between low risk males at age 18 with good and poor adaptation at age 31/32

Variables	Low risk males at 18 with good outcomes at 31/32 (N: 104)		Low risk males at 18 with poor outcomes at 31/32 (N: 22)		
	Mean	SD	Mean	SD	p
Stressful life events reported for ages 18–32	3.2	2.2	5.0	3.0	.05
	%		%		
Trouble with boss	18.7		41.2		.05
Trouble with in-laws	3.3		17.6		.05
Marital separation	5.5		41.2		.001
Divorce	3.3		58.8		.001
Status at 31/32					
Currently unemployed	1.1		17.6		.01
No additional schooling beyond high school	6.6		29.4		.01
Evaluation of father: ambivalent or negative	13.0		53.8		.001
Satisfaction with relationship with own child(ren): ambivalent or negative	10.4		40.0		.01
Siblings provide emotional support	60.7		21.4		.01

Table 8. Significant differences between low risk males at age 18 with good and poor adaptation at age 31/32 (continued)

Variables	Low risk males at 18 with good outcomes at 31/32 (N: 104)		Low risk males at 18 with poor outcomes at 31/32 (N: 22)		
	%		%		*p*
Siblings share interests, activities	44.0		14.3		.05
Siblings are role models, share values	41.7		7.1		.01
Friends are role models, share values	60.7		33.3		.05
Satisfaction with relationship with friends: ambivalent	9.9		38.5		.01
Feeling about self at present stage of life:					
Ambivalent	24.4		47.1		.01
Unhappy	0.0		11.8		
EAS Temperament Survey for Adults	(N: 91)		(N: 17)		
	Mean	SD	Mean	SD	*p*
Distress	2.10	.64	2.53	.69	.05
Anger	2.31	.63	2.69	.61	.05

Table 9. Significant differences between low risk females at age 18 with good and poor adaptation at age 31/32

Variables	Low risk females at 18 with good outcomes at 31/32 (N: 119)		Low risk females at 18 with poor outcomes at 31/32 (N: 18)		
	Mean	SD	Mean	SD	*p*
Stressful life events reported for ages 18–32	4.2	2.3	5.8	2.7	.05
	%		%		
Breakup of long-term relationship after 18	30.2		57.1		.05
Marital separation	7.8		50.0		.001
Marital reconciliation	3.4		21.4		.05
Divorce	4.3		71.4		.001
Financial problems	25.0		57.1		.05
Status at 31/32					
Marital satisfaction: ambivalent	10.0		50.0		.05
Conflict resolution: discuss and arrive at joint resolution	61.2		14.3		.05
Evaluation of mother: ambivalent or negative	16.0		30.8		.05
Satisfaction with relationship with own child(ren): ambivalent	8.2		30.0		.05

Table 9. Significant differences between low risk females at age 18 with good and poor adaptation at age 31/32 (continued)

Variables	Low risk females at 18 with good outcomes at 31/32 (N: 119)		Low risk females at 18 with poor outcomes at 31/32 (N: 18)		
	%		%		*p*
Satisfaction with relationship with own child(ren): ambivalent	8.2		30.0		.05
Satisfaction with relationship with siblings: can't think of anything positive	3.1		30.8		.001
Feeling about self at present stage of life:					
Ambivalent	7.9		53.8		.001
Unhappy	0.0		7.7		
EAS Temperament Survey for Adults	(N: 116)		(N: 14)		
	Mean	SD	Mean	SD	*p*
Sociability	3.52	.66	3.29	1.1	.01
Distress	2.28	.59	2.66	1.1	.01
Anger	2.39	.67	2.68	1.0	.05
Fear	2.39	.58	2.41	1.0	.01

Table 10. Significant differences between teenage mothers whose status had improved by age 26 and those whose status had not improved

Variables	Improved (N: 10)		Unimproved (N: 10)		
	Mean	SD	Mean	SD	*p*
N of negative adjectives checked to describe child's behavior at 2-yr. exam (i.e., anxious, dependent, insecure, passive, slow, withdrawn)	1.0	1.0	3.1	2.6	.05
N of negative adjectives checked to describe caretaker's interaction with child at 2-yr. exam (i.e., distant, indifferent, hostile, restrictive, punitive)	2.2	1.9	3.8	1.1	.05
	%		%		
Mother worked long-term (ages 2–10)	60.0		20.0		.10
Problems in relationship with father (ages 10–18)	20.0		60.0		.10
Feeling of security as part of family: strong (ages 10–18)	60.0		20.0		.10
	Mean	SD	Mean	SD	*p*
Locus of Control Scale (age 18)	13.7	4.8	20.0	1.4	.10
CPI scales					
Socialization (age 18)	21.8	2.3	16.0	1.4	.05

Table 10. Significant differences between teenage mothers whose status had improved by age 26 and those whose status had not improved (continued)

Variables	Improved (N: 10)		Unimproved (N: 10)		
	Mean	SD	Mean	SD	*p*
Capacity for status (age 26)	17.9	4.1	13.3	3.1	.01
Responsibility (age 26)	25.6	3.7	21.3	4.8	.05
Flexibility (age 26)	9.0	2.2	6.1	3.6	.05
	%		%		*p*
Additional schooling beyond high school	40.0		0.0		.05
Employment. unskilled	30.0		70.0		.10
Serious financial worries	30.0		90.0		.05
Conflict with spouse/mate	20.0		70.0		.05
Separation/divorce	10.0		80.0		.01
Additional children	40.0		80.0		.10
Sources of child care:					
Parents, relatives	30.0		90.0		.05
In-laws, babysitters	60.0		10.0		.05
Sources of help:					
Siblings	80.0		40.0		.10
Friends	100.0		40.0		.01
Trouble with police	10.0		50.0		.10
Alcohol problems: self or mate	10.0		50.0		.10

Table 11. Proportion of delinquents engaging in specific delinquent acts as recorded in police and/or family court files by age 18

	Males (N: 77) %	Females (N: 26) %
Larceny, second degree	32.8	31.4
Larceny, first degree	6.0	5.7
Burglary, second degree	17.9	8.6
Burglary, first degree	13.4	5.7
Assault and battery	14.9	17.1
Malicious injury	9.0	2.9
Car theft	6.0	2.9
Narcotic drug offense	16.7	0.0
Sexual misconduct	0.0	5.7
Forgery	4.5	0.0

Table 12. Proportion of offenders arrested for criminal acts as recorded in court files of state of Hawaii by age 32

	Males (N: 26) %	Females (N: 5) %
Narcotic drug offenses	38.5	20.0
Assault, battery	38.5	20.0
Theft, burglary	31.0	40.0
Driving under the influence of alcohol	31.0	0.0
Criminal contempt of court	12.0	20.0
Disorderly conduct	8.0	0.0
Terrorist threat	8.0	0.0
Rape, sodomy	8.0	0.0

Table 13. Background characteristics that differentiated between male and female delinquents whose deviant behavior persisted at age 32

Variables	Males (N: 21) %	Females (N: 8) %
Congenital defect	14.3	37.5
Parent alcoholic, mentally ill, or retarded	19.0	75.0
Birth of sibling before index child was 2 yrs.	38.1	87.5
Sister with developmental disability	0.0	42.9
Brother with developmental disability	4.8	28.6
Teenage parent	0.0	50.0
Chronic conflict between parents in teens	0.0	37.5
Problems in relationship with father in teens	23.8	62.5
Problems in relationship with mother in teens	9.5	37.5
Poor peer relationships in teens	0.0	25.0

Table 14. Significant differences between delinquents with and without criminal court records by age 32

Variables	Delinquents without criminal court records by age 32 (N: 62)		Delinquents with criminal court records by age 32 (N: 27)		
	Mean	SD	Mean	SD	*p*
Cattell IQ (age 2)	96.3	12.9	89.4	15.0	.05
Vineland SQ (age 2)	116.9	12.4	108.7	16.8	.05
	%		%		
Teacher's Behavior Checklist (age 10)					
Temper tantrums, uncontrollable emotions	1.6		14.3		.05
Extremely irritable	0.0		14.3		.01
Bullying	1.6		17.9		.01
Frequent lying	1.6		14.3		.05

Table 14. Significant differences between delinquents with and without criminal court records by age 32 (continued)

Variables	Delinquents without criminal court records by age 32 (N: 62)	Delinquents with criminal court records by age 32 (N: 27)	
	%	%	*p*
Parents' Behavior Checklist (age 10)			
Frequent lying	3.2	17.9	.05
Need for mental health care (age 10)	12.7	35.7	.02
Police record (ages 10–18)			
Car theft, larceny, burglary	46.0	75.0	.02
Stressful life events			
Mother absent: separation, divorce (ages 2–10)	8.2	25.9	.05
Father absent: separation, divorce (ages 10–18)	13.6	42.3	.01

Table 15. Consequences of early deviant behavior: males at age 32

Outcome variables at age 32	No problems by 18 (N: 206) %	Delinquent by 18 (N: 38) %	Mental health problems only by 18 (N: 11) %	Delinquent *and* mental health problems by 18 (N: 12) %
Criminal record	.5	21.7	7.7	46.7**
Divorce	4.3	13.0*	0.0	26.7**
Family court record	5.4	10.9	0.0	26.7**
Mental health problems	.5	0.0	15.4**	40.0**
Overall adaptation:				
2 or more serious coping problems	5.9	31.3**	33.3**	91.7**
1 minor coping problem	28.7	37.5**	50.0**	8.3**
No coping problems	65.3	31.3**	16.7**	0.0**

*Level of significant difference: $p < .05$.
**Level of significant difference: $p < .01$.

Table 16. Consequences of early deviant behavior: females at age 32

Outcome variables at age 32	No problems by 18 (N: 233) %	Delinquent only by 18 (N: 9) %	Mental health problems only by 18 (N: 21) %	Delinquent *and* mental health problems by 18 (N: 13) %
Criminal record	0.5	7.7	0.0	13.3**
Divorce	8.0	8.3	7.7	0.0
Family court record	4.1	7.7	3.8	33.3**
Mental health problems	2.3	0.0	19.2**	13.3**
Overall adaptation:				
2 or more serious coping problems	11.5	25.0	26.3**	41.7**
1 minor coping problem	23.0	37.5*	42.1*	50.0**
No coping problems	65.6	37.5*	31.6**	8.3**

*Level of significant difference: $p < .05$.
**Level of significant difference: $p < .01$.

Table 17. First admissions to psychiatric care between ages 18 and 32

Age period	Diagnosis	Previous problems	Perinatal stress score
Males			
18–19	Chronic schizophrenia	Need for remedial education by 10; delinquency record by 18	1
20–24	Mental retardation (car theft)	Delinquency record by 18; schizophrenic father	2
20–24	Paranoid schizophrenic	Need for remedial education by 10; delinquency record by 18; schizophrenic mother	0
20–24	Social maladjustment (narcotic drug offense)	Educable mentally retarded; delinquency record by 18	0
25–30	Sanity test (attempted murder)	Need for remedial education by 10	0
25–30	Marital maladjustment	Need for remedial education and mental health care by 10	0
30–32	Depression	Father diagnosed as depressed	3
30–32	Adjustment reaction of adulthood	Need for remedial education by 10	2

Table 17. First admissions to psychiatric care between ages 18 and 32 (continued)

Age period	Diagnosis	Previous problems	Perinatal stress score
Males			
30–32	Adjustment reaction of adulthood	No previous problems	0
Females			
18–19	Marital maladjustment	No previous problems	1
18–19	Schizophrenia	Learning disability; need for mental health care by 10	2
20–24	Depression	No previous problems	0
20–24	Acute schizophrenia	Need for remedial education by 10	2
25–30	Paranoid schizophrenia	Mental health problems and delinquency record by 18	3
25–30	Paranoid schizophrenia	Mental health problems by 18	3
30–32	Transitional situational disturbance (divorce)	No previous problems	1
30–32	Adjustment reaction to adult life	No previous problems	0

Table 18. Stressful life events that differentiated significantly between males with and without coping problems at age 31/32

Stressful life events	Males without problems (N: 128) %	Males with problems (N: 111) %
Birth–12 months		
Prolonged disruptions of family life	0.0	6.4
Prolonged separation from mother	5.7	14.9
Birth–2 years		
Mother pregnant or birth of sibling	14.4	30.9
2–10 years		
Mother alcoholic, mentally ill	2.2	7.3
Mother absent (divorced, separated)	0.0	7.2
Father absent (divorced, separated)	0.0	10.0
Sibling died	0.0	1.8
Mother remarried, stepfather moved in	0.0	6.3
Chronic conflict between parents	3.3	10.9
Sibling(s) left home	4.4	18.2
Child changed schools (ages 6–10)	1.1	5.5
11–18 years		
Parental mental health problems	3.3	8.1
Mother absent (divorced, separated)	1.8	7.6
Father absent (divorced, separated)	1.8	12.0
Foster home placement	0.0	3.3
School problems	33.9	66.3
Financial problems	3.6	17.4

Table 18. Stressful life events that differentiated significantly between males with and without coping problems at age 31/32 (continued)

Stressful life events	Males without problems (N: 128) %	Males with problems (N: 111) %
18–32 years		
Death of father	2.2	20.8
Death of mother	0.0	6.5
Remarriage of parents	0.0	7.8
Loss of a job	15.4	20.8
Breakup of long-term relationship	22.0	35.1
Trouble with in-laws	3.3	15.6
Marital separation	1.1	24.7
Marital reconciliation	0.0	7.8
Divorce before 32	0.0	29.9

Table 19. Stressful life events that differentiated significantly between females with and without coping problems at age 31/32

Stressful life events	Females without problems (N: 199) %	Females with problems (N: 90) %
Birth–2 years		
Mother pregnant or birth of sibling	21.2	40.0
2–10 years		
Mother died	0.0	1.1
Mother absent (divorced, separated)	0.0	3.4
Father absent (divorced, separated)	1.6	11.2
Mother remarried, stepfather moved in	0.0	3.3
Sibling handicapped	0.0	6.7
11–18 years		
Father alcoholic or mentally ill	1.4	7.7
Mother absent (divorced, separated)	0.0	12.3
Father absent (divorced, separated)	2.9	13.8
Foster home placement	2.9	13.8
Chronic conflict between parents	2.9	12.3
Father remarried, stepmother moved in	0.0	4.6
Death of sibling	0.0	1.5
Sibling(s) left home	0.0	4.6
School problems	30.4	53.8
Poor peer relationships	2.9	12.3
Problems in family relationships	11.6	36.9
Problems in relationship with mother	5.8	24.6
Problems in relationship with father	2.9	29.2
Teenage pregnancy	11.6	26.2
Teenage marriage	2.9	13.8
Financial problems	17.4	33.8

Table 19. Stressful life events that differentiated significantly between females with and without coping problems at age 31/32 (continued)

Stressful life events	Females without problems (N: 199) %	Females with problems (N: 90) %
18–32 years		
Father alcoholic or mentally ill	0.0	5.9
Divorce of parents	2.5	5.3
Marital separation	6.8	31.6
Divorce before age 32	0.0	38.2
Financial problems	22.0	42.1

Table 20. Stressors: standardized canonical discriminant function coefficients for individuals with and without two or more serious coping problems at age 31/32

Stressors	Males*	Females**
Mother not married when child born	0.59	0.07
(Low) SES at birth	0.07	0.09
Perinatal stress	0.15	0.09
Prolonged disruptions in family (age 1)	0.49	0.02
Prolonged separation from mother (age 1)	0.46	0.14
Birth of sibling before age 2	0.36	0.09
(Low) physical status (age 2)	0.49	0.24
(Low) intellectual status (age 2)	0.22	0.35
(Low) psychological status (age 2)	0.09	0.54
Mother alcoholic or mentally ill (ages 2–10)	0.21	0.13
Mother died (ages 2–10)	0.00	0.40
Mother absent: divorced, separated (ages 2–10)	0.24	0.02
Father absent: divorced, separated (ages 2–10)	0.33	0.71
Death of sibling (ages 2–10)	0.11	0.15
Mother remarried (ages 2–10)	0.10	0.11
Chronic conflict between parents (ages 2–10)	0.01	0.43
Sibling left home (ages 2–10)	0.25	0.08
Child changed schools (ages 6–10)	0.35	0.14
Sibling handicapped (before age 10)	0.18	0.04
(Low) SES (age 10)	0.17	0.11
Physical handicap (age 10)	0.08	0.10
Need for remedial education (age 10)	0.31	0.30
Need for mental health care (age 10)	0.47	0.08
Father alcoholic or mentally ill (ages 11–18)	0.04	0.14
Mother absent: divorced, separated (ages 11–18)	0.49	0.22
Father absent: divorced, separated (ages 11–18)	0.06	0.03
Foster home placement (ages 11–18)	0.89	0.20
Chronic conflict between parents (ages 11–18)	0.21	0.13
Death of sibling (ages 11–18)	0.06	0.09
Parent remarried (ages 11–18)	0.79	0.00
Sibling left home (ages 11–18)	0.00	0.05

Table 20. Stressors: standardized canonical discriminant function coefficients for individuals with and without two or more serious coping problems at age 31/32 (continued)

Stressors	Males*	Females**
Conflict with peers (ages 11–18)	0.01	0.40
Conflict with mother (ages 11–18)	0.19	0.25
Conflict with father (ages 11–18)	0.30	0.22
Teenage parenthood (ages 11–18)	0.00	0.35
Teenage marriage (ages 11–18)	0.31	0.54
Financial problems (ages 11–18)	0.18	0.56
Delinquency record (ages 11–18)	0.01	0.01
Mental health problems (ages 11–18)	0.50	0.05
School problems (ages 11–18)	0.73	0.26

*43 males with 2 or more serious coping problems; 91 males without any coping problems.

**34 females with 2 or more serious coping problems; 118 females without any coping problems.

Table 21. Stressors: standardized canonical discriminant function coefficients for individuals with and without a divorce by age 32

Stressors	Males*	Females**
Mother not married when child born	0.04	0.39
(Low) SES at birth	0.33	0.25
Perinatal stress	0.26	0.14
Prolonged disruptions in family (age 1)	0.33	0.04
Prolonged separation from mother (age 1)	0.11	0.13
Birth of sibling before age 2	0.28	0.08
(Low) physical status (age 2)	0.31	0.21
(Low) intellectual status (age 2)	0.06	0.54
(Low) psychological status (age 2)	0.12	0.64
Mother alcoholic or mentally ill (ages 2–10)	0.14	0.47
Mother died (ages 2–10)	0.40	0.42
Father absent: divorced, separated (ages 2–10)	0.28	0.33
Death of sibling (ages 2–10)	0.00	0.15
Chronic conflict between parents (ages 2–10)	0.02	0.27
Sibling left home (ages 2–10)	0.26	0.06
Child changed schools (ages 6–10)	0.05	0.11
Sibling handicapped (before age 10)	0.09	0.21
(Low) SES (age 10)	0.18	0.06
Physical handicap (age 10)	0.24	0.22
Need for remedial education (age 10)	0.35	0.39
Need for mental health care (age 10)	0.04	0.10
Father alcoholic or mentally ill (ages 11–18)	0.04	0.33
Mother absent: divorced, separated (ages 11–18)	0.72	0.28
Father absent: divorced, separated (ages 11–18)	0.10	0.05
Foster home placement (ages 11–18)	0.00	0.20
Chronic conflict between parents (ages 11–18)	0.28	0.03
Death of sibling (ages 11–18)	0.03	0.11
Parent remarried (ages 11–18)	0.52	0.12

Table 21. Stressors: standardized canonical discriminant function coefficients for individuals with and without a divorce by age 32 (continued)

Stressors	Males*	Females**
Sibling left home (ages 11–18)	0.00	0.21
Conflict with peers (ages 11–18)	0.01	0.28
Conflict with mother (ages 11–18)	0.06	0.39
Conflict with father (ages 11–18)	0.07	0.53
Teenage parenthood (ages 11–18)	0.23	0.40
Teenage marriage (ages 11–18)	0.00	0.44
Financial problems (ages 11–18)	0.10	0.51
Delinquency record (ages 11–18)	0.07	0.07
Mental health problems (ages 11–18)	0.01	0.40
School problems (ages 11–18)	0.80	0.16

*41 males with a divorce; 91 males without a divorce or any other coping problems.

**32 females with a divorce; 118 females without a divorce or any other coping problems.

Table 22. Stressors: standardized canonical discriminant function coefficients for males with and without criminal records by age 32*

Stressors	
Mother not married when child born	0.86
(Low) SES at birth	0.16
Perinatal stress	0.07
Prolonged disruptions in family (age 1)	0.77
Prolonged separation from mother (age 1)	0.25
Birth of sibling before age 2	0.48
(Low) physical status (age 2)	0.66
(Low) intellectual status (age 2)	0.43
(Low) psychological status (age 2)	0.16
Mother alcoholic or mentally ill (ages 2–10)	0.01
Mother absent: divorced, separated (ages 2–10)	1.27
Father absent: divorced, separated (ages 2–10)	0.02
Death of sibling (ages 2–10)	0.22
Chronic conflict between parents (ages 2–10)	0.09
Sibling left home (ages 2–10)	0.79
Child changed schools (ages 6–10)	0.65
Sibling handicapped (before age 10)	0.29
(Low) SES (age 10)	0.23
Physical handicap (age 10)	0.15
Need for remedial education (age 10)	0.08
Need for mental health care (age 10)	0.40
Father alcoholic or mentally ill (ages 11–18)	0.12
Mother absent: divorced, separated (ages 11–18)	0.73
Father absent: divorced, separated (ages 11–18)	0.23
Foster home placement (ages 11–18)	1.66
Chronic conflict between parents (ages 11–18)	0.22
Death of sibling (ages 11–18)	0.07
Parent remarried (ages 11–18)	1.00

Table 22. Stressors: standardized canonical discriminant function coefficients for males with and without criminal records by age 32* (continued)

Stressors	
Conflict with peers (ages 11–18)	0.09
Conflict with mother (ages 11–18)	0.20
Conflict with father (ages 11–18)	0.44
Teenage marriage (ages 11–18)	0.50
Financial problems (ages 11–18)	0.14
Delinquency record (ages 11–18)	0.27
Mental health problems (ages 11–18)	0.64
School problems (ages 11–18)	0.77

*26 males with criminal records; 92 males without criminal records or any other coping problems.

Table 23. Stressors: standardized canonical discriminant function coefficients for individuals with and without mental health problems by age 32*

Stressors	
Mother not married when child born	0.58
(Low) SES at birth	0.18
Perinatal stress	0.02
Prolonged disruptions in family (age 1)	0.05
Prolonged separation from mother (age 1)	0.01
Birth of sibling before age 2	0.12
(Low) physical status (age 2)	0.08
(Low) intellectual status (age 2)	0.01
(Low) psychological status (age 2)	0.01
Mother alcoholic or mentally ill (ages 2–10)	0.24
Mother absent: divorced, separated (ages 2–10)	0.22
Father absent: divorced, separated (ages 2–10)	0.85
Death of sibling (ages 2–10)	0.03
Mother remarried (ages 2–10)	0.35
Chronic conflict between parents (ages 2–10)	0.16
Sibling left home (ages 2–10)	0.16
Child changed schools (ages 6–10)	0.03
Sibling handicapped (before age 10)	0.18
(Low) SES (age 10)	0.17
Physical handicap (age 10)	0.05
Need for remedial education (age 10)	0.03
Need for mental health care (age 10)	0.01
Father alcoholic or mentally ill (ages 11–18)	0.01
Mother absent: divorced, separated (ages 11–18)	0.01
Father absent: divorced, separated (ages 11–18)	0.03
Foster home placement (ages 11–18)	1.22
Chronic conflict between parents (ages 11–18)	0.05
Death of sibling (ages 11–18)	0.06
Parent remarried (ages 11–18)	1.13
Conflict with peers (ages 11–18)	0.23
Conflict with mother (ages 11–18)	0.02

Table 23. Stressors: standardized canonical discriminant function coefficients for individuals with and without mental health problems by age 32* (continued)

Stressors	
Conflict with father (ages 11–18)	0.07
Teenage parenthood (ages 11–18)	0.41
Teenage marriage (ages 11–18)	0.03
Financial problems (ages 11–18)	0.08
Delinquency record (ages 11–18)	0.03
Mental health problems (ages 11–18)	0.88
School problems (ages 11–18)	0.14

*25 individuals with a record of mental health problems; 209 individuals without any coping problems.

Table 24. Protective factors in high risk males:* correlations with ratings of adult adaptation

Variables	Overall adaptation (age 31/32)	Work	Interpersonal relationships	Self-evaluation
Father's age at birth of child		.30		
Mother's education	.38			
Infant "very active" (age 1)		.28		
Percentage of positive adjectives describing mother (age 1)	.26			
Percentage of positive adjectives describing child (age 2)	.31			
Percentage of positive adjectives describing caregiver (age 2)	.32	.42		
Health status (birth–2 years)	.24		.32	.28
Number of stressful life events (birth–2 years)		−.24		
PMA IQ (age 10)	.31			
PMA Reasoning factor R (age 10)	.31			
STEP Reading score (age 10)	.29			
Number of behavior problems checked by teacher (age 10)				−.28
Number of behavior problems checked by parents (age 10)		−.28	−.41	−.24
Emotional Support Rating (ages 2–10)	.25	.28		
Number of stressful life events (ages 2–10)			−.25	
Number of adults in household other than parents (by age 10)			.52	.29
Number of adults outside family with whom child likes to be (age 10)	.25	.21		

Table 24. Protective factors in high risk males:* correlations with ratings of adult adaptation (continued)

Variables	Overall adaptation (age 31/32)	Work	Interpersonal relationships	Self-evaluation
Structure and rules in household (ages 11–18)	.35			
Source of help: teacher (age 11–18)	.36		.22	
Number of stressful life events (ages 11–18)	−.38	−.30	−.24	
Attitude toward school (age 17/18)	.38	.32	.40	.33
Realism of educational and vocational plans (age 17/18)	.43		.34	.31
Quality of social life (age 17/18)	.37		.40	.30
Self-esteem rating (age 17/18)	.24			
Locus of Control Scale (age 17/18)		.26	.42	.26
Number of sources of support (ages 18–32)	.24			.37
Sources of support: spouse (ages 18–32)	.22		.32	.48
Source of support: parents (ages 18–32)	.40		.30	
Source of support: siblings (ages 18–32)	.38			
Source of support: faith (ages 18–32)	.29			.25
Locus of Control Scale (age 32)			.26	.32
Activity (age 32)	.25			
Distress (age 32)	−.24		−.46	

*N: 49.

Table 25. Protective factors in high risk females:* correlations with ratings of adult adaptation

Variables	Overall adaptation (age 31/32)	Work	Interpersonal relationships	Self-evaluation
Father's age at birth of child	.21			
Father's education	.57		.51	.31
Baby "affectionate, cuddly" (age 1)	.23			
Baby free of distressing habits (age 1)	.23	.29		
Percentage of positive adjectives describing mother (age 1)			.22	

Table 25. Protective factors in high risk females:* correlations with ratings of adult adaptation (continued)

Variables	Overall adaptation (age 31/32)	Work	Interpersonal relationships	Self-evaluation
Percentage of positive adjectives describing child (age 2)	.23			.38
Percentage of positive adjectives describing caregiver (age 2)				.33
Cattell Development Quotient (age 2)	.25			
Health status (birth–age 2)			.30	
PMA IQ (age 10)	.30	.28		.35
PMA Reasoning factor R (age 10)	.32	.25	.23	
STEP Reading score (age 10)		.45		.31
Health status (ages 2–10)		.28		
Mother holds steady job (ages 2–10)	.46	.22	.29	
Emotional Support Rating (ages 2–10)		.28		
Number of children in household by age 10	.25			
Number of adults in household other than parents (age 10)	.20			
Assigned household chores and responsibilities (ages 11–18)	.20		.23	
Structure and rules in household (ages 11–18)	.22			
Source of help: teacher (ages 11–18)	.24			
Number of stressful life events (ages 11–18)	−.49			−.29
CPI: Responsibility Scale (age 17/18)		.29		.32
CPI: Socialization Scale (age 17/18)		.28		.45
Realism of educational/vocational plans (rating) (age 17/18)	.36			.36
Quality of social life (age 17/18)	.28	.29		.35
Self-esteem rating (age 17/18)	.41	.44		.39
Achievement motivation rating (age 17/18)	.27	.53		.34
Locus of Control Scale (age 17/18)	.26	.27		.48
Locus of Control Scale (age 32)				.21
Activity (age 32)	.39		.28	
Sociability (age 32)	.21			
Distress (age 32)		−.26		

*N: 55

Table 26. Protective factors: standardized canonical discriminant function coefficients for high risk males and females

Protective factors	High risk males (N: 49)	High risk females (N: 55)
Educational level of opposite-sex-parent	0.72	0.39
Activity level (age 1)	0.73	0.06
Baby free of distressing habits (age 1)	0.58	0.58
Baby "cuddly, affectionate" (age 1)	0.14	0.40
Baby "good natured, easygoing" (age 1)	1.14	0.12
Percentage of positive adjectives describing mother (age 1)	0.07	0.47
Percentage of positive adjectives describing child (age 2)	0.51	0.68
Percentage of positive adjectives describing caregiver (age 2)	0.76	0.32
Family stability rating (age 2)	0.45	0.01
PMA IQ (age 10)	0.34	1.33
PMA nonverbal Reasoning factor (age 10)	0.18	1.18
STEP Reading score (age 10)	0.16	0.14
Emotional support rating (age 10)	0.28	0.18
Number of children in family (age 10)	−0.51	−0.35
Number of adults in home other than parents (age 10)	0.08	0.45
Number of adults outside family with whom child likes to be (age 10)	0.47	0.15
Mother has steady employment (age 10)	0.11	0.73
Overall attitude toward school (age 17/18)	0.24	0.29
Achievement motivation (age 17/18)	0.51	0.32
Realism of educational plans (rating) (age 17/18)	0.65	0.90
Quality of social life (age 17/18)	0.34	0.12
Self-esteem rating (age 17/18)	0.05	0.54
Locus of Control Scale (age 17/18)	0.72	0.17
Sources of help: teachers (age 17/18)	0.71	0.00
Rules in household (age 17/18)	0.52	0.26
Regular household chores (age 17/18)	0.15	0.09
Number of sources of support (age 32)	1.38	0.37
Sociability (age 32)	0.27	0.18
Distress (age 32)	−1.09	−0.36
Activity (age 32)	0.01	0.29

Table 27. Stressful life events: loading patterns of latent variables (LV) for males and females

	Manifest variables linked to latent variables (LV)	Males (N: 239)	Females (N: 239)
LV 1	*Poverty (birth–age 2)*	1.00	1.00
LV 2	*Disruption of family unit (birth–age 2)*		
	Mother not married when child born	.28	.73
	Prolonged disruptions of family life (age 1)	.58	.72
	Prolonged separation from mother (age 1)	.19	.04
	Mother pregnant or birth of sibling before age 2	.74	.62

Table 27. Stressful life events: loading patterns of latent variables (LV) for males and females (continued)

	Manifest variables linked to latent variables (LV)	Males (N: 239)	Females (N: 239)
LV 3	*Illness/handicap in child (birth–age 2)*		
	Moderate to severe perinatal stress	.12	.27
	Number of illnesses (birth–age 2)	.60	.75
	Below normal physical development or handicap (age 2)	.82	.60
LV 4	*Deviant outcomes (age 2)*		
	Below normal intellectual status	.95	.97
	Below normal psychological status	.82	.62
LV 5	*Disruption of family unit (ages 2–10)*		
	Mother died	.04	.04
	Mother absent permanently (divorced, separated)	.72	.39
	Father absent permanently (divorced, separated)	.86	.93
	Sibling died	.27	.19
	Sibling left home	.45	.44
LV 6	*Illness/handicap in family (ages 2–10)*		
	Number of illnesses	.68	.15
	Child handicapped	.48	.24
	Sibling handicapped	.68	.95
LV 7	*Chronic discord (ages 2–10)*		
	Mother alcoholic, mentally ill, or retarded	.58	.30
	Mother remarried, conflict with stepfather	.55	.79
	Chronic parental conflict	.77	.69
LV 8	*Poverty (ages 2–10)*	1.00	1.00
LV 9	*Deviant outcomes (age 10)*		
	Need for remedial education; placement in special class or institution	.82	.87
	Need for (in- or outpatient) mental health care	.71	.77
LV 10	*Poverty (ages 11–18)*	1.00	1.00
LV 11	*Disruption of family unit (ages 11–18)*		
	Mother absent permanently (divorced, separated)	.68	.53
	Father absent permanently (divorced, separated)	.81	.60
	Foster home placement	.52	.50
	Sibling died	.00	.19
	Parent remarried	.61	.38
	Sibling left home	.00	.39
	Teenage marriage	.00	.75
LV 12	*Chronic discord (ages 11–18)*		
	Father alcoholic, mentally ill, or retarded	.20	.22
	Chronic parental conflict	.07	.49
	Conflict with peers	.15	.43
	Conflict with mother	.89	.84
	Conflict with father	.90	.82
LV 13	*Deviant outcomes (age 17/18)*		
	Delinquency record	.74	.75
	Mental health problem	.70	.79
	School failure	.72	.64
	Teenage pregnancy	.00	.64

Table 27. Stressful life events: loading patterns of latent variables (LV) for males and females (continued)

	Manifest variables linked to latent variables (LV)	Males (N: 239)	Females (N: 239)
LV 14	*Disruptions of family unit (ages 18–32)*		
	Death of mother	.62	.64
	Death of father	.87	.24
	Divorce of parents	.15	.69
LV 15	*Chronic discord (ages 18–32)*		
	Breakup of long-term relationship	.50	.13
	Marital separation	.82	.99

Table 28. Protective factors: loading patterns of latent variables (LV) for high risk males and females

	Manifest variables linked to latent variables (LV)	High risk males (N: 49)	High risk females (N: 55)
LV 1	*Parental education*		
	Father's education	.71	.89
	Mother's education	.91	.55
LV 2	*Infant's temperament (age 1)*		
	Affectionate, cuddly	.43	.39
	Good-natured (girls only)	.00	.80
	Very active	.87	.46
	Free of distressing habits	−.09	−.56
LV 3	*Infant's health (birth–age 2)*		
	Perinatal stress	−.39	−.56
	Number of illnesses (birth–age 2)	−.85	−.54
	Physical status (age 2)	.57	.73
LV 4	*Sources of support (birth–age 2)*		
	Family stability rating	.81	.68
	Percentage of positive adjectives describing mother (age 1)	.57	.71
	Percentage of positive adjectives describing caregiver (age 2)	.67	.80
LV 5	*Toddler's autonomy/social maturity (age 2)*		
	Cattell IQ	.87	.68
	Vineland SQ	.57	.71
	Percentage of positive adjectives describing child	.67	.80
LV 6	*Sources of support (ages 2–10)*		
	Emotional support rating	.85	.82
	Number of adults outside home with whom child likes to associate	.69	.24
	Mother steadily employed	.53	.78
LV 7	*Number of stressful life events (birth–age 10)*	−1.00	−1.00
LV 8	*Child's scholastic competence* (age 10)		
	PMA IQ	.96	.95
	PMA Reasoning factor R	.81	.87
	STEP Reading score	.88	.69

Table 28. Protective factors: loading patterns of latent variables (LV) for high risk males and females (continued)

	Manifest variables linked to latent variables (LV)	High risk males (N: 49)	High risk females (N: 55)
LV 9	*Child's behavior problems (age 10)*		
	In class: teacher report	.58	.86
	At home: parents' report	.80	.87
LV 10	*Sources of support (ages 11–18)*		
	Number of sources of help (including teacher)	.48	.12
	Rating of quality of social life with peers	.79	.81
	Rating of feeling of security as part of family	.61	.79
	Structure and rules provided by family	.19	.35
LV 11	*Number of stressful life events (ages 11–18)*	−1.00	−1.00
LV 12	*Self-esteem, efficacy (ages 17/18)*		
	Realism of educational/vocational plans (rating)	.85	.85
	Self-esteem rating	.87	.86
	Locus of Control	.22	.74
LV 13	*Sources of support (ages 18–32)*		
	Number of sources listed by young adult	.55	.89
	Spouse/mate	.35	.52
	Elders (parents, in-laws)	.85	.91
	Sibling	.75	.29
	Faith/prayer	.31	.09
LV 14	*Number of stressful life events (ages 18–32)*	−1.00	−1.00
LV 15	*EAS Temperament Survey for Adults (age 32)*		
	Activity	.74	.79
	Distress	−.88	.62
	Sociability	.20	.36

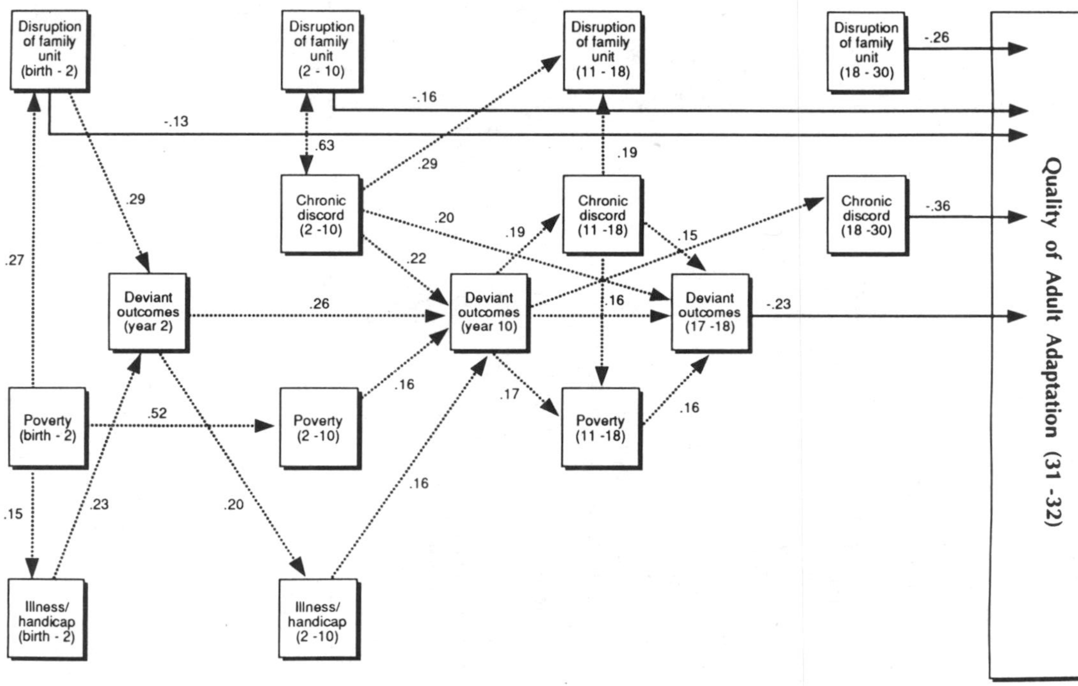

Figure A1. Paths relating stressful life events and deviant outcomes in childhood and adolescence to quality of adult adaptation: males

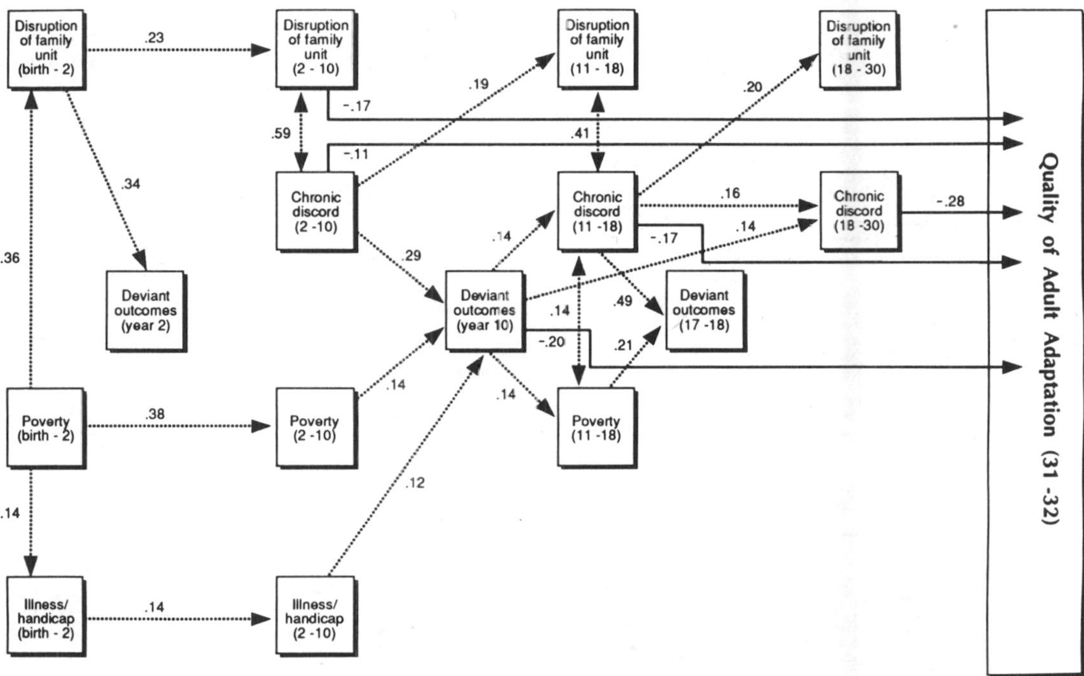

Figure A2. Paths relating stressful life events and deviant outcomes in childhood and adolescence to quality of adult adaptation: females

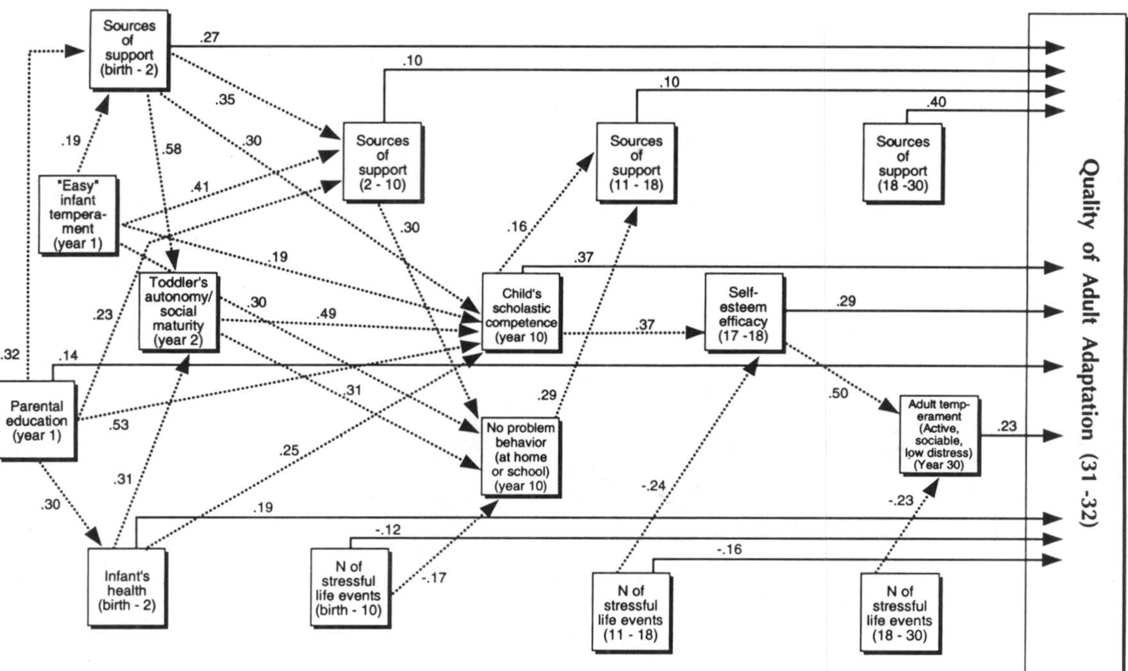

Figure A3. Paths relating protective factors and number of stressful life events to quality of adult adaptation: high risk males

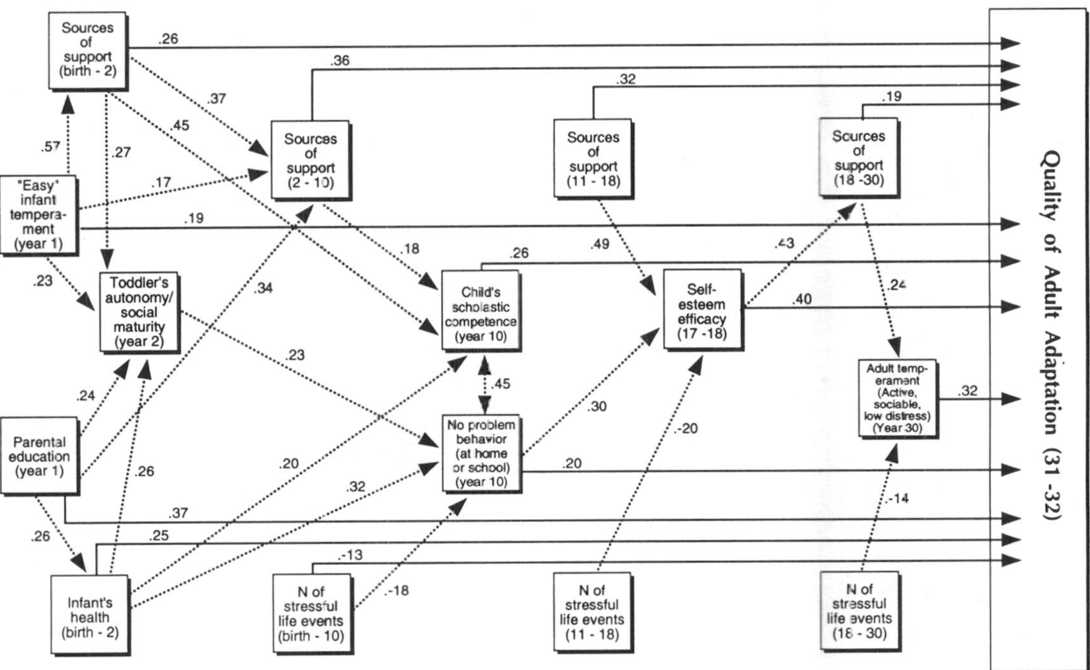

Figure A4. Paths relating protective factors and number of stressful life events to quality of adult adaptation: high risk females

Summary of Data Base: Kauai Longitudinal Study

Variables	*Source*
Demographic Characteristics	
Age of parents	Birth records
Educational level of parents	School records
IQ of parents who attended school on Kauai	School records
Record of parental mental health problems	Study files and mental health register, State of Hawaii
Socioeconomic status at birth, age 2, and age 10	Parental occupation, plantation pay scale
Number of persons in household by age 10	Home interviews by social and public health workers
Number of adults besides parents by age 10	Home interviews by social and public health workers
Number of children by age 10	Home interviews by social and public health workers
At birth	
Prernatal and perinatal stress score	Evaluation by pediatrician on basis of recorded events during prenatal, labor, delivery, and neonatal periods
1 Year	
Stressful life events	Social service records; postpartum interview
Mother's coping skills (adjective checklist)	1-year home interview by public health nurse
Mother's perception of infant's temperamental characteristics (activity level, responsiveness, nervous habits, temper, distressing habits)	Mother's assessment during 1-year home visit
2 Years	
Cattell IQ	Developmental examinations by psychologists
Vincland SQ	Developmental examinations by psychologists
Examiner's assessment of toddler's behavior patterns (adjective checklist)	Developmental examinations by psychologists
Examiner's assessment of quality of parent-child interaction (adjective checklist)	Developmental examinations by psychologists
Examiner's rating of toddler's psychological status	Developmental examinations by psychologists
Physical status of child	Pediatrician's rating
Stressful life events between birth and age 2	Interview with primary caretaker; social service records

2–10 Years

Medical problems and acquired physical handicaps	Public health, M.D., and hospital records
Readiness and achievement test results	School records (K-grade 5)
Grades	School records (K-grade 5)
Behavior problems	Teacher checklist, mental health service records, parent checklist
Stressful life events	Social service records, 10-year home interview
Rating of educational stimulation provided at home	Ratings by clinical psychologist
Rating of emotional support at home	Ratings by clinical psychologist

10 Years

PMA IQ and factor scores (R.V.S.P.N.)	Group tests
Classroom behavior	Teacher checklist
Needs assessment: long-term remedial education, special class placement, long-term mental health care, and medical care	Panel of pediatrician, psychologist, and public health nurse

10–18 Years

Repeated or serious delinquency	Police and family court records
Teenage pregnancy or abortion	Hospital records
Mental-health problems	Mental health service records
SCAT (verbal, quantitative, total) scores	School records (grades 8-10, 12)
STEP (reading, writing, mathematics) scores	School records (grades 8-10, 12)
Stressful life events	Biographical questionnaire, social service records

18 Years

CPI sub-scales	Group tests
Locus of Control Scale (Nowicki)	Group tests
Interview ratings	Individual interview with youth

18–32 Years

Mental health problems	Mental health register
Criminal, civil records	Circuit court records
Family court records	Circuit court records
Military records	U.S. Veterans Administration

31/32 Years

Structured interview and questionnaire
(on work, marriage, family life)
Life Event Checklist
EAS Temperament Survey for Adults
Locus of Control Scale (Rotter)

Summary of Scoring System for Prenatal-Perinatal Complications

Mild (Score 1)	*Moderate* (Score 2)	*Severe* (Score 3)
mild: pre-eclampsia, essential hypertension, renal insufficiency, or anemia; controlled diabetes or hypothyroidism; possitve Wasserman and no treatment; acute genitourinary infection 3rd trimester; untreated pelvic tumor producing dystocia; treated asthma	marked: pre-eclampsia, essential hypertension, renal insufficiency, or anemia; diabetes under poor control; decompensated cardiovascular disease requiring treatment; untreated thyroid dysfunction; confirmed rubella 1st trimester; nonobstetrical surgery: general anesthesia, abdominal incision or hypotension	eclampsia; renal or diabetic coma; treated pelvic tumor
2nd or 3rd trimester vaginal bleeding; placental infarct; marginal placenta previa; premature rupture of membranes; amnionitis; abnormal fetal heart rate; meconium stained amniotic fluid (excl. breech); confirmed polyhydramnios	vaginal bleeding with cramping; central placenta previa; partial placenta abruptio; placental or cord anomalies	complete placenta abruptio; congenital syphilis of the newborn
rapid, forceful, or prolonged unproductive labor; frank breech or persistent occiput posterior; twins; elective Cesarean section; low forceps with complications; cord prolapsed or twisted and oxygen administered to newborn	chin, face, brow, or footling presentation; emergency Cesarean section; manual or forceps rotation, mid forceps or high forceps or breech and oxygen administered under 5 minutes	transverse lie; emergency Cesarean section; manual rotation, mid forceps or high forceps or breech extraction and oxygen administered 5 minutes or more

Summary of Scoring System for Prenatal-Perinatal Complications (continued)

Mild (Score 1)	*Moderate* (Score 2)	*Severe* (Score 3)
breathing delayed 1–3 minutes; intermittent central cyanosis and oxygen administered under 1 minute; cry weak or abnormal; bradycardia	breathing delayed 3–5 minutes; gasping; intermittent central cyanosis and oxygen administered over 1 minute; cry delayed 5–15 minutes	breathing delayed over 5 minutes; no respiratory effort; persistent cyanosis and oxygen administered continuously; cry delayed over 15 minutes
birth injury excl. central nervous system; jaundice; hemmorrhagic disease mild; pneumonia, rate of respiration under 40 and oxygen administered intermittently; birth weight 1,800–2,500 gm and oxygen administered intermittently or incubator or other special care; oral antibiotic to newborn; abnormal tone or Moro reflex; irritability	major birth injury and temporary central nervous system involvement; spasms; pneumonia, rate of respiration over 40 and oxygen administered intermittently; apnea and oxygen administered intermittently or resuscitation under 5 minutes; birth weight 1,800–2,500 gm, fair suck and oxygen administered or incubator; antibiotics administered intravenously; cry absent	major birth injury and persistent central nervous system involvement; exchange transfusion; seizure; hyaline membrane disease; pneumonia, rate of respiration over 60 and oxygen administered continuously, resuscitation over 5 minutes; birth weight under 1,800 gm and oxygen administered or special feeding; meningitis; absent Moro reflex

Instruments Used in the 31/32-Year Follow-up

Code No. ________

Interview

Fact Sheet

Name ________

Address ________

Phone ________

Sex: M F

Current marital status: Married ____
Divorced ____
Single ____

Children:

Name:	Sex:		Birthdate:
________	M	F	________
________	M	F	________
________	M	F	________
________	M	F	________
________	M	F	________
________	M	F	________
________	M	F	________

*Work**

1. What kind of work do you do? How long have you been there?
2. What other kind of jobs have you had?
3. How satisfied have you been with your working situation(s)?
4. What was positive about your work experience? What was stressful?
5. How have you managed? What helped?
6. (If married or steady relationship) what effect did your work have on your family (or social) life?

Finances

7. Has your income generally been sufficient for your lifestyle?
8. Have you had financial worries or concerns? About what?
9. How did you manage? What helped?

Let's go back a bit.

Education

10. After you left high school, what additional education did you have? What kind?
11. How well did you do? How satisfied were you with your achievement?
12. What was positive about school?
13. What was difficult or stressful?
14. How did you manage? What helped?

Work (Spouse/Mate)

15. When did you get married (or establish long-term relationship)?
16. Does your spouse work?
17. What does s/he do?
18. On the whole, how satisfied is s/he with working?
19. What is positive about his/her working? What is stressful?
20. How did you manage? What helped?

Relationship with Spouse/Mate

21. Tell me about your spouse (mate). What kind of a person is s/he (temperament, activities, strong or weak points)?

22. What kind of things about him/her satisfy or please you?
23. What kind of things bother you (personally, in relationship)?
24. What kind of things do you and s/he disagree on? How much?
25. How do you resolve it?
26. Have you had any worries or concerns about your relationship with your spouse/mate?
27. How have you handled it? What helped you handle it?
28. What expectations do you have for your marriage (relationship)?

For Persons Who Have Been Divorced

29. How long did your previous marriage (relationship) last?
30. What mainly seemed to be the problem between you?
31. How has the divorce affected your present marriage (relationship)?
32. Has the divorce affected the relationship between you and your children, if any? How?

Children

33. Tell me about your child(ren)? What is each like?
34. What pleases you about them?
35. What worries (displeases) you about them?
36. What are your hopes for them?
37. What has been the most positive aspect of being a parent?
38. What has been the most difficult/stressful aspect of being a parent?
39. How did you manage? What helped?
40. How do you share child-rearing responsibilities? What do you think of him/her as parent?
41. What are some of your ideas about child-rearing, i.e.:
    41a. How do you feel about rules and regulations?
    41b. What kind of discipline do you believe in? How do you manage your children?
    41c. What are your thoughts about independence/dependence?

Parents

42. Are your mother/father still alive?
43. If deceased, when and how?
44. How much contact do you have with your parent(s)?
45. What kind of person is (was) your mother?
46. What has been positive about your relationship with your mother?
47. What has been stressful?
48. What kind of person is (was) your father?
49. What has been positive about your relationship with your father?
50. What has been stressful?
51. How did you manage?
52. What was helpful? Supportive?
53. Are there any specific problems in your parents' lives that have affected you?

In-laws

54. Are your mother-in-law, father-in-law still alive?
55. If deceased, when and how?
56. How much contact do you have with your in-laws?
57. What kind of person is (was) your mother-in-law?
58. What has been positive about your relationship with your mother-in-law?
59. What has been stressful?
60. What kind of person is (was) your father-in-law?
61. What has been positive in your relationship with your father-in-law?
62. What has been stressful or difficult in your relationship with your father-in-law?

63. How did you manage? What helped?
64. Are there any specific problems in your in-laws' lives that have affected you?

Siblings
65. How about your brother(s) and sister(s)? What part have they played in your life since you left high school?
66. What has been positive about your relationship with them (or a particular sibling)?
67. What has been difficult and/or stressful?
68. How did you manage? What was helpful?
69. Have any of your siblings had problems in their lives that have affected you?

Friends
70. Do you have any close friends?
71. What has been positive in your relationship with your friends?
72. Are there any problems your friends have had that were difficult/stressful for you (have affected your life)?
73. How did you manage? What was helpful?

Self
74. Now let's talk a little bit about you. How has your health been?
75. Any hobbies? Recreational activities?
76. What do you feel are your strong points?
77. What do you feel are your weak points?
78. Do you have any special goals or objectives that you are working toward?
79. Everybody worries about some things. What kinds of things worry you? How much?
80. What major problems have you had to face or deal with since you left high school?
81. What has helped you (most) in dealing with stressful things in your life?
82. Looking back so far, what has been the most critical thing that happened to you in your life?
83. How do you generally feel about yourself as a person at this stage in your life?

*Space was provided below each question so that the interviewer could jot down a full response.

Date ________ Code No. ________

Questionnaire

Address ______________
Phone ________
Sex _____ M _____ F
Current marital status:
- _____ Single
- _____ Married
- _____ Divorced
- _____ Widowed
- _____ Remarried

Children:
Name ______________________________ Sex _____ Birthdate ________
Name ______________________________ Sex _____ Birthdate ________
Name ______________________________ Sex _____ Birthdate ________
Name ______________________________ Sex _____ Birthdate ________
Name ______________________________ Sex _____ Birthdate ________
Name ______________________________ Sex _____ Birthdate ________
No Children _____

What is your present job?
List past jobs since leaving high school:

______________________ ______________________
______________________ ______________________
______________________ ______________________

How satisfied are you with your work?
- _____ Mostly satisfied
- _____ Somewhat satisfied/Somewhat dissatisfied
- _____ Mostly dissatisfied

What has been difficult or stressful about your work?
- _____ Not interesting
- _____ Poor work conditions
- _____ Social, interprersonal difficulties at work (with co-workers, boss)
- _____ Interferes with family (social) life
- _____ Financial (poor pay, lack of advancement)
- _____ Other: Describe ______________________
- _____ No difficulties

What did you do about it? What helped you?
Did you have any more schooling beyond high school?
- _____ Yes
- _____ No

If yes, what kind?
- _____ Technical training (i.e., mechanic, secretarial)
- _____ Junior college
- _____ Four year college
- _____ Graduate or professional school
- _____ Other: Describe ______________________

How satisfied were you with your acievement in school?
- _____ Mostly satisfied
- _____ Somewhat satisfied/Somewhat dissatisfied
- _____ Mostly dissatisfied

What was difficult or stressful about school?
What did you do about it? What helped you?
How do you feel about your marriage or relationship?

- ______ Mostly satisfied
- ______ Somewhat satisfied/Somewhat dissatisfied
- ______ Mostly dissatisfied
- ______ Have no current relationship

What has been difficult or stressful in this relationship?
What did you do about it? What helped you?
If divorced, what problems led to the breakup of your marriage?
If you have children, what has been difficult or stressful in raising them?
What did you do about it? What helped you?
What has been satisfying about being a parent?
How satisfied are you with your present relationship with your children?

- ______ Mostly satisfied
- ______ Somewhat satisfied/Somewhat dissatisfied
- ______ Mostly dissatisfied

Are your parents still alive?

- ______ Yes ______ No: Your father
- ______ Yes ______ No: Your mother

How satisfied are you with your present relationship with . . .

Your father:

- ______ Mostly satisfied
- ______ Somewhat satisfied/Somewhat dissatisfied
- ______ Mostly dissatisfied

Your mother:

- ______ Mostly satisfied
- ______ Somewhat satisfied/Somewhat dissatisfied
- ______ Mostly dissatisfied

What has been difficult or stressful in your relationship with . . .
Your father?
Your mother?
What did you do about it? What helped you?
If married, what has been difficult or stressful in your relationship with your in-laws?
What did you do about it? What helped you?
If you have brothers or sisters, how satisfied are you with your relationship with them?

- ______ Mostly satisfied
- ______ Somewhat satisfied/Somewhat dissatisfied
- ______ Mostly dissatisifed

Check the positive aspects of your relationship with your siblings.

- ______ Financial support
- ______ Emotional support
- ______ Shared interests, activities
- ______ Models, shared values
- ______ Providers of child care
- ______ Other: Specify ____
- ______ Can't think of any

How many close friends do you have?

- ______ Many
- ______ A few
- ______ One
- ______ None

How satisfied are you with your relationship(s) with your friends?
_____ Mostly satisfied
_____ Somewhat satisfied/Somewhat disatisfied
_____ Mostly dissatisfied
Check the positive aspects of your relationship with your friends.
_____ Financial support
_____ Emotional support
_____ Shared interests, activities
_____ Models, shared values
_____ Providers of child care
_____ Other: Specify ______________________________
_____ Can't think of any
Do you have any major health problems?
_____ Yes
_____ No
If so, what health problems?
What do you do for recreation and hobbies?
What do you consider your strong points?
What do you consider your weak points?
What do you most want to accomplish in life?
Everyone worries about something. What kinds of things worry you most?
What has helped you most in dealing with difficulties and stresses in your life?
Have you gotten help from another person or agency when you had a problem?
_____ Yes
_____ No
If so, who? Check sources of help:
_____ Spouse/mate
_____ Parents
_____ Siblings
_____ Other family members
_____ Friends
_____ Neighbors
_____ Teachers, mentors
_____ Co-workers
_____ Boss
_____ Minister
_____ Mental health professional(s)
_____ Self-help organiztions
_____ Other: Specify ______________________________
What has been the most important thing that has happened in your life so far?
What has been the best period of your life so far? Why?
What has been the worst period of your life? Why?
How do you feel generally about yourself as a person at this stage of life?
_____ Happy, delighted
_____ Mostly satisfied
_____ Mixed (about equally satisfied and dissatisifed with different areas of life)
_____ Mostly dissatisfied
_____ Unhappy

Date ___________ Code No. ___________

Life Event Checklist

PLEASE CHECK ANY OF THESE EVENTS THAT HAVE OCCURRED IN YOUR LIFE:

	Before Age 18 (indicate approximate age)	Between Age 18 and Today (indicate approximate age)
Prolonged absence of mother	______	______
Prolonged absence of father	______	______
Serious illness of mother	______	______
Serious illness of father	______	______
Mother alcoholic, mentally ill	______	______
Father alcoholic, mentally ill	______	______
Death of father	______	______
Death of mother	______	______
Divorce of parents	______	______
Remarriage of parents	______	______
Chronic family discord	______	______
Brother or sister with handicap	______	______
Death of brother or sister	______	______
Problems in school	______	______
Change of schools	______	______
Loss of job	______	______
Trouble with boss	______	______
Breakup of long-term relationship with boy/girlfriend	______	______
Trouble with in-laws	______	______
Marital separation	______	______
Marital reconciliation	______	______
Divorce	______	______
Pregnancy	______	______
Death of child	______	______
Death of spouse, mate	______	______
Death of close friend	______	______
Personal illness or injury	______	______
Financial problems	______	______
Problems with substance abuse (drugs or alcohol)	______	______
Change of residence	______	______

Scoring System for Ratings of Adult Adaptation

Fourteen items were included in the ratings of the quality of adult adaptation. They dealt with accomplishments and satisfaction in the work and school areas, with the quality of the individual's interpersonal relationships, and with the individual's state of health and well-being. The ratings were based on both the individual's own assessment and on community records. Interrater agreement on the overall ratings of adult adaptation was 91.2 percent.

In the *work/school* area 1 point was assigned if the individual had obtained additional schooling beyond high school, 2 points were assigned if he or she had not sought any additional schooling. Satisfaction with schooling was rated on a 3-point scale, ranging from 1 (satisfied) to 2 (ambivalent) to 3 (dissatisfied). One point was assigned if the individual was currently employed, 2 points were assigned if he or she was currently unemployed. Satisfaction with current employment was rated on a 3-point scale, ranging from 1 (satisfied) to 2 (ambivalent) to 3 (dissatisfied). The range of possible scores in this area was from 4 (best score) to 10 (worst score).

In the area of *interpersonal relationships*, 1 point was assigned if the individual was married, remarried, or in a long-term committed relationship; 2 points were assigned if he or she was divorced and not remarried or had no committed relationship as a single person. The quality of marital relationships, of relationships with children, mother and father, and siblings and friends were each rated on a 3-point scale, ranging from 1 (satisfied) to 2 (ambivalent) to 3 (dissatisfied, conflict ridden). The range of possible scores in this area was from 7 (best score) to 20 (worst score).

In the *self-evaluation*, 1 point was assigned if the individual was free of any debilitating health or mental-health problems, 2 points were assigned if there was evidence of psychosomatic or psychiatric problems. One point was assigned if the individual could rely on two or more sources of emotional support (spouse or mate, friends, kith, and kin); 2 points were assigned if he or she relied exclusively on only one source of emotional support; 3 points were assigned if he or she did not report any outside source of emotional support. The individual's satisfaction with his/her present state of life was scored on a 5-point scale, ranging from 1 (happy, delighted) to 2 (mostly satisfied) to 3 (ambivalent) to 4 (mostly dissatisfied) to 5 (unhappy). The range of possible scores in this area was from 3 (best score) to 10 (worst score).

Total scores ranging from 14 to 20 defined the best outcomes, those for individuals who had coped successfully in early adulthood. Total scores ranging from 23 to 31 were assigned to individuals with minor coping problems; total scores ranging from 32 to 40 defined the worst outcomes, those for individuals with multiple coping problems in their early 30s.

References

Aldwin, C., and D. Stokols. (1988). The effects of environmental change on individuals and groups: Some neglected issues in stress research. *Journal of Environmental Psychology, 5*, 57–75.

Anthony, E. J. (1974) The syndrome of the psychologically invulnerable child. In E. J. Anthony and C. Koupernik, eds., *The Child and His Family*, vol. 3: *Children at Psychiatric Risk* (pp. 529–544). New York: John Wiley.

Anthony, E. J. (1987). Children at high risk for psychosis growing up successfully. In E. J. Anthony and B. J. Cohler, eds., *The Invulnerable Child* (pp. 147–184). New York: Guilford.

Anthony, E. J., and B. J. Cohler, eds. (1987). *The Invulnerable Child*. New York: Guilford.

Antonovsky, A. (1979). *Health, Stress, and Coping: New Perspectives on Mental and Physical Well-Being*. San Francisco: Jossey-Bass.

Antonovsky, A. (1987). *Unravelling the Mystery of Health: How People Manage Stress and Stay Well*. San Francisco: Jossey-Bass.

Aptekar, L. (1988). *Street Children of Cali*. Durham, N.C.: Duke University Press.

Ayala-Canales, C. E. (1984). The impact of El Salvador's civil war on orphan and refugee children. M.S. thesis in Child Development, University of California, Davis.

Bandura, A. (1977). Self-efficacy: Toward a unifying theory of behavioral change. *Psychological Review, 84*, 191–215.

Bandura, A. (1982). The psychology of chance encounters and life paths. *American Psychologist, 37*, 747–755.

Bellah, R. N., R. Madson, W. M. Sullivan, A. Swidler, and S.M. Tipton. (1985). *Habits of the Heart: Individualism and Commitment in American Life*. Berkeley: University of California Press.

Bleuler, M. (1978). *The Schizophrenic Disorders: Long-term Patient and Family Studies*. New Haven: Yale University Press.

Bleuler, M. (1984). Different forms of childhood stress and patterns of adult psychiatric outcome. In N. S. Watt, E. J. Anthony, L. C. Wynne, and J. E. Rolf, eds., *Children at Risk for Schizophrenia: A Longitudinal Perspective* (pp. 537–542). New York: Cambridge University Press.

Block, J. (1971). *Lives through Time*. Berkeley: Bancroft Books.

Boothby, N. (1983). The horror, the hope. *Natural History, 92*, 64–71.

Bronfenbrenner, U. (1979). *The Ecology of Human Development*. Cambridge, Mass.: Harvard University Press.

Brown, G. W., T. O. Harris, and A. Bifulco. (1986). The long-term effect of early loss of parent. In M. Rutter, C. E. Izard, and P. S. Read, eds., *Depression in Young People* (pp. 251–296). New York: Guilford.

Buka, T. S., L. P. Lipsitt, and M. T. Tsuang. (1987). Birth complications and psychological deviancy: A 25 year prospective study. Poster presentation at the 9th Biennial Meeting of the International Society for the Study of Behavioral Development. Tokyo.

Buss, A. H., and R. Plomin. (1984). *Temperament: Early Developing Personality Traits*. Hillsdale, N.J.: Erlbaum.

Caspi, A., G. H. Elder, and D. J. Bem. (1988). Moving away from the world: Life course patterns of shy children. *Developmental Psychology, 24*, 824–831.

Chess, S., and A. Thomas. (1984). *Origins and Evolution of Behavior Disorders from Infancy to Early Adult Life*. New York: Brunner/Mazel.

Cline, H. (1980). Criminal behavior over the lifespan. In O. G. Brim and J. Kagan, eds., *Constancy and Change in Human Behavior* (pp. 641–674). Cambridge, Mass.: Harvard University Press.

Cohler, B. J. (1987). Adversity, resilience, and the study of lives. In E. J. Anthony and B. J. Cohler, eds., *The Invulnerable Child* (pp. 363–424). New York: Guilford.

Compas, B. E. (1987a). Stress and life events during childhood and adolescence. *Clinical Psychology Review, 1*, 275–302.

Compas, B. E. (1987b). Coping with stress during childhood and adolescence. *Psychological Bulletin, 101*(3), 393–403.

Current Population Survey (1986). Machine readable data file, prepared and distributed by the Bureau of Census for the Bureau of Labor Statistics. Washington, D.C.: Bureau of the Census, March.

Danzig, R., and P. Scanton. (1986). *National Service: What Would It Mean?* Lexington, Mass.: D. C. Heath.

Dell, P., and A. Applebaum. (1977). Trigenerational enmeshment: Unresolved ties of single parents to family of origin. *American Journal of Orthopsychiatry, 47*, 52–59.

Dohrenwend, B. S., and B. P. Dohrenwend, eds. (1974). *Stressful Life Events: Their Nature and Effects*. New York: John Wiley.

Douglas, J. W. B., and S. Mann. (1979). Personal communication. Cited in N. Garmezy and M. Rutter, eds. (1983), *Stress, Coping, and Development in Children* (p. 35). New York: McGraw-Hill.

Dunn, J., and C. Kendrick. (1980). The arrival of a sibling: Changes in patterns of interaction between mother and first-born child. *Journal of Child Psychology and Psychiatry, 21*, 119–132.

Dunn, J., C. Kendrick, and R. MacNamee. (1981). The reaction of first-born children to the birth of a sibling: Mothers' reports. *Journal of Child Psychology and Psychiatry, 22*, 1–8.

Eichorn, D., and D. Stern. (1989). *Adolescence and Work: Influences of Social Structure, Labor Market, and Culture*. Hillsdale, N.J.: Erlbaum.

Elder, G. H. (1974). *Children of the Great Depression*. Chicago: University of Chicago Press.

Elder, G. H. (1986). Military times and turning points in men's lives. *Developmental Psychology, 22*(2), 233–245.

Elder, G. H., ed. (1985). *Life Course Dynamics: Trajectories and Transitions, 1968–1980*. Ithaca, N.Y.: Cornell University Press.

Elder, G. H., A. Caspi, and T. Van Nguyen. (1985). Resourceful and vulnerable children. In R. Silbereisen and H. Eyferth, eds., *Development in Context* (pp. 167–186). Berlin: Springer.

Elder, G. H., K. Liker, and C. E. Cross. (1984). Parent-child behavior in the Great Depression: Life course and intergenerational influences. In T. B. Baltes and O. G. Brim, Jr., eds., *Lifespan Development and Behavior, 6* (pp. 109–158). New York: Academic Press.

Elder, G. H., T. Van Nguyen, and A. Caspi. (1985). Linking family hardships to children's lives. *Child Development, 56*, 361–375.

Ensminger, M. E., S. G. Kellam, and B. R. Rubin. (1983). School and family origins of delinquency: Comparisons by sex. In K. Van Dusen and S. A. Mednick, eds., *Prospective Studies of Crime and Delinquency* (pp. 73–97). Boston/The Hague: Kluwer-Nijhoff.

Erikson, E. H. (1959). Identity and the life cycle. *Psychological Issues, 1*, 1–171.

Farrington, D. P. (1983). Offending from 10 to 25 years of age. In K. T. Van Dusen and S. A. Mednick, eds., *Prospective Studies of Crime and Delinquency* (pp. 17–38). Boston/The Hague: Kluwer/Nijhoff.

Farrington, D. P. (1987). Early precursors of frequent offending. In J. G. Wilson and G. C. Loury, eds., *From Children to Citizens*, vol. 3: *Families, Schools, and Delinquency Prevention* (pp. 27–50). New York/Berlin: Springer.

Farrington, D. P. (1989). Long-term prediction of offending and other life outcomes. In H. Wegener, F. Loesel, and J. Haisch, eds., *Criminal Behavior and the Justice System* (pp. 26–39). New York: Springer.

Farrington, D. P., B. Gallagher, L. Morley, R. J. St. Ledger, and D. J. West. (1988a). Are there successful men from criminogenic backgrounds? *Psychiatry, 51*, 116–130.

Farrington, D. P., B. Gallagher, L. Morley, R. J. St. Ledger, and D. J. West. (1988b). A 24 year follow-up of men from vulnerable backgrounds. In R. L. Jenkins, eds., *The Abandonment of Delinquent Behavior: The Turnaround* (pp. 155–173). New York: Praeger.

Felsman, J. K. (1984). Abandoned children: A reconsideration. *Children Today, 13*, 13–18.

Felsman, J. K., and G. E. Vaillant. (1987). Resilient children as adults: A 40 year study. In E. J. Anthony and B. J. Cohler, eds., *The Invulnerable Child* (pp. 289–314). New York: Guilford.

Fiske, M., and D. Chiriboga. (1990). *Change and Continuity in Adult Life*. San Francisco: Jossey-Bass.

Freedman, M. (1989, March–April). Fostering intergenerational relationships for at-risk youth. *Children Today*, 10–15.

Furstenberg, F. F., J. Brooks-Gunn, and L. Chase-Lansdale. (1989). Teenaged pregnancy and child-bearing. *American Psychologist, 44*, 313–320.

Furstenberg, F. F., J. Brooks-Gunn, and S. P. Morgan. (1987). *Adolescent Mothers in Later Life*. Cambridge: Cambridge University Press.

Garmezy, N. (1983). Stressors of childhood. In N. Garmezy and M. Rutter, eds., *Stress, Coping, and Development in Children* (pp. 43–84). New York: McGraw-Hill.

Gilbert, E. S. (1968). On discrimination using qualitative variables. *Journal of the American Statistical Association, 63*, 1399–1412.

Gilligan, C. (1982). *In a Different Voice: Psychological Theory and Women's Development*. Cambridge, Mass.: Harvard University Press.

Glueck, S., and E. Glueck. (1968). *Delinquents and Non-Delinquents in Perspective*. Cambridge, Mass.: Harvard University Press.

Gonsalves, A. M. (1982). Follow-up of teenage mothers at age 26: A longitudinal study on the island of Kauai. M.S. thesis in Child Development, University of California, Davis.

Gove, W. R. (1979). Sex differences in the epidemiology of mental disorders: Evidence and explanation. In E. S. Gomberg and V. Franks, eds., *Gender and Disordered Behavior: Sex Differences in Psychopathology* (pp. 23–70). New York: Brunner/Mazel.

Havighurst, R. J. (1972). *Developmental Tasks and Education*, 3d ed. New York: David McKay.

Havighurst, R. J., P. H. Bowman, G. P. Liddle, C. V. Mathews, and C. V. Pierce. (1962). *Growing Up in River City*. New York: Wiley.

Hetherington, E. M., M. Stanley-Hagan, and E. R. Anderson. (1989). Marital transitions: A child's perspective. *American Psychologist, 44*, 303–312.

Hobcraft, J. N., J. W. McDonald, and S. L. Rutstein. (1985). Demographic determinants of infant and child mortality: A comparative analysis. *Population Studies, 39*, 363–385.

Horowitz, F. D. (1987). *Exploring Developmental Theories: Toward a Structural/Behavioral Model of Development*. Hillsdale, N.J.: Erlbaum.

Horowitz, F. D. (1989). Using developmental theory to guide the search for the effects of biological risk factors on the development of children. *American Journal of Clinical Nutrition, 50*, 589–597.

Katz, S. (1990). Personal communication.

Kellam, S. G., R. Adams, C. H. Brown, and M. E. Ensminger. (1982). The long-term evolution of the family structure of teenage and older mothers. *Journal of Marriage and the Family, 44*, 539–554.

Levinson, D. J. (1986). A conception of adult development. *American Psychologist, 41*, 3–13.

Levitt, E. (1971). Research on psychotherapy with children. In A. E. Bergen and S. L. Garfield, eds., *Handbook of Psychotherapy and Behavior Change* (pp. 474–494). New York: John Wiley.

Lohmöller, J. B. (1984). *LVPLS Program Manual with Partial Least-square Estimates*. Cologne: Zentralarchiv für Empirische Sozial Forschung.

Long, J. V., and G. E. Vaillant. (1984). Natural history of male psychological health, XI: Escape from the underclass. *American Journal of Psychiatry, 141*, 341–346.

Lowenthal, M. Fiske, M. Thurnher, and D. Chiriboga. (1977). *Four Stages of Life*. San Francisco: Jossey-Bass.

Luthar, S. S., and E. Zigler (1991). Vulnerability and competence: A review of research on resilience in childhood. *American Journal of Orthopsychiatry, 61*, 6–22.

McCord, J. (1979). Some child-rearing antecedents of criminal behavior in adult men. *Journal of Personality and Social Psychology, 37*, 1477–1486.

McCord, J. (1982). A longitudinal view of the relationship between paternal absence and crime. In J. Gunn and D. P. Farrington, eds., *Abnormal Offenders, Delinquency, and the Criminal Justice System* (pp. 113–128). New York: John Wiley.

McCord, J. (1983a). A forty year perspective on the effects of child abuse and neglect. *Child Abuse and Neglect, 7*, 265–270.

McCord, J. (1983b). A longitudinal study of aggression and antisocial behavior. In K. T. Van Dusen and S. A. Mednick, eds., *Prospective Studies of Crime and Delinquency* (pp. 269–275). Boston/The Hague: Kluwer-Nijhoff.

McCord, J. (1986). Instigation and insulation: How families affect antisocial aggression. In D. Olweus, J. Block, and M. Radke-Yarrow, eds., *Development of Antisocial and Prosocial Behavior: Research, Theories, and Issues* (pp. 343–357). New York: Academic Press.

Magnusson, D. (1988). *Individual Development from an Interactional Perspective: A Longitudinal Study*. Hillsdale, N.J.: Erlbaum.

Masten, A. (1990). Resilience in development: Implications of the study of successful adaptation for developmental psychopathology. In D. Cicchetti, ed., *Rochester Symposium on Developmental Psychopathology, 1*. Hillsdale, N.J.: Erlbaum.

Masten, A. S., and N. Garmezy. (1985). Risk, vulnerability, and protective factors in developmental psychopathology. In D. B. Lahey and A. E. Kazdin, eds., *Advances in Clinical Child Psychology, 8* (pp. 1–51). New York: Plenum Press.

Mednick, S. A., R. Cudeck, J. J. Griffith, S. A. Talovic, and F. Schulsinger. (1984). The Danish high risk project (1962–1982): Recent methods and findings. In N. S. Watt, E. J. Anthony, L. C. Wynne, and J. E. Rolf, eds., *Children at Risk for Schizophrenia: A Longitudinal Perspective* (pp. 21–42). Cambridge: Cambridge University Press.

Moore, T. (1975). Stress in normal childhood. In L. Levi, ed., *Society, Stress, and Disease: Childhood and Adolescence* (pp. 170–180). London: Oxford University Press.

Moskovitz, S. (1983). *Love despite Hate: Child Survivors of the Holocaust and Their Adult Lives*. New York: Schocken.

Neighbors, H. W., J. S. Jackson, P. J. Bowman, and G. Gurin (1983). Stress, coping, and black mental health: Preliminary findings from a national study. In *Innovations in Prevention* (pp. 5–29). Binghamtom, N.Y.: Haworth.

Ness, R. C., and R. M. Wintrop. (1980). The emotional impact of fundamentalist religious participation. *American Journal of Orthopsychiatry, 50*, 303–315.

Norusis, M. J. (1985). *SPSS: Advanced Statistics Guide*. New York: McGraw-Hill.

O'Connell Higgins, R. (1985). Psychological resilience and the capacity for intimacy: How the wounded might "love well." Ed.D. dissertation, Harvard University.

Osofsky, J. D. (1990). Risk and protective factors for teenage mothers and their infants. *Newsletter of the Society for Research in Child Development*, Winter issue, pp. 1–2.

Patterson, G. R., B. DeBaryshe, and E. Ramsey. (1989). A developmental perspective on antisocial behavior. *American Psychologist, 44*, 329–335.

Purdy, B. A., C. G. Simari, and G. Colon. (1983). Religiosity, ethnicity, and mental health: Interface the 80s. *Counseling and Values, 27*, 112–122.

Quinton, D., M. Rutter, and C. Liddle. (1984). Institutional rearing, parenting difficulties, and marital support. *Psychological Medicine, 14*, 107–124.

Rachman, S. (1979). The concept of required helpfulness. *Behavior Research and Therapy, 17*, 1–6.

Robins, L. N. (1966). *Deviant Children Grown Up*. Baltimore, Md.: William and Wilkins. (1974 ed., New York: Krieger).

Robins, L. N. (1978). Study of childhood predictors of adult outcome: Replication from longitudinal studies. *Psychological Medicine, 8*, 611–622.

Robins, L. N. (1983). Some methodological problems and research directions in the study of the effect of stress on children. In N. Garmezy and M. Rutter, eds., *Stress, Coping, and Development in Children* (pp. 335–346). New York: McGraw-Hill.

Robins, L. N. (1986). The consequences of conduct disorder in girls. In D. Olweus, J. Block, and M. Radke-Yarrow, eds., *Development of Antisocial and Prosocial Behavior* (pp. 385–408). New York: Academic Press.

Rotter, J. (1966). General expectancies for internal or external control of reinforcement. *Psychological Monographs, 80*(1), Whole No. 609.

Rutter, M. (1983). Stress, coping, and development: Some issues and some questions. In N. Garmezy and M. Rutter, eds., *Stress, Coping, and Development in Children* (pp. 1–42). New York: McGraw-Hill.

Rutter, M. (1985). Resilience in the face of adversity: Protective factors and resistance to psychiatric disorders. *British Journal of Psychiatry, 147*, 598–611.

Rutter, M. (1987). Psychosocial resilience and protective mechanisms. *American Journal of Orthopsychiatry, 57*, 316–331.

Rutter, M. (1989). Pathways from childhood to adult life. *Journal of Child Psychology and Psychiatry*. *30*, 23–51.

Rutter, M., and D. Quinton. (1984). Long-term follow-up of women institutionalized in childhood: Factors promoting good functioning in adult life. *British Journal of Developmental Psychology, 18*, 225–234.

Scarr, S., and K. McCartney. (1983). How people make their own environments: A theory of genotype → environment effects. *Child Development, 54*, 424–435.

Schorr, L. B. (with D. Schorr). (1988). *Within Our Reach: Breaking the Cycle of Disadvantage*. New York: Doubleday.

Sellman, W. S. (1990, June/July). Military service for low aptitude recruits. Leg up or let down? *Science Agenda*, 14–15. Washington, D.C.: American Psychological Association.

Snarey, J. R., and G. E. Vaillant. (1985). How lower and working class youth become middle class adults: The association between ego defense mechanisms and upward social mobility. *Child Development, 56*, 899–910.

Super, C., and S. Harkness. (1986). The developmental niche: A conceptualization of the interface between child and culture. *International Journal of Behavioral Development, 9*, 545–569.

Tress, W. (1986). *Das Raetsel der seelischen Gesundheit: Traumatische Kindheit und frueher Schutz gegen Psychogene Stoerungen*. Goettingen: Verlag fuer medizinische Psychologie im Verlag Vandenhoeck und Ruprecht.

Tuma, J. M. (1989). Mental health services for children: The state of the art. *American Psychologist, 44*, 188–199.

Vaillant, G. E. (1977). *Adaptation to Life*. Boston: Little, Brown.

Vaillant, G. E. (1983). *The Natural History of Alcoholism*. Cambridge, Mass.: Harvard University Press.

Vaillant, G. E., and E. S. Milofsky. (1980). Natural history of male psychological health, IX: Empirical evidence for Erikson's model of the life cycle. *American Journal of Psychiatry, 137*, 1348–1359.

Vaillant, G. E., and E. S. Milofsky. (1982). Natural history of male alcoholism, IV: Paths to recovery. *Archives of General Psychiatry, 39*, 127–133.

Vaillant, G. E., and C. O. Vaillant. (1981). Natural history of male psychological health, X: Work as a predictor of positive mental health. *American Journal of Psychiatry, 138*, 1433–1440.

Viederman, M. (1979). Monica: A 25 year longitudinal study of the consequences of trauma in infancy. *Journal of the American Psychoanalytic Association, 27*, 107–126.

Wadsworth, M. (1979). *Roots of Delinquency*. London: Martin Robertson.

Wallerstein, J. S. (1985). Children of divorce: Preliminary report of a 10 year follow-up of older children and adolescents. *Journal of the American Academy of Child Psychiatry, 28*(5), 545–553.

Wallerstein, J., and S. Blakeslee. (1989). *Second Chances: Men, Women, and Children: A Decade after Divorce*. New York: Ticknor and Fields.

Werner, E. E. (1984). *Child Care: Kith, Kin, and Hired Hands*. Baltimore, Md.: University Park Press.

Werner, E. E. (1985). Stress and protective factors in children's lives. In A. R. Nichol, ed., *Longitudinal Studies in Child Psychology and Psychiatry* (pp. 335–356). Chichester, England: John Wiley.

Werner, E. E. (1986). The concept of risk from a developmental perspective. In B. K. Keogh, ed., *Advances in Special Education*, vol. 4: *Developmental Problems in Infancy and the Preschool Years* (pp. 1–23). Greenwich, Conn.: JAI Press.

Werner, E. E. (1987). Vulnerability and resiliency in children at risk for delinquency: A longitudinal study from birth to young adulthood. In J. D. Burchard and S. N. Burchard, eds., *The Prevention of Delinquent Behavior* (pp. 16–43). Beverly Hills, Calif.: Sage.

Werner, E. E. (1988). Vulnerability and resiliency: A longitudinal study of Asian-Americans from birth to age 30. *Proceedings of the 9th Biennial Meeting of the International Society for the Study of Behavioral Development*. Tokyo.

Werner, E. E. (1989). Children of the Garden Island. *Scientific American, 260*(4), 106–111.

Werner, E. E. (1990). Protective factors and individual resilience. In S. Meisel and J. Shonkoff, eds., *Handbook of Early Intervention* (pp. 97–116). Cambridge: Cambridge University Press.

Werner, E. E., J. M. Bierman, and F. E. French. (1971). *The Children of Kauai*. Honolulu: University of Hawaii Press.

Werner, E. E., and R. S. Smith. (1977). *Kauai's Children Come of Age*. Honolulu: University of Hawaii Press.

Werner, E. E., and R. S. Smith. (1982). *Vulnerable but Invincible: A Longitudinal Study of Resilient Children and Youth*. New York: McGraw-Hill; paperback ed., 1989, New York: Adams, Bannister, Cox.

West, D. J. (1982). *Delinquency: Its Roots, Careers, and Prospects*. London: Heinemann.

Widom, C. S., and A. Ames. (1988). Biology and female crime. In T. E. Moffitt and S. A. Mednick, eds., *Biological Contributions to Crime Causation* (pp. 308–331). Dordrecht, Martinus Nijhoff.

Wolfgang, M. E., R. M. Figlio, and T. Sellin. (1972). *Delinquency in a Birth Cohort*. Chicago: University of Chicago Press.

Wolfgang, M. E., T. P. Thornberry, and R. M. Figlio. M. (1987). *From Boy to Man—From Delinquency to Crime*. Chicago: University of Chicago Press.

Index